PENGUIN POETRY LIBRARY

THE SELECTED POEMS OF
THOMAS HARDY

Thomas Hardy was born at Higher Bockhampton, near Dorches-
ter, on 2 June 1840. He was educated locally at the village school
and later in Dorchester. At sixteen he was articled to the
Dorchester architect and church restorer, John Hicks, although
he continued his studies under the guidance of Horace Moule, a
Cambridge graduate, whose later suicide affected Hardy and his
writing deeply. In 1862 he went to London to pursue his archi-
tectural career and also began writing at this time. He returned to
Dorset in 1867 to become assistant to John Hicks, at the same
time beginning his first novel, *The Poor Man and the Lady*, of
which only fragments remain. In 1870 Hardy was sent to St
Juliot in Cornwall and it was here that he met his first wife,
Emma Gifford, whom he married in 1874; in the same year *Far
from the Madding Crowd* was published and met with consider-
able success. In the previous three years he had published
Desperate Remedies (1871), *Under the Greenwood Tree* (1872) and
A Pair of Blue Eyes (1873). In 1878 Hardy moved back to
London and in this year *The Return of the Native* appeared. His
reputation as a writer grew and he became a well-known figure in
London's literary circles. In 1885 he returned to Dorset to live at
Max Gate and over the next three years he published *The Mayor
of Casterbridge* (1886), which many regard as his greatest tragic
novel, *The Woodlanders* (1887) and his first collection of short
stories, *Wessex Tales* (1888). In 1891 *Tess of the D'Urbervilles*
appeared and in 1895 his last novel, *Jude the Obscure*. During the
latter part of his life Hardy devoted himself to poetry, publishing
his first collection of verse, *Wessex Poems*, in 1898. He also
worked on his autobiography, *The Early Life of Thomas Hardy*
(published posthumously in 1928), at the same time burning his
old letters, notebooks and private papers. Thomas Hardy died on
11 January 1928.

David Wright's collected poems, *To the Gods the Shades*, ap-
peared in 1976. He has edited *The Penguin Book of English
Romantic Verse*, *The Penguin Book of Everyday Verse*, *Longer
Contemporary Poems*, Thomas Hardy's *Under the Greenwood
Tree*, Edward Thomas' *Selected Poems and Prose*, translated
Beowulf and *The Canterbury Tales*, and published an auto-
biography, *Deafness*.

Selected Poems

Thomas Hardy

EDITED WITH AN
INTRODUCTION AND NOTES BY
DAVID WRIGHT

PENGUIN BOOKS

Penguin Books Ltd, Harmondsworth, Middlesex, England
Viking Penguin Inc., 40 West 23rd Street, New York, New York 10010, U.S.A.
Penguin Books Australia Ltd, Ringwood, Victoria, Australia
Penguin Books Canada Ltd, 2801 John Street, Markham, Ontario, Canada L3R 1B4
Penguin Books (N.Z.) Ltd, 182–190 Wairau Road, Auckland 10, New Zealand

—

First published 1978
Reprinted 1980, 1981, 1983, 1984, 1986, 1987

—

—

Made and printed in Great Britain by
Richard Clay Ltd, Bungay, Suffolk
Set in Monotype Ehrhardt

CONTENTS

1839   Thomas Hardy, builder and mason of Higher Bockhampton near Dorchester, marries Jemima Hand, cook and servantmaid, at Melbury Osmund on 22 December.

1840   Their eldest son Thomas Hardy born at Higher Bockhampton, 2 June.

1848   He attends village school at Bockhampton built by the lady of the manor, Mrs Julia Martin of Kingston Maurward. His mother gives him Dryden's *Virgil*, Johnson's *Rasselas*. First visit to London about this time.

1849–56   Goes to school at Dorchester to learn Latin. Sees traditional harvest-supper and dance in Kingston Maurward barn. Plays fiddle at weddings and dances; begins learning French and German; reads the novels of Harrison Ainsworth and Dumas père.

1856–62   He is articled to one of his father's employers, the architect and church-restorer John Hicks, whose office in Dorchester is next door to the school kept by the Rev. William Barnes, the Dorset poet and philologist. Witnesses the public execution of Martha Brown outside Dorchester County Gaol. Horace Moule, a university-educated classical scholar and eight years Hardy's senior, becomes his mentor. Studies Greek dramatists with Moule. Reads Darwin's *Origin of Species* (1859). Writes his first poem, *Domicilium*.

1862–7   Leaves Dorchester for London in the year of the exhibition of 1862. Works as assistant-architect to Arthur Blomfield. Attends operas and theatre, explores London, visits National Gallery almost daily, dances at Willis's Rooms, sees Cremorne and the Argyle. Reads Spencer, Huxley, J. S. Mill, Shelley, Browning, Scott and Swinburne. In 1865 publishes his first article, 'How I Built Myself a House' (*Chambers' Journal*). Buys Walker's *Rhyming Dictionary* and begins sending poems to periodicals (they are rejected).

1867–70   Returns to Higher Bockhampton to assist Hicks at Dorchester. Begins his first novel (now lost) *The Poor Man and the Lady*. May have had an understanding with his cousin Tryphena Sparks, the model for Fancy Day and Sue Bridehead. (She went to London to train as a teacher in 1870, married seven

7

years later, and died in 1890.) Completes *The Poor Man* in 1868; it is accepted by Chapman and Hall, but their reader, George Meredith, advises Hardy not to publish. Hicks dies, and Hardy moves to Weymouth to work for his successor, Crickmay. Begins writing *Desperate Remedies*. In 1870 Crickmay sends Hardy to St Juliot, Cornwall, to make plans for the restoration of the church. Here he meets his future wife, Emma Lavinia Gifford, the rector's sister-in-law.

1870–85   Publishes *Desperate Remedies* in 1871, followed by *Under the Greenwood Tree*, 1872, and *A Pair of Blue Eyes*, 1873. Leslie Stephen serializes *Far from the Madding Crowd* in the *Cornhill Magazine*. Horace Moule commits suicide at Cambridge. Publication and success of *Far from the Madding Crowd* in 1874. Hardy marries Emma Lavinia Gifford at St Peter's Church, Paddington, and encouraged by her abandons architecture for novel-writing. They take a short continental honeymoon and after brief residences at Surbiton, Swanage and Yeovil, settle at Sturminster Newton in 1876. In this year *The Hand of Ethelberta* is published. 1878 sees publication of *The Return of the Native* and the end of Hardy's 'Sturminster Newton idyll'. They remove to Upper Tooting. Hardy joins Savile Club and becomes a well-known literary figure in London, attending parties and 'crushes'. In 1880 publishes *The Trumpet-Major*, falls seriously ill and is bedridden for six months while writing *A Laodicean*. In 1881 Hardy publishes *A Laodicean*, and takes a house at Wimborne Minster. Visits Paris in 1882 after publication of *Two on a Tower*. Moves to Dorchester in 1883 to supervise the building of his house at Max Gate, taking occupation in 1885.

1885–97   The next three years see the publication of *The Mayor of Casterbridge*, 1886, *The Woodlanders*, 1887, and his first collection of short stories, *Wessex Tales*, 1888. In the spring of 1887 the Hardys tour Italy, visiting Genoa, Pisa, Florence, Rome, Venice, and Milan, returning via London, where Hardy meets Browning and Arnold. From now on they usually visit London in the spring, and sometimes the Continent or Scotland. *A Group of Noble Dames* and *Tess of the D'Urbervilles* are published in 1891; and in the following year Hardy's father dies. In 1893 the Hardys visit Dublin at the invitation of Mrs Henniker (authoress, a daughter of Richard Monckton Milnes). In 1894 publishes *Life's Little Ironies*. About this time strain manifests itself in Hardy's home life, especially during the writing of *Jude the Obscure* (published 1896). Hardy resolves to write no more novels, though he publishes *The Well-Beloved* (written ten years earlier) in 1897.

1898–1912   In 1898 Hardy publishes his first collection of verse, *Wessex Peoms*, and in 1902 *Poems of the Past and the Present*. In this year he begins *The Dynasts*, of which the first part appears in 1904, the year of his mother's death. Two subsequent parts are published in 1906 and 1908, in which year he also brings out a selection of William Barnes's poems. In 1909 he publishes *Time's Laughingstocks*, and in the following year is awarded the Order of Merit and the freedom of Dorchester. He makes a final revision of his novels in 1912, and in November his wife suddenly dies.

1913–28   In March 1913 Hardy makes a pilgrimage to St Juliot and his wife's birthplace at Plymouth. He marries in February 1914 Florence Emily Dugdale, whom he had met through Mrs Henniker in 1904 and who had acted as his secretary and general assistant since 1912. In 1913 receives honorary degree of Litt. D. from Cambridge University (in 1920 Oxford University was to follow suit) and publishes *A Changed Man and Other Tales*. In 1914 publishes *Satires of Circumstances* (including 'Poems of 1912–13'). In 1915 his sister Mary dies. *Moments of Vision* published 1917; *Late Lyrics and Earlier*, 1922; and in 1923 a verse play, *The Famous Tragedy of the Queen of Cornwall*. *Human Shows*, the last collection of poems to appear in his lifetime, is published in 1925. During these years he works at his autobiography, *The Early Life of Thomas Hardy*, supposedly written by Florence Emily Hardy (published posthumously in 1928); at the same time burning his old letters, notebooks and private papers. Dies 11 January 1928, and his ashes are laid in Poets' Corner of Westminster Abbey at the same time that his heart is buried in the grave of his first wife at Stinsford, next to the tombs of his parents. This year sees the publication of his posthumous collection of poems, *Winter Words*.

INTRODUCTION

WHEN Thomas Hardy's first book of poems made its appearance in 1898, just a hundred years after the publication of *Lyrical Ballads*, no one remarked the coincidence. To Hardy's contemporaries, apart from a few pleasing ballads and lyrics like 'A Dance at the Phoenix,' 'Friends Beyond' and 'I Look into my Glass', *Wessex Poems* was no more than a curiosity, the by-product of a famous elder novelist.

Yet this collection, and still more its successor in 1902, can be seen as a beginning of the end of Victorian poetry, and even to presage the tone of the coming century. Not that Hardy had set out, like Wordsworth and Coleridge, to make a poetic revolution. He was too unassuming a character for that. Though he noted, around 1900: 'There is no new poetry; but the new poet – if he carry the flame on further (and if not he is no new poet) – comes with a new note. And that new note it is that troubles the critical waters.' All that Hardy had in mind to do was to make poems. This he did, persistently, out of whatever material came to hand. For Hardy there was no subject unfit for verse.

Hardy was always a poet. He once told his friend Sydney Cockerell that he would never have written a line of prose if he could have earned his living at poetry. Many of the poems in his first collection had been written thirty or more years earlier, while he was still an apprentice architect; in fact all his books contain poems, or rewritten poems, dating from the 1860s. They sit remarkably well with his later poetry, for Hardy developed very little. It is often difficult to tell whether a poem is early or late, except in so far that a late poem is less likely to wear a crabbed syntax or consciously poetical hat than an early one. He did attain more skill – another thing from dexterity – and in his great period from 1910 to 1920, when he was in his seventies, a plainness and directness not easily to be found in English poetry after the seventeenth century. But there are few other poets of the language who changed less over so long a career.

Hardy's becoming a novelist was an accident, whereas from the start poetry was his vocation. Born in 1840, the son of a country builder and mason, he wrote his first poem when he was seventeen. 'Domicilium' is a remarkably good exercise in Wordsworthian blank verse as well as being a prototypical Hardy poem: local to himself, a description and history of the house where he was born, it sets the scene for the rest of his work.

At the time that he wrote it he was apprenticed to an architect in Dorchester whose offices were next door to the school run by William Barnes, the Dorset poet. Forty years older than himself, Barnes was one of the very few contemporary poets to whom Hardy refers in his writings, and the only one to whom he ever acknowledged a direct debt. Barnes remains a poet still largely neglected and badly underrated. One reason is the unfamiliar dialect in which he wrote, although his Dorset is far easier to follow than Burns's Lowland Scotch. Barnes was a self-taught philologist, widely learned, and one of the very few Victorian poets to write a language derived from common speech rather than books. His influence on Hardy cannot be overestimated. But it was not until Hardy was in his twenties, living in London and working as an assistant to the architect Arthur Bloomfield, that he began to involve himself seriously in poetry. For a time he read nothing else 'as in verse was concentrated the essence of all imaginative and emotional literature'. Hardy, like Barnes, was a great self-educator; among other things he more or less taught himself – though aided by his friend and mentor, the scholar H. M. Moule, whose influence on Hardy as a young man was profound – to read the New Testament and the Greek dramatists in the original. He bought a Walker's *Rhyming Dictionary* and embarked on the somewhat bizarre task of turning the Book of Ecclesiastes into Spenserian stanzas. As for the *Rhyming Dictionary*, Robert Gittings has noted that Hardy added new words to its lists of rhymes, some of which show that Hardy's pronunciation was not always the standard English he claimed – e.g. he rhymed 'groat' with 'ought' and 'bought'.

However, the poems he produced were all rejected by the magazine editors to whom they were sent. It was clear that bread was not to be won with verses – and if the poems Hardy sent out were, as is probable, in the vein of the early sonnet called 'Hap', then no wonder Victorian editors found them rebarbative. Hardy had been reading the progressives in the *Saturday Review*, besides Darwin, and Mill, and Spencer, and Huxley, to say nothing of *Essays and Studies*; all the new rationalists. It ended with his losing his faith; though as he himself remarked, Hardy always remained 'churchy'. After all, his father and grandfather had been leading bandsmen of the village choir at Stinsford church; it was in his blood. But from the beginning Hardy's attitude to his Maker seems to have been one of greater or lesser umbrage, as if personally affronted by the impersonality and in-difference of what he later designated as 'It' (a nasty crack, that pronoun) or 'The Immanent Will' which he believed to have no consciousness, if indeed it existed at all. These notions, which partly derived from Schopenhauer and partly from the extreme gentleness and compassion of his own nature, he never quite successfully assimilated into his poetry.

Meanwhile Hardy had begun to be bothered, while working at the drawing-board, by floating specks in front of his eyes. He felt that he should find some other means of earning a living than architecture. Novel-writing seemed the best answer. His first attempt was accepted but not published; his second was published, but failed; the third, *Under the Greenwood Tree*, attracted the right sort of attention. Within a couple of years of its publication Hardy was fairly launched as a successful novelist. In 1867, for reasons of health, he had left London for Dorset, where he continued working as an architect while writing novels. Then in 1870 Hardy's employer sent him to restore the parish church of St Juliot in Cornwall. Here he met and fell in love with his future wife, Emma Lavinia Gifford. Emma encouraged and helped Hardy, transcribing fair copies of his novels, and they were eventually married in 1874 on the strength of the success of Hardy's fourth novel, *Far from the Madding Crowd*. With Emma's moral backing Hardy abandoned architecture and became a professional novelist, which he remained till the publication of *Jude the Obscure* in 1896.

Hardy is said to have given up novel-writing in disgust at the reception of this book, which provided a field day for the prurient and for wits who renamed it *Jude the Obscene*. There was also domestic pressure; his wife had violently objected to *Tess of the D'Urbervilles*, and had done what she could to prevent the publication of *Jude*. A famous anecdote has her travelling up from Dorset to call on Richard Garnett, Keeper of Printed Books at the British Museum, to invoke his help in suppressing it. By this time strain was showing in the Hardy marriage. The public outcry over *Jude* added to Hardy's gloom, which found expression in the three poems called 'In Tenebris', written between 1895 and 1896. At any rate Hardy never wrote another novel. By then he did not need to. For the rest of his life he was able to live quite comfortably in the big ugly house that he had built for himself and Emma at Max Gate outside Dorchester, on income from the royalties of novels, none of which ever went out of print.

It is hard to feel that he took the novel seriously as an art form, great as his contribution to it was. This is not to say that Hardy did not study its techniques or that he thought little of his novels. But his attitude to novel-writing suggests that he looked on it as a trade or craft rather than an art. At any rate he was not above attempting the contemporary equivalent of a thriller (e.g. *Desperate Remedies*, which is in the Wilkie Collins tradition) and made no bones about amputating or altering even a masterpiece like *Tess* for magazine publication. Looking at his life as a whole, it seems clear that Hardy wrote his novels primarily to make the money on which to live while he wrote poetry.

Nor was it a bad training. Speaking of Hardy's *Collected Poems* in 1937, Ezra Pound remarked: 'Now *there* is clarity. There *is* the harvest of having written twenty novels first.' Not that Hardy had ever entirely stopped writing poems. The leanest years for his poetry seem to have been in the 1870s, when he was busy establishing himself as a novelist. There is only one poem dated between 1872 and 1882 in the *Collected Poems*. But as only a small proportion of Hardy's poems bear dates, this does not mean that no others were written during those years. After the publication of *Jude* the only year without a dated poem is 1903, when Hardy was engaged in writing his epic dramatic poem, *The Dynasts*. Between 1898 and his death in 1928 he produced eight collections of poems, not counting *The Dynasts* or his verse play *The Queen of Cornwall*. His *Complete Poems*, published in 1976, total nearly nine hundred and fifty.

Such productiveness is an attribute though not necessarily an indication of a major poet. Certainly Hardy aimed at becoming one. Between 1902 and 1907 he immersed himself in his long-planned epic verse-drama *The Dynasts*, which is in bulk almost equal to the *Collected Poems*. Alas, like Tennyson's *Idylls of the King* or Browning's *The Ring and the Book*, this is a work that obeys the will of its poet rather than of his muse. Hardy's Napoleonic panorama is an expression of poetic ambition. Admirable in places, as a poem it is neither cohering nor coherent, though saved from unreadability, not to say mediocrity, by the magnificent prose scene-settings, which in fact do the job that Hardy's plain journeyman blank verse fails, if it was ever meant, to achieve. In design it eclipses C. M. Doughty's contemporaneous epic, *The Dawn in Britain*, which is in many ways a more remarkable magnum opus. But though Doughty's epic loses itself in sheer length, the rumbling Saxon diapason of its blank verse reverberates as Hardy's does not; as a poem, *The Dawn* is the more impressive failure.

But whatever one may think of *The Dynasts* (and there are plenty of people who regard it as a masterwork), there is no doubt that Hardy is one of the major poets of the twentieth century – paradoxically; for he was born in 1840, only three years later than that very nineteenth-century poet, Algernon Charles Swinburne. Ezra Pound, who had more to do than most with the modern movement in poetry, recognized Hardy's contemporaneity well enough; though it is only comparatively recently that the real stature and influence of Hardy's poetry has come to be understood and appraised Not that it has ever been really neglected. Like Yeats's, Hardy's poetry has always been widely popular with ordinary people while retaining the admiration of a literary élite. But, perhaps deliberately, Hardy made himself difficult to assess – at least for the latter – by his haphazard jumbling of the contents of his various collections of poetry, all of which contain poems written at widely differing dates (sometimes as much as half a century apart) besides offering a kaleidoscope of forms and metres – traditional ballads, sonnets, triolets, sapphics, fourteeners, blank verse – as well as a ragbag of subjects, with autobiographical pieces lying confusedly and confusingly alongside dramatic monologues of imagined or imaginary characters; and partly because of his very idiosyncratic diction, which is often as not neither the language of common speech nor of books, but a tongue that never was on sea or land: a Hardyese made up of rare or archaic words, poeticisms, dialect, and above all his own compounds and coinages. William Archer once remarked that Hardy seemed 'to lose all sense of local and historical perspective in language, seeing all the words in the dictionary on one plane . . . and regarding them all as equally available and appropriate for any and every literary purpose'. But he added, quite truly: 'Hardy's anarchic attitude towards language freed him for patterns of diction which are odd but often successful'. All this makes Hardy sound as if he were a difficult poet to read; the paradox is, he is not. It is only difficult to make up one's mind how good, and/or how bad, almost any particular poem of Hardy's is.

Hardy's strength is in his weakness: that he was a home-made poet. If one excepts the Irish poet, the late Patrick Kavanagh, Hardy was the last of the autochthonous provincial poets of the line of Burns and John Clare. Like them he is not primarily a literate poet, by which I mean that like theirs his first approach to poetry was by way of an indigenous oral culture of songs and ballads, rather than the printed page. Hardy was one of the last English poets to be brought up in a pre-industrial world, even if, as he says in the autobiographical *Early Life of Thomas Hardy*, the Dorchester of his youth 'had advanced to railways and photographs and daily London papers'. However, 'not living there, but walking every day from a world of shepherds and ploughmen in a hamlet not three miles off, he saw rustic and borough doings in a juxtaposition peculiarly close'. And Hardy records that as a youth his was 'a life twisted of three strands – the professional life, the scholar's life, and the rustic life', for he would be reading the *Iliad* and the *Aeneid* from 6 a.m. to

8 a.m., working all day in an architect's office, and in the evening rushing off 'with his fiddle under his arm, sometimes in company with his father as first violin and uncle as 'cellist, to play at country dances, reels and hornpipes at an agriculturist's wedding, christening, or Christmas party ... the Hardys still being traditionally string-bandsmen available on such occasions'. Thus Hardy (like Clare, whose father was a well-known ballad-singer with a repertoire of more than a hundred songs) was brought up in contact with a live traditional culture, the oral poetry of the people. It was a culture which in England survived almost unchanged from the Middle Ages up to the agricultural revolution and enclosure of the commons in the early nineteenth century and is now petrified in the collections of folk songs compiled by Cecil Sharp *et al.*

One obvious consequence is to be found in Hardy's mastery and development of the use of refrain and repetition in his poetry. W. B. Yeats's use of ballad-refrains – e.g. in his 'Crazy Jane' lyrics – seems embarrassingly artificial, even phoney, in comparison with the organic construction of such refrain- and repetition-built poems of Hardy's as 'The Five Students', 'The Change', 'Lines to a Movement in Mozart's E-Flat Symphony', 'An Ancient to Ancients', ' "Who's in the Next Room?" ', and that masterpiece of impressionism, 'During Wind and Rain'.

From the folk-songs that he heard, homespun and effective, Hardy may have absorbed some of his principles of style. 'The whole secret of a living style and the difference between it and a dead style, lies in having not too much style – being, in fact, a little careless, or rather seeming to be, here and there ... Inexact rhymes and rhythms now and then are far more pleasing than correct ones.' He also attributed much of his metrical technique to his training as an architect:

Years earlier he had decided that too regular a beat was bad art. He had fortified himself in this opinion by thinking of the analogy of architecture, between which art and that of poetry he had discovered, to use his own words, that there existed a close and curious parallel, both arts, unlike some others, having to carry a rational content inside their artistic form. He knew that in architecture cunning irregularity

17

is of enormous worth, and it is obvious that he carried on into his verse, perhaps in part unconsciously, the Gothic art-principle in which he had been trained – the principle of spontaneity, resulting in the 'unforeseen' (as it has been called) character of his metres and stanzas, that of stress rather than of syllable, poetic texture rather than poetic veneer; the latter kind of thing, under the name of 'constructed ornament' being what he, in common with every Gothic student, had been taught to avoid as the plague. He shaped his poetry accordingly, introducing metrical pauses, and reversed beats.

(The Later Years of Thomas Hardy)

An example of the kind of thing that he meant could be the elaborately constructed orchestration of the stanza-form, rhyme-scheme and metre of such a poem as the magnificent 'Honeymoon Time at an Inn':

While their large-pupilled vision swept the scene there,
    Nought seeming imminent,
  Something fell sheer, and crashed, and from the floor
  Lay glittering at the pair with a shattered gaze,
While their large-pupilled vision swept the scene there,
    And the many-eyed thing outleant.

With a start they saw that it was an old-time pier-glass
    Which had stood on the mantel near,
  Its silvering blemished, – yes, as if worn away
  By the eyes of the countless dead who had smirked at it
Ere these two ever knew that old-time pier-glass
    And its vague and vacant leer.

As he looked, his bride like a moth skimmed forth, and kneeling
    Quick, with quivering sighs,
  Gathered the pieces under the moon's sly ray,
  Unwitting as an automaton what she did;
Till he entreated, hasting to where she was kneeling,
    'Let it stay where it lies!'

Note how the first and fifth lines of each stanza end on the same word, and how the third and fourth lines do not rhyme at all (except in the last two stanzas of the complete poem). There are many others to which one might point, e.g. 'To My Father's Violin', 'Copying Architecture in an Old Minster', 'An East-End Curate', 'The Monument Maker', 'A Hurried Meeting', and what is probably Hardy's finest elegiac lyric, 'After a Journey'. But the intricate structure of many of Hardy's poems probably owes even more to the influence and example of his neighbour William Barnes, who in his dialect poems employed very sophisticated verse-forms drawn from other literatures, e.g. the Persian *ghazel*, Italian *terza rima*, Welsh *cynghanned* (a repetitive consonantal pattern) and *union* (internal rhyming). The latter is introduced in compliment to Barnes in the fine elegy that Hardy wrote for him, 'The Last Signal'.

In another poem, 'The Collector Cleans His Picture', Hardy directly reflects the Anglo-Saxon-orientated vocabulary that Barnes advocated, in which Latinate words are shunned in favour of equivalents made up of native Anglo-Saxon roots – for example, in this poem Hardy uses 'housegear' for 'furniture' and 'brushcraft' for 'painting'. This is of course artificial and idiosyncratic; the example of Barnes perhaps over-encouraged Hardy to invent words like 'unbloom', 'byss' (abyss), 'lip' (speak), and even more grotesque compounds and coinages. But Barnes was right, as C. H. Sisson remarks in a notable essay, 'in turning his back on the literary effects of "the money-making mind, which looks on the works of God mainly, if not only, as sources of wealth" ' and using a language (the spoken Dorset speech) 'that was a genuine common store, made to express what those who spoke it could understand. Each man took as much of it as answered his share of the world, what he had directly by sight and hearing and touch. It is as far as possible from the meretricious speech of public and commercial media which all but the most sophisticated are ashamed now not to talk'.

This has a bearing on Hardy's development. Though he wrote no more than a handful of Dorset dialect poems himself ('The Bride-Night Fire' is one; it is also one of his earliest poems) it is this language – Hardy himself insisted that it was a language, not merely a dialect – that formed a large part of the verbal environment in which he grew up. It is one of the reasons why Hardy escapes his period, why he is not a Victorian like Swinburne, his almost exact contemporary; why his poetry escapes the thinness that afflicted most English poetry after the death of Byron in 1824. This thinness was a post-romanticism, a preference for abstracts rather than objects, for fancies, decorativeness, moralizing; for waffling about unrealities, or if not quite that, realities at a decent or comfortable remove. It reflects the urbanization of life by a new industrial society, the rise of middle classes who owed most of their prosperity to their function as middlemen, who operated at a remove from the actual sources of wealth. The language of most Victorian poets reflected a similar disassociation from reality: in the main theirs was the diction of the written, not spoken, word. Not surprisingly it was an age of failed major poets: Tennyson, Browning, Arnold, Swinburne. It was partly thanks to the literarysm of their diction which, like the glass panes of a greenhouse, let in the light but kept out the cold air, that their poetry was so full of exotic blooms. One could maintain that the true indigenous line of English poetry through most of the nineteenth century went underground: that it is not really to be found in the work of the major figures, despite their often admirable achievements, but in that of less publicized and sometimes unpublished poets – John Clare for one, William Barnes for another, and Thomas Hardy for a third.

Another reason why Hardy escaped Victorianism is because he recorded its commonplaces as none of his contemporaries managed, or perhaps even wanted, to do – even Browning, one of Hardy's main influences, or the underrated Coventry Patmore. Hardy was one of the few to communicate its evanescent detail:

> The evening sunlit cliffs, the talk,
> Hailings and halts,
> The keen sea-salts,
> The band, the Morgenblätter waltz

('At a Seaside Town in 1869')

Read the nine hundred odd of Hardy's poems, and despite or because of the occasional melodramatics – poems like 'The Chapel-Organist', 'The Contretemps' (Hardy's vulgar curiosity and weakness for ungentlemanly speculation is one strength), despite or because of his frontal attacks on the obvious (another strength), despite or because of the many costume poems (mostly set in the eighteenth century), one ends by knowing, almost as a participant, what the nineteenth century was like to be alive in; one sees it, smells it, hears it, feels it. Not as a nostalgic Then, or 'period', but as part of the immortal present and continuous Now of human consciousness. As Hardy remarked, 'I hold that the mission of poetry is to record impressions, not convictions.' He added, 'Wordsworth in his later writings fell into the error of recording the latter. So also did Tennyson, and so do many other poets when they grow old. *Absit omen.*'

Absit omen indeed. The poems that record Hardy's convictions – e.g. 'God's Funeral', 'Panthera', even 'In Tenebris', or the Immanent Will machinery of *The Dynasts* with its chorus of Spirits, are not Hardy's best. As for the last-named, Hardy himself put his finger on what was wrong with that ambitious work: 'A widely appreciative mind mostly fails to achieve a great work out of pure far-sightedness. The very clearness with which he discerns remote possibilities is, from its nature, scarcely ever consistent with the microscopic vision demanded for tracing the narrow path that leads to them.' The other poems mentioned are among those in which Hardy tended to rationalize or explain – e.g. 'In Tenebris' – his famous pessimism, rather than embody it as he does in much more effective poems like 'In Front of the Landscape', 'Autumn in King's Hintock Park', or 'The Five Students'. Hardy was inclined rather pettishly to disclaim being a pessimist; the truth was, he had a somewhat melancholic disposition and rather enjoyed it. This was quite evident to his second wife, Florence Emily Hardy. In a letter to Edmund Gosse she remarked: 'T. H. . . . is now, this afternoon writing a poem with great spirit: always a sign of well-being with him. Needless to say, it is an intensely dismal poem.' As Hardy knew perfectly well, he was not a philosophical but an impressionist poet – the 'microscopic vision' is what makes Hardy's poetry unique. 'He was a man who used to notice such things' – for example:

You stand so stock-still that your ear-ring shakes
At each pulsation that the vein there makes.

('At Wynyard's Gap')

The imagination working and engaged, but the eye unwaveringly fixed upon the object. The key to Hardy's poetry is in his own statement: 'Unadjusted impressions have their value, and the road to a true philosophy of life seems to lie in humbly recording diverse readings of its phenomena as they are forced upon us by chance and change.'

Hardy's poems are exactly that – unadjusted impressions, a record of diverse readings of the phenomena of life. That microscopic vision ensures that almost no poem, however flawed, is without interest or fails to contribute, like an apparently random dot of colour in a pointilliste painting, to Hardy's image of the world. And, as has been said, Hardy made any and everything a subject of poetry. His range is, in fact, remarkable. He could be classed as a 'nature' poet on the strength of such pieces as the well-known 'The Darkling Thrush'; or a rural poet in the line of Barnes and Clare (e.g. 'An Unkindly May', 'A Trampwoman's Tragedy'); a poet of London ('Recollections of a Dancing Man', 'The Woman I Met', 'Beyond the Last Lamp', 'An East End Curate'); a poet of travel (cf. the sequence of poems recording his Italian tour of 1887), or above all, a topographical poet. He could even be classified as a 'war poet', that specifically twentieth-century phenomenon. Hardy was in fact the first of them, as his Boer War poems attest; while his Great War poems stand beside Rosenberg's, Owen's, and Kipling's.

So one could go on; but it is as a poet of love and marriage that Hardy is unique. More than three hundred of his poems are on this subject. These poems of Hardy's are unparalleled in this or any other language, except perhaps in Shakespeare's sonnets – which do not treat of marriage. The latter is a theme hardly ever handled in poetry outside satire and comedy: in English literature only in Chaucer (the 'marriage-debate' in *The Canterbury Tales*); in Coventry Patmore's *The Angel in the House* and in his less successful *The Victories of Love*; and in

George Meredith's *Modern Love*. Only Chaucer approaches Hardy in realism and psychological insight. Patmore is too saccharine and Meredith too self-absorbed; in the last analysis both of them are too sentimentally gentlemanly (though Meredith rants a bit) to handle so abrasive a topic. Hardy has the passion, the detached subjectivity, the lack of inhibitory good manners, and enough of the pure wonder of observing human behaviour, that are needed to deal honestly with this most tendentious of themes.

He once remarked that his autobiography could be found in his poems. It is certainly true that the history of Hardy's loves and marriage is there to read in his eight collections of verse; but so shuffled and randomly dispersed by that devious and secretive man that, except in his great sequence 'Poems of 1912–13' (how non-committal a title!), the story they tell is exceptionally difficult to decipher – in fact impossible without some previous background knowledge of Hardy's life. And so far as his love-life is concerned, he left little other evidence than the poems; for before his death he made a bonfire of his private papers at Max Gate, followed by another lit by his widow soon after he died.

Apart from a few childish infatuations with village girls, and a romantic attachment to Mrs Julia Martin, the lady of the manor of Kingston Maurward, Hardy's first serious love affair (if one discounts a rejected proposal of marriage to a Dorchester girl when he was twenty-two) seems to have been with his cousin Tryphena Sparks, the daughter of Hardy's mother's sister. This began in 1867, when he came back to live with his parents at Higher Bockhampton near Dorchester after spending five years in an architect's office in London. The two may have become engaged. It is probable that Tryphena Sparks was partly the model for Fancy Day in *Under the Greenwood Tree* and also for Sue Bridehead in *Jude the Obscure*. At the time she was a pupil-teacher in the National School at Puddletown, a village two or three miles from Hardy's home. In 1869 she went to a training college for teachers in London, and became head-mistress of Plymouth Public Free School in 1872. Five years later she married a hotel keeper called Charles Gale, bore him four children, and died in 1890. Hearing the news of her death Hardy wrote the poem he called 'Thoughts of Phena', which refers to her as 'my lost prize'. These are all the facts about Tryphena that are certainly known; but according to Lois Deacon and Terry Coleman's *Providence and Mr Hardy* (1966) Hardy had an illegitimate son by Tryphena in 1868 – a boy called 'Randy' who was somehow brought up in concealment by the Sparks family. In 1873, according to these authors, Tryphena broke off the engagement and returned his ring to Hardy, who gave it to Emma Lavinia Gifford when he married her in 1874. These 'facts' depend on the evidence of Tryphena's daughter, who was eleven years old when her mother died, and who, just before her own death at the age of eighty-six, identified the photograph of an unknown boy in the family album as that of Hardy's son. No documentary record of the birth or death of 'Randy' has been found anywhere, and if he existed it is quite incredible that there should have been no gossip about him; even more that there should be no reference to such a child in Hardy's prose or verse. Remembering Hardy's discursiveness about anything that touched him emotionally, and his grief at his own childlessness, the theory that 'Randy' may have been 'Father Time' in *Jude the Obscure*, or 'the journeying boy' of 'Midnight on the Great Western', seems self-defeating. However, it is certain that Hardy was emotionally involved with Tryphena, and Lois Deacon and Terry Coleman have done a useful job in identifying many Hardy poems that refer to her, despite a predilection for unearthing Tryphena from under almost every other stanza that Hardy wrote.

In 1870 occurred the great event in Hardy's life, when he travelled to St Juliot, a remote parish on the north coast of Cornwall, to make drawings for the restoration of its church. He stayed at the vicarage, and there met and fell in love with the vicar's sister-in-law, Emma Lavinia Gifford: an event celebrated in 'The Wind's Prophecy', 'When I Set Out for Lyonesse', 'The Discovery', 'She Opened the Door'. Hardy was then about thirty and Emma not much younger; she may have felt she was in danger of being left on the shelf, especially as she lived in so remote a place with few eligible suitors bar the odd curate. It was a wild landscape, barren and magnificent; she took Hardy riding to show it to him (she was a fine horsewoman). Together they visited Tintagel and Beeny Cliffs near Boscastle. Like Hardy, Emma was musical; she played the harmonium in the church of St Juliot. Hardy was to erect a tablet to commemorate this not long after her death. But Emma was a rung or two above Hardy in the social scale – a matter of more import then than now. An uncle of hers became an Archdeacon; whereas one of Hardy's Puddletown cousins was a servantmaid, and others were workfolk. Nonetheless it was Emma's uncle, the future Archdeacon, who married them in 1874 when Hardy's ship came home with the success of *Far from the Madding Crowd*.

The marriage was happy enough to begin with. They honeymooned on the Continent and set up house in London, later moving to Sturminster Newton, where they spent their two happiest years together (cf. 'A Two Years' Idyll', 'The Musical Box'). Then things began to go wrong between them. There was no child; Emma's social snobbery became pronounced – she would not invite Hardy's parents or sisters to their house at Max Gate. She made it clear that she had married beneath her, but at the same time was exasperated by Hardy's social success in London, where his fame made him welcome at the houses of the great. Then Emma's conventional piety was outraged by the views expressed in Hardy's novels and poems. She took up writing herself, published poems in the local paper, and came to believe, or at any rate to claim, that she had more talent than her husband. Towards the end of her life there is reason to suppose that her mind may have been disturbed. Hardy implies as much in a sinister poem, 'The Interloper'. Near the end of their marriage the Hardys were in effect living separate lives at Max Gate, meeting only at meals; for Hardy (according to his second wife) there were 'long evenings spent alone in his study, insult and abuse his only enlivenment'. Yet Emma Hardy was a generous hostess, well liked by her friends and neighbours; the servants at Max Gate preferred her to the withdrawn and rather stingy master of the house.

Hardy found consolation of sorts elsewhere. He began an *amitie amoureuse* with Mrs Arthur Henniker. She wrote novels, and was the daughter of Richard Monckton Milnes, Lord Houghton, the friend of poets and the first biographer of Keats. This affair began in 1893 when the Hardys first met her in Dublin, and is referred to in 'A Thunderstorm in Town', 'At an Inn' and 'A Broken Appointment'. As the poems indicate, it is unlikely ever to have been consummated; but they remained friends till Mrs Henniker died in 1923.

The last of Hardy's loves was Florence Emily Dugdale, who was introduced to him by Mrs Henniker in 1904. She became his secretary and, according to servants' gossip, his mistress. Hardy married her fifteen months after the death of his first wife. The poems 'After the Visit', 'To Meet or Otherwise' and 'A Jog-Trot Pair' are about Florence.

The sudden and unexpected death of Emma in November 1912 was a profound shock to Hardy. The death of a person close to him was always likely to broach emotions that had lain maturing, as it were, while the person lived. As Hardy said of himself, 'I have a faculty . . . for burying an emotion in heart or brain for forty years, and exhuming it at the end of that time as fresh as when interred'. Thus his poems about Tryphena Sparks were written after her death in 1890, when he had probably not seen her for two decades. In the same way Emma's death opened up all Hardy's intense feeling for her. The life they had shared, their remembered love, their courting in Cornwall forty years before, filled his mind. Gentleness was the dominant trait in Hardy's make-up (it was the cruelty in God and Nature that he could not forgive) and instead of feeling relief at her death, he felt he had failed Emma by his later coldness and lack of understanding. The sequence, 'Poems of 1912–13', that he wrote immediately after her death was, he claimed, 'an expiation', though in an excellent essay *Hardy's Virgilian Purples* (which explodes, by the way, the condescending idea that Hardy, who for all his provincial unbringing had a better grounding in the classics than most of us, was in any way a *naif*) Donald Davie points out that these poems are an examination of the nature of sexual passion and *exclude* remorse. This is true. In 'Poems of 1912–13' and in the hundred and more poems that Hardy wrote about himself and Emma in the years following her death, his recreation of their love and its impairment is detached and clear-sighted though full of intense feeling; there is sentiment but not sentimentality. He tells truths without pretending to 'the truth' which in the matter of the relationship between people is no more than illusion.

These poems are Hardy's masterwork – yet so lacking in pretension (as C. H. Sisson has pointed out, 'it is Hardy's lack of pretension – more in evidence in his verse than in his prose – which is his profoundest contribution to the literature of the twentieth century') that although admired, even now their uniqueness is scarcely appraised.

Hardy's poetry seems to come closer to us the further the age he lived in recedes. As a 'modern poet' (already the phrase has a period air) he was, as Ezra Pound himself recognized, Pound's forerunner. Hardy's odd, disruptive, but elaborately plotted rhythms, and his singular, at times grotesque vocabulary and syntax, are so idiosyncratic that it has taken time to appreciate the fact. In the 1930s Michael Roberts opened his enormously influential *Faber Book of Modern Verse* not with Hardy but Hardy's contemporary G. M. Hopkins, then all the rage for his sprung-rhythm and surrealistic-looking handling of imagery. Yet it is Hopkins who now seems to have faded into the Victorian background, to belong with the stained-glass of Burne-Jones; while it is a shock to remember that Hardy was only three years younger than Swinburne. For all his peculiar turns of phrase and wrenchings of speech, Hardy hasn't dated like his Victorian contemporaries. Not because he lived longer into the twentieth century but because he aimed, not at perfection of form, finish, or verbal dexterity but – in words written by Hardy about his master, William Barnes, though they might have come from an imagist manifesto – at 'closeness of phrase to vision'.

DAVID WRIGHT

A NOTE ON THE SELECTION

ALMOST no poem Hardy wrote is wholly uninteresting. Of all poets, it is Hardy who best repays re-reading over the years. Poems that seem slight or merely awkward at first glance, are found to contain resonances that take time and one's own increasing experience of life to discover. This makes the job of selection difficult; not least because one man's Hardy is often as not another man's bathos. As this selection, generous as the publishers have been with their allocation of space, admits less than half of Hardy's entire output (if *The Dynasts*, which is represented here, be taken into account) I don't expect not to have left out poems that other readers would certainly have included, though quite sure that each reader would find a different omission with which to castigate the editor.

Another poser has been the arrangement of the poems. Had it been possible, a chronological order should have been attempted. But even a rough and ready dating of the composition of Hardy's poems is beset with problems. So I have made a loose arrangement of the poems more or less thematically, beginning with a handful of the very earliest ones dated by the poet. These are followed by poems bearing upon his family and background, leading to his narrative and anecdotal verse; thence to poems dealing with the South African, Napoleonic, and First World War, followed by his more sombre and reflective pieces. The selection ends with the largely autobiographic poems referring to Hardy's early loves, his courtship of Emma Gifford and the difficulties of their marriage, followed by the sequence 'Poems of 1912–13' and the elegiac pieces he wrote after her death. In this loosely narrative arrangement Hardy's autobiography displays itself in his poems, as he said it would.

DAVID WRIGHT

HARDY's Wessex is so familiar that it is hard to realize how odd it is that a novelist should have tied himself by so many strings to a particular tract of territory. Many novelists have set their scenes in real places, or have written with some features of a familiar landscape always before them. But Hardy has done something different. Almost every step taken by his characters is taken along real roads or over real heaths; the towns and villages, the hills, even many of the houses, are identifiable. It is as if Hardy's imagination could not work unless with solid ground under its feet, with solid objects to be seen around it. Many of the characters, there is little doubt, contain more or less of one real person, more or less of another, with elements drawn purely from imagination or from the accumulated layers of experience, which comes to much the same thing. But with the topography, Hardy was rarely satisfied with anything less than a one-to-one correspondence between the fictional and the real.

While the detail of Hardy's topographical nomenclature may become tedious, the fact that the landscape is identifiable does give the novels a special quality, as of a day-dream, with half-real figures moving over a real world. One might say – if it can be said with respect – that it is this which leaves the novels with a touch of the magazine-story still, in which the ingenuous reader may lose himself – or herself – in vicarious adventures. And part of the immense popularity of Hardy certainly derives from the interest of the places written about, and particularly the more picturesque.

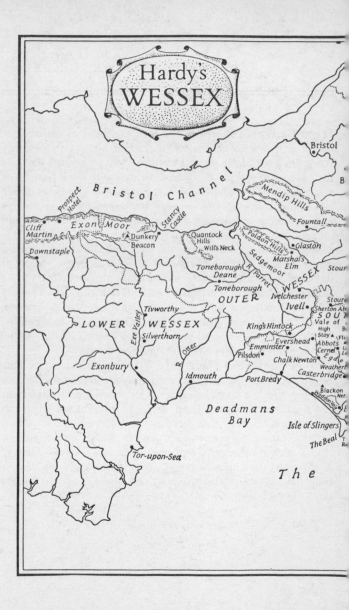

Hardy's WESSEX

Bristol

Bristol Channel

Prospect Hotel

Mendip Hills

Cliff Martin

Exon Moor

Stancy Castle

Fountall

Downstaple

Dunkery Beacon

Quantock Hills
Will's Neck

Poldon Hills

Glaston

Sedgemoor

Marshal's Elm

R. Parret

Toneborough Deane

WESSEX

Stour

Toneborough

OUTER

Ivelchester

Stour

Tivworthy

Ivell

Sherton Ab

SOU

LOWER

WESSEX

Vale of

Ere Valley

Silverthorn

King's Hintock

High Stoy

Flin

Abbots

R. Otter

Evershead

Cernel

Egd

Le

Exonbury

Pilsdon

Emminster

Chalk Newton

Weather

Idmouth

Port Bredy

Casterbridge

Blackon
Net

Deadmans Bay

Isle of Slingers

Wa

The Beal

T
Re

Tor-upon-Sea

The

R. Thames
Lumsdon
Christminster

NORTH

The Brown House
Alfredston
Cresscombe
Marygreen

MID
WESSEX

Marlbury Downs
Kennetbridge
Gaymead
Aldbrickham
Castle Royal

Batton Castle
Inkpen Beacon

WESSEX
Quartershot

The Great Plain
Stoke Barehills
Icenway House

Weydon Priors

Stonehenge
UPPER
WESSEX

Melchester
Wintoncester

Fernel Hall
Deansleigh Park

Wingreen
Chase
The Slopes
Trantridge Cross

ottsford
orum
Chaseborough
Lornton Inn
The Great
Badbury Rings
Yewsholt
Bramshurst
Forest

nd
Warborne
Southampton

Chene Manor
Haveripool
Solentsea
Portsmouth

ath
ys
Sandbourne

Anglebury
The Island

gate
Knollsea

Cove

hannel

N

0   10   20   30 miles

Fictitious names: Exonbury
Real names: Portsmouth

H. A. Shelley

Key to Place-Names

HARDY'S NAME	REAL NAME
Abbot's-Cernel	Cerne Abbas
Abbotsea	Abbotsbury
Aldbrickham	Reading
Alfredston	Wantage
Anglebury	Wareham
Badbury Rings	A hill near Wimborne Minster
Bubmouth	Weymouth
Bulbarrow	A hill near Sturminster Newton
Casterbridge	Dorchester
Chalk Hewton	Maiden Newton
Chaseborough	Cranborne
Christminster	Oxford
Cresscombe	Letcombe Basset
Damer's Wood	Came Wood near Dorchester
Dogbury	A hill near High Stoy
Durnover	Fordington
Egdon Heath	A composite of the heaths between Bournemouth and Dorchester
Emminster	Beaminster
Evershead	Evershot
Exonbury	Exeter
Fensworth	Letcombe Regis
Flintcombe-Ash	Nettlecombe-Tout
Greenhill	Woodbury Hill near Bere Regis
Hope Cove	Church Hope
Kennetgridge	Newbury
Kingsbere and *King's-Bere*	Bere Regis
Leddenton	Gillingham
Longpuddle	Piddlehinton (also called by Hardy *Upper Longpuddle*)
Lulwind Cove	Lulworth Cove
Lumsdon	Cumnor

HARDY'S NAME	REAL NAME
Marlott	Marnhull
Marygreen	Fawley
Melchester	Salisbury
Mellstock	Stinsford and Lower and Higher Bockhampton
Middleton Abbey	Milton Abbas
Nether-Moynton	Owermoigne
Norcombe Hill	A hill near Toller Down
Nuttlebury	Hazelbury Bryan
Oxwell Hall	Poxwell
Port Bredy	Bridport
Pos'ham	Portisham
Quartershot	Aldershot
Rainbarrow	Rainbarrows, a mound north of the Dorchester-Wareham road
Ridgeway	A road between Dorchester and Weymouth
Roy Town	Troy Town
St Aldhelm's Head	St Alban's Head
Sandbourne	Bournemouth
Shaston	Shaftesbury
Sherton	Sherborne
Shottsford and *Shottsford Forum*	Blandford
Stoke-Barehills	Basingstoke
Stourcastle	Sturminster Newton
Upper Longpuddle	Piddlehinton
Weatherbury	Puddletown
Wellbridge	Wool
Wintonchester	Winchester
Yalbury Wood	Yellowham Wood

POEMS

CONTENTS

CONTENTS

CONTENTS

CONTENTS

CONTENTS

CONTENTS

From THE DYNASTS

*

CONTENTS

CONTENTS

CONTENTS

CONTENTS

CONTENTS

Domicilium [1]

It faces west, and round the back and sides
High beeches, bending, hang a veil of boughs,
And sweep against the roof. Wild honeysucks
Climb on the walls, and seem to sprout a wish
(If we may fancy wish of trees and plants)
To overtop the apple-trees hard by.

Red roses, lilacs, variegated box
Are there in plenty, and such hardy flowers
As flourish best untrained. Adjoining these
Are herbs and esculents; and farther still
A field; then cottages with trees, and last
The distant hills and sky.

Behind, the scene is wilder. Heath and furze
Are everything that seems to grow and thrive
Upon the uneven ground. A stunted thorn
Stands here and there, indeed; and from a pit
An oak uprises, springing from a seed
Dropped by some bird a hundred years ago.

                In days bygone –
Long gone – my father's mother, who is now
Blest with the blest, would take me out to walk.
At such a time I once inquired of her
How looked the spot when first she settled here.
The answer I remember. 'Fifty years
Have passed since then, my child, and change has marked
The face of all things. Yonder garden-plots
And orchards were uncultivated slopes
O'ergrown with bramble bushes, furze and thorn:
That road a narrow path shut in by ferns,
Which, almost trees, obscured the passer-by.

'Our house stood quite alone, and those tall firs
And beeches were not planted. Snakes and efts
Swarmed in the summer days, and nightly bats
Would fly about our bedrooms. Heathcroppers
Lived on the hills, and were our only friends;
So wild it was when first we settled here.'

Hap

IF but some vengeful god would call to me
From up the sky, and laugh: 'Thou suffering thing,
Know that thy sorrow is my ecstasy,
That thy love's loss is my hate's profiting!'

Then would I bear it, clench myself, and die,
Steeled by the sense of ire unmerited;
Half-eased in that a Powerfuller than I
Had willed and meted me the tears I shed.

But not so. How arrives it joy lies slain,
And why unblooms the best hope ever sown?
– Crass Casualty obstructs the sun and rain,
And dicing Time for gladness casts a moan . . .
These purblind Doomsters had as readily strown
Blisses about my pilgrimage as pain.

1866

Discouragement

To see the Mother, naturing Nature, stand
All racked and wrung by her unfaithful lord,
Her hopes dismayed by his defiling hand,
Her passioned plans for bloom and beauty marred.

Where she would mint a perfect mould, an ill;
Where she would don divinest hues, a stain,
Over her purposed genial hour a chill,
Upon her charm of flawless flesh a blain:

Her loves dependent on a feature's trim,
A whole life's circumstance on hap of birth,
A soul's direction on a body's whim,
Eternal Heaven upon a day of Earth,
Is frost to flower of heroism and worth,
And fosterer of visions ghast and grim.

Westbourne Park Villas, 1863–7
(From old MS.)

A Young Man's Epigram on Existence

A SENSELESS school, where we must give
Our lives that we may learn to live!
A dolt is he who memorizes
Lessons that leave no time for prizes.

16 W.P.V., 1866

Her Definition

I LINGERED through the night to break of day,
Nor once did sleep extend a wing to me,
Intently busied with a vast array
Of epithets that should outfigure thee.

Full-featured terms – all fitless – hastened by,
And this sole speech remained: 'That maiden mine!' –
Debarred from due description then did I
Perceive the indefinite phrase could yet define.

As common chests encasing wares of price
Are borne with tenderness through halls of state,
For what they cover, so the poor device
Of homely wording I could tolerate,
Knowing its unadornment held as freight
The sweetest image outside Paradise.

W.P.V., Summer: 1866

To an Actress[2]

I READ your name when you were strange to me,
Where it stood blazoned bold with many more;
I passed it vacantly, and did not see
Any great glory in the shape it wore.

O cruelty, the insight barred me then!
Why did I not possess me with its sound,
And in its cadence catch and catch again
Your nature's essence floating therearound?

Could *that* man be this I, unknowing you,
When now the knowing you is all of me,
And the old world of then is now a new,
And purpose no more what it used to be –
A thing of formal journeywork, but due
To springs that then were sealed up utterly?

1867

1967

IN five-score summers! All new eyes,
New minds, new modes, new fools, new wise;
New woes to weep, new joys to prize;

With nothing left of me and you
In that live century's vivid view
Beyond a pinch of dust or two;

A century which, if not sublime,
Will show, I doubt not, at its prime,
A scope above this blinkered time.

– Yet what to me how far above?
For I would only ask thereof
That thy worm should be my worm, Love!

16 Westbourne Park Villas, 1867

54

Neutral Tones

WE stood by a pond that winter day,
And the sun was white, as though chidden of God,
And a few leaves lay on the starving sod;
　　　－ They had fallen from an ash, and were gray.

Your eyes on me were as eyes that rove
Over tedious riddles of years ago;
And some words played between us to and fro
　　　On which lost the more by our love.

The smile on your mouth was the deadest thing
Alive enough to have strength to die;
And a grin of bitterness swept thereby
　　　Like an ominous bird a-wing . . .

Since then, keen lessons that love deceives,
And wrings with wrong, have shaped to me
Your face, and the God-curst sun, and a tree,
　　　And a pond edged with grayish leaves.

1867

Her Initials

UPON a poet's page I wrote
Of old two letters of her name;
Part seemed she of the effulgent thought
Whence that high singer's rapture came.
－ When now I turn the leaf the same
Immortal light illumes the lay,
But from the letters of her name
The radiance has waned away!

1869

Coming Up Oxford Street: Evening

THE sun from the west glares back,
And the sun from the watered track,
And the sun from the sheets of glass,
And the sun from each window-brass;
Sun-mirrorings, too, brighten
From show-cases beneath
The laughing eyes and teeth
Of ladies who rouge and whiten.
And the same warm god explores
Panels and chinks of doors;
Problems with chymists' bottles
Profound as Aristotle's
He solves, and with good cause,
Having been ere man was.

Also he dazzles the pupils of one who walks west,
A city-clerk, with eyesight not of the best,
Who sees no escape to the very verge of his days
From the rut of Oxford Street into open ways;
And he goes along with head and eyes flagging forlorn,
Empty of interest in things, and wondering why he was born.

As seen 4 July 1872

After a Romantic Day

THE railway bore him through
An earthen cutting out from a city:
There was no scope for view,
Though the frail light shed by a slim young moon
Fell like a friendly tune.

Fell like a liquid ditty,
And the blank lack of any charm
Of landscape did no harm.
The bald steep cutting, rigid, rough,
And moon-lit, was enough

For poetry of place: its weathered face
Formed a convenient sheet whereon
The visions of his mind were drawn.

Life and Death at Sunrise

(NEAR DOGBURY GATE, 1867)

THE hills uncap their tops
Of woodland, pasture, copse,
And look on the layers of mist
At their foot that still persist:
They are like awakened sleepers on one elbow lifted,
Who gaze around to learn if things during night have shifted.

A waggon creaks up from the fog
With a laboured leisurely jog;
Then a horseman from off the hill-tip
Comes clapping down into the dip;
While woodlarks, finches, sparrows, try to entune at one time,
And cocks and hens and cows and bulls take up the chime.

With a shouldered basket and flagon
A man meets the one with the waggon,
And both the men halt of long use.
'Well,' the waggoner says, 'what's the news?'
' – 'Tis a boy this time. You've just met the doctor trotting back.
She's doing very well. And we think we shall call him "Jack".

'And what have you got covered there?'
He nods to the waggon and mare.
'Oh, a coffin for old John Thinn:
We are just going to put him in.'
' – So he's gone at last. He always had a good constitution.'
' – He was ninety-odd. He could call up the French Revolution.'

57

One We Knew[3]

(M.H. 1772–1857)

SHE told how they used to form for the country dances –
'The Triumph', 'The New-rigged Ship' –
To the light of the guttering wax in the panelled manses,
And in cots to the blink of a dip.

She spoke of the wild 'poussetting' and 'allemanding'
On carpet, on oak, and on sod;
And the two long rows of ladies and gentlemen standing,
And the figures the couples trod.

She showed us the spot where the maypole was yearly planted,
And where the bandsmen stood
While breeched and kerchiefed partners whirled, and panted
To choose each other for good.

She told of that far-back day when they learnt astounded
Of the death of the King of France:
Of the Terror; and then of Bonaparte's unbounded
Ambition and arrogance.

Of how his threats woke warlike preparations
Along the southern strand,
And how each night brought tremors and trepidations
Lest morning should see him land.

She said she had often heard the gibbet creaking
As it swayed in the lightning flash,
Had caught from the neighbouring town a small child's shrieking
At the cart-tail under the lash . . .

With cap-framed face and long gaze into the embers –
We seated around her knees –
She would dwell on such dead themes, not as one who remembers,
But rather as one who sees.

She seemed one left behind of a band gone distant
So far that no tongue could hail:

Past things retold were to her as things existent,
Things present but as a tale.

20 May 1902

The Choirmaster's Burial[4]

He often would ask us
That, when he died,
After playing so many
To their last rest,
If out of us any
Should here abide,
And it would not task us,
We would with our lutes
Play over him
By his grave-brim
The psalm he liked best –
The one whose sense suits
'Mount Ephraim' –
And perhaps we should seem
To him, in Death's dream,
Like the seraphim.

As soon as I knew
That his spirit was gone
I thought this his due,
And spoke thereupon.
'I think,' said the vicar,
'A read service quicker
Than viols out-of-doors
In these frosts and hoars.
That old-fashioned way
Requires a fine day,
And it seems to me
It had better not be.'

Hence, that afternoon,
Though never knew he
That his wish could not be,
To get through it faster
They buried the master
Without any tune.

But 'twas said that, when
At the dead of next night
The vicar looked out,
There struck on his ken
Thronged roundabout,
Where the frost was graying
The headstoned grass,
A band all in white
Like the saints in church-glass,
Singing and playing
The ancient stave
By the choirmaster's grave.

Such the tenor man told
When he had grown old.

A Church Romance⁵

(MELLSTOCK: CIRCA 1835)

SHE turned in the high pew, until her sight
Swept the west gallery, and caught its row
Of music-men with viol, book, and bow
Against the sinking sad tower-window light.

She turned again; and in her pride's despite
One strenuous viol's inspirer seemed to throw
A message from his string to her below,
Which said: 'I claim thee as my own forthright!'

Thus their hearts' bond began, in due time signed.
And long years thence, when Age had scared Romance,
At some old attitude of his or glance

That gallery-scene would break upon her mind,
With him as minstrel, ardent, young, and trim,
Bowing 'New Sabbath' or 'Mount Ephraim'.

The Roman Road

THE Roman Road runs straight and bare
As the pale parting-line in hair
Across the heath. And thoughtful men
Contrast its days of Now and Then,
And delve, and measure, and compare;

Visioning on the vacant air
Helmed legionaries, who proudly rear
The Eagle, as they pace again
     The Roman Road.

But no tall brass-helmed legionnaire
Haunts it for me. Uprises there
A mother's form upon my ken,
Guiding my infant steps, as when
We walked that ancient thoroughfare,
     The Roman Road.

The Ghost of the Past[6]

WE two kept house, the Past and I,
  The Past and I;
Through all my tasks it hovered nigh,
  Leaving me never alone.
It was a spectral housekeeping
  Where fell no jarring tone,
As strange, as still a housekeeping
  As ever has been known.

As daily I went up the stair
  And down the stair,
I did not mind the Bygone there –
  The Present once to me;

Its moving meek companionship
    I wished might ever be,
There was in that companionship
    Something of ecstasy.

It dwelt with me just as it was,
    Just as it was
When first its prospects gave me pause
    In wayward wanderings,
Before the years had torn old troths
    As they tear all sweet things,
Before gaunt griefs had torn old troths
    And dulled old rapturings.

And then its form began to fade,
    Began to fade,
Its gentle echoes faintlier played
    At eves upon my ear
Than when the autumn's look embrowned
    The lonely chambers here,
When autumn's settling shades embrowned
    Nooks that it haunted near.

And so with time my vision less,
    Yea, less and less
Makes of that Past my housemistress,
    It dwindles in my eye;
It looms a far-off skeleton
    And not a comrade nigh,
A fitful far-off skeleton
    Dimming as days draw by.

Heredity

I AM the family face;
Flesh perishes, I live on,
Projecting trait and trace
Through time to times anon,
And leaping from place to place
Over oblivion.

The years-heired feature that can
In curve and voice and eye
Despise the human span
Of durance – that is I;
The eternal thing in man,
That heeds no call to die.

The Pedigree

I

I BENT in the deep of night
Over a pedigree the chronicler gave
As mine; and as I bent there, half-unrobed,
The uncurtained panes of my window-square let in the watery
        light
Of the moon in its old age:
And green-rheumed clouds were hurrying past where mute and
        cold it globed
Like a drifting dolphin's eye seen through a lapping wave.

II

So, scanning my sire-sown tree,
And the hieroglyphs of this spouse tied to that,
With offspring mapped below in lineage,
Till the tangles troubled me,
The branches seemed to twist into a seared and cynic face
    Which winked and tokened towards the window like a Mage
    Enchanting me to gaze again thereat.

III

It was a mirror now,
And in it a long perspective I could trace
Of my begetters, dwindling backward each past each
    All with the kindred look,
    Whose names had since been inked down in their place
    On the recorder's book,
Generation and generation of my mien, and build, and brow.

63

IV

And then did I divine
That every heave and coil and move I made
Within my brain, and in my mood and speech,
    Was in the glass portrayed
As long forestalled by their so making it;
The first of them, the primest fuglemen of my line,
Being fogged in far antiqueness past surmise and reason's reach.

V

    Said I then, sunk in tone,
'I am merest mimicker and counterfeit! –
    Though thinking, *I am I,*
    And what I do I do myself alone.'
–The cynic twist of the page thereat unknit
Back to its normal figure, having wrought its purport wry,
    The Mage's mirror left the window-square,
And the stained moon and drift retook their places there.
1916

Old Furniture

I KNOW not how it may be with others
    Who sit amid relics of householdry
That date from the days of their mothers' mothers,
    But well I know how it is with me
        Continually.

I see the hands of the generations
    That owned each shiny familiar thing
In play on its knobs and indentations,
    And with its ancient fashioning
        Still dallying:

Hands behind hands, growing paler and paler,
    As in a mirror a candle-flame
Shows images of itself, each frailer
    As it recedes, though the eye may frame
        Its shape the same.

On the clock's dull dial a foggy finger,
    Moving to set the minutes right
With tentative touches that lift and linger
      In the wont of a moth on a summer night,
        Creeps to my sight.

On this old viol, too, fingers are dancing –
    As whilom – just over the strings by the nut,
The tip of a bow receding, advancing
      In airy quivers, as if it would cut
        The plaintive gut.

And I see a face by that box for tinder,
    Glowing forth in fits from the dark,
And fading again, as the linten cinder
      Kindles to red at the flinty spark,
        Or goes out stark.

Well, well. It is best to be up and doing,
    The world has no use for one to-day
Who eyes things thus – no aim pursuing!
      He should not continue in this stay,
        But sink away.

Middle-Age Enthusiasms[7]

TO M.H.

WE passed where flag and flower
Signalled a jocund throng;
We said: 'Go to, the hour
Is apt!' – and joined the song;
And, kindling, laughed at life and care,
Although we knew no laugh lay there.

We walked where shy birds stood
Watching us, wonder-dumb;
Their friendship met our mood;
We cried: 'We'll often come:
We'll come morn, noon, eve, everywhen!'
– We doubted we should come again.

We joyed to see strange sheens
    Leap from quaint leaves in shade;
A secret light of greens
    They'd for their pleasure made.
We said: 'We'll set such sorts as these!'
– We knew with night the wish would cease.

'So sweet the place,' we said,
    'Its tacit tales so dear,
Our thoughts, when breath has sped,
    Will meet and mingle here!' . . .
'Words!' mused we. 'Passed the mortal door,
Our thoughts will reach this nook no more.'

On One Who Lived and Died Where He Was Born[8]

WHEN a night in November
    Blew forth its bleared airs
An infant descended
    His birth-chamber stairs
    For the very first time,
    At the still, midnight chime;
All unapprehended
    His mission, his aim. –
Thus, first, one November,
An infant descended
        The stairs.

On a night in November
    Of weariful cares,
A frail aged figure
    Ascended those stairs
    For the very last time:
    All gone his life's prime,
All vanished his vigour,

66

And fine, forceful frame:
Thus, last, one November
Ascended that figure
    Upstairs.

On those nights in November –
    Apart eighty years –
The babe and the bent one
    Who traversed those stairs
    From the early first time
    To the last feeble climb –
That fresh and that spent one –
    Were even the same:
Yea, who passed in November
As infant, as bent one,
    Those stairs.

Wise child of November!
    From birth to blanched hairs
Descending, ascending,
    Wealth-wantless, those stairs;
    Who saw quick in time
    As a vain pantomime
Life's tending, its ending,
    The worth of its fame.
Wise child of November,
Descending, ascending
    Those stairs!

To My Father's Violin

DOES he want you down there
In the Nether Glooms where
The hours may be a dragging load upon him,
    As he hears the axle grind
    Round and round
Of the great world, in the blind
    Still profound

Of the night-time? He might liven at the sound
Of your string, revealing you had not forgone him.

In the gallery west the nave,
But a few yards from his grave,
Did you, tucked beneath his chin, to his bowing
Guide the homely harmony
Of the quire
Who for long years strenuously –
Son and sire –
Caught the strains that at his fingering low or higher
From your four thin threads and eff-holes came outflowing.

And, too, what merry tunes
He would bow at nights or noons
That chanced to find him bent to lute a measure,
When he made you speak his heart
As in dream,
Without book or music-chart,
On some theme
Elusive as a jack-o'-lanthorn's gleam,
And the psalm of duty shelved for trill of pleasure.

Well, you cannot, alas,
The barrier overpass
That screens him in those Mournful Meads hereunder,
Where no fiddling can be heard
In the glades
Of silentness, no bird
Thrills the shades;
Where no viol is touched for songs or serenades,
No bowing wakes a congregation's wonder.

He must do without you now,
Stir you no more anyhow
To yearning concords taught you in your glory;
While, your strings a tangled wreck,
Once smart drawn,

Ten worm-wounds in your neck,
    Purflings wan
With dust-hoar, here alone I sadly con
Your present dumbness, shape your olden story.

1916

Bereft⁹

    In the black winter morning
No light will be struck near my eyes
While the clock in the stairway is warning
For five, when he used to rise.
        Leave the door unbarred,
        The clock unwound,
        Make my lone bed hard –
        Would 'twere underground!

    When the summer dawns clearly,
And the appletree-tops seem alight,
Who will undraw the curtain and cheerly
Call out that the morning is bright?

    When I tarry at market
No form will cross Durnover Lea
In the gathering darkness, to hark at
Grey's Bridge for the pit-pat o' me.

    When the supper crock's steaming,
And the time is the time of his tread,
I shall sit by the fire and wait dreaming
In a silence as of the dead.
        Leave the door unbarred,
        The clock unwound,
        Make my lone bed hard –
        Would 'twere underground!

1901

She Hears the Storm

THERE was a time in former years –
　　While my roof-tree was his –
When I should have been distressed by fears
　　At such a night as this!

I should have murmured anxiously,
　　'The pricking rain strikes cold;
His road is bare of hedge or tree,
　　And he is getting old.'

But now the fitful chimney-roar,
　　The drone of Thorncombe trees,
The Froom in flood upon the moor,
　　The mud of Mellstock Leaze,

The candle slanting sooty-wick'd,
　　The thuds upon the thatch,
The eaves-drops on the window flicked,
　　The clacking garden-hatch,

And what they mean to wayfarers,
　　I scarcely heed or mind;
He has won that storm-tight roof of hers
　　Which Earth grants all her kind.

After the Last Breath[10]

(J.H. 1813–1904)

THERE'S no more to be done, or feared, or hoped;
None now need watch, speak low, and list, and tire;
No irksome crease outsmoothed, no pillow sloped
　　Does she require.

Blankly we gaze. We are free to go or stay;
Our morrow's anxious plans have missed their aim;
Whether we leave to-night or wait till day
　　Counts as the same.

70

The lettered vessels of medicaments
Seem asking wherefore we have set them here;
Each palliative its silly face presents
    As useless gear.

And yet we feel that something savours well;
We note a numb relief withheld before;
Our well-beloved is prisoner in the cell
    Of Time no more.

We see by littles now the deft achievement
Whereby she has escaped the Wrongers all,
In view of which our momentary bereavement
    Outshapes but small.

1904

The Self-Unseeing

HERE is the ancient floor,
Footworn and hollowed and thin,
Here was the former door
Where the dead feet walked in.

She sat here in her chair,
Smiling into the fire;
He who played stood there,
Bowing it higher and higher.

Childlike, I danced in a dream;
Blessings emblazoned that day;
Everything glowed with a gleam;
Yet we were looking away!

A Wet Night

I PACE along, the rain-shafts riddling me,
Mile after mile out by the moorland way,
And up the hill, and through the ewe-leaze gray
Into the lane, and round the corner tree;

Where, as my clothing clams me, mire-bestarred,
And the enfeebled light dies out of day,
Leaving the liquid shades to reign, I say,
'This is a hardship to be calendared!'

Yet sires of mine now perished and forgot,
When worse beset, ere roads were shapen here,
And night and storm were foes indeed to fear,
Times numberless have trudged across this spot
In sturdy muteness on their strenuous lot,
And taking all such toils as trifles mere.

The House of Hospitalities

HERE we broached the Christmas barrel,
    Pushed up the charred log-ends;
Here we sang the Christmas carol,
    And called in friends.

Time has tired me since we met here
    When the folk now dead were young,
Since the viands were outset here
    And quaint songs sung.

And the worm has bored the viol
    That used to lead the tune,
Rust eaten out the dial
    That struck night's noon.

Now no Christmas brings in neighbours,
    And the New Year comes unlit;
Where we sang the mole now labours,
    And spiders knit.

Yet at midnight if here walking,
    When the moon sheets wall and tree,
I see forms of old time talking,
    Who smile on me.

Logs on the Hearth[11]

A MEMORY OF A SISTER

THE fire advances along the log
        Of the tree we felled,
Which bloomed and bore striped apples by the peck
    Till its last hour of bearing knelled.

The fork that first my hand would reach
        And then my foot
In climbings upward inch by inch, lies now
    Sawn, sapless, darkening with soot.

Where the bark chars is where, one year,
        It was pruned, and bled –
Then overgrew the wound. But now, at last,
    Its growings all have stagnated.

My fellow-climber rises dim
        From her chilly grave –
Just as she was, her foot near mine on the bending limb,
    Laughing, her young brown hand awave.

December 1915

Molly Gone[12]

NO more summer for Molly and me;
        There is snow on the tree,
    And the blackbirds plump large as the rook are, almost,
        And the water is hard
Where they used to dip bills at the dawn ere her figure was lost
        To these coasts, now my prison close-barred.

No more planting by Molly and me
        Where the beds used to be
    Of sweet-william; no training the clambering rose
        By the framework of fir
Now bowering the pathway, whereon it swings gaily and blows
        As if calling commendment from her.

73

No more jauntings by Molly and me
   To the town by the sea,
Or along over Whitesheet to Wynyard's green Gap,
   Catching Montacute Crest
To the right against Sedgmoor, and Corton-Hill's far-distant cap,
   And Pilsdon and Lewsdon to west.

No more singing by Molly to me
   In the evenings when she
Was in mood and in voice, and the candles were lit,
   And past the porch-quoin
The rays would spring out on the laurels; and dumbledores hit
   On the pane, as if wishing to join.

Where, then, is Molly, who's no more with me?
   – As I stand on this lea,
Thinking thus, there's a many-flamed star in the air,
   That tosses a sign
That her glance is regarding its face from her home, so that there
   Her eyes may have meetings with mine.

In the Garden [13]

(M.H.)

WE waited for the sun
To break its cloudy prison
(For day was not yet done,
And night still unbegun)
Leaning by the dial.

After many a trial –
We all silent there –
It burst as new-arisen,
Throwing a shade to where
Time travelled at that minute.

Little saw we in it,
But this much I know,
Of lookers on that shade,
Her towards whom it made
Soonest had to go.

1915

Paying Calls[14]

I WENT by footpath and by stile
   Beyond where bustle ends,
Strayed here a mile and there a mile
   And called upon some friends.

On certain ones I had not seen
   For years past did I call,
And then on others who had been
   The oldest friends of all.

It was the time of midsummer
   When they had used to roam;
But now, though tempting was the air,
   I found them all at home.

I spoke to one and other of them
   By mound and stone and tree
Of things we had done ere days were dim,
   But they spoke not to me.

Transformations

PORTION of this yew
Is a man my grandsire knew,
Bosomed here at its foot:
This branch may be his wife,
A ruddy human life
Now turned to a green shoot.

These grasses must be made
Of her who often prayed,
Last century, for repose;
And the fair girl long ago
Whom I often tried to know
May be entering this rose.

So, they are not underground,
But as nerves and veins abound
In the growths of upper air,
And they feel the sun and rain,
And the energy again
That made them what they were!

At Middle-Field Gate in February

THE bars are thick with drops that show
    As they gather themselves from the fog
Like silver buttons ranged in a row,
And as evenly spaced as if measured, although
    They fall at the feeblest jog.

They load the leafless hedge hard by,
    And the blades of last year's grass,
While the fallow ploughland turned up nigh
In raw rolls, clammy and clogging lie –
    Too clogging for feet to pass.

How dry it was on a far-back day
    When straws hung the hedge and around,
When amid the sheaves in amorous play
In curtained bonnets and light array
    Bloomed a bevy now underground!

Bockhampton Lane

Voices from Things Growing in a Churchyard[15]

THESE flowers are I, poor Fanny Hurd,
      Sir or Madam,
A little girl here sepultured.
Once I flit-fluttered like a bird
Above the grass, as now I wave
In daisy shapes above my grave,
      All day cheerily,
      All night eerily!

– I am one Bachelor Bowring, 'Gent',
      Sir or Madam;
In shingled oak my bones were pent;
Hence more than a hundred years I spent
In my feat of change from a coffin-thrall
To a dancer in green as leaves on a wall,
      All day cheerily,
      All night eerily!

– I, these berries of juice and gloss,
      Sir or Madam,
Am clean forgotten as Thomas Voss;
Thin-urned, I have burrowed away from the moss
That covers my sod, and have entered this yew,
And turned to clusters ruddy of view,
      All day cheerily,
      All night eerily!

– The Lady Gertrude, proud, high-bred,
      Sir or Madam,
Am I – this laurel that shades your head;
Into its veins I have stilly sped,
And made them of me; and my leaves now shine,
As did my satins superfine,
      All day cheerily,
      All night eerily!

– I, who as innocent withwind climb,
      Sir or Madam,

Am one Eve Greensleeves, in olden time
Kissed by men from many a clime,
Beneath sun, stars, in blaze, in breeze,
As now by glowworms and by bees,
      All day cheerily,
      All night eerily!*

– I'm old Squire Audeley Grey, who grew,
      Sir or Madam,
Aweary of life, and in scorn withdrew;
Till anon I clambered up anew
As ivy-green, when my ache was stayed,
And in that attire I have longtime gayed
      All day cheerily,
      All night eerily!

– And so these maskers breathe to each
      Sir or Madam
Who lingers there, and their lively speech
Affords an interpreter much to teach,
As their murmurous accents seem to come
Thence hitheraround in a radiant hum,
      All day cheerily,
      All night eerily!

Jubilate

'The very last time I ever was here,' he said,
'I saw much less of the quick than I saw of the dead.'
– He was a man I had met with somewhere before,
But how or when I now could recall no more.

'The hazy mazy moonlight at one in the morning
Spread out as a sea across the frozen snow,
Glazed to live sparkles like the great breastplate adorning
The priest of the Temple, with Urim and Thummim aglow.

* It was said her real name was Eve Trevillian or Trevelyan; and that she
was the handsome mother of two or three illegitimate children, *circa* 1784–95.

'The yew-tree arms, glued hard to the stiff stark air,
Hung still in the village sky as theatre-scenes
When I came by the churchyard wall, and halted there
At a shut-in sound of fiddles and tambourines.

'And as I stood hearkening, dulcimers, hautboys, and shawms,
And violoncellos, and a three-stringed double-bass,
Joined in, and were intermixed with a singing of psalms;
And I looked over at the dead men's dwelling-place.

'Through the shine of the slippery snow I now could see,
As it were through a crystal roof, a great company
Of the dead minueting in stately step underground
To the tune of the instruments I had before heard sound.

'It was "Eden New", and dancing they sang in a chore,
"We are out of it all! – yea, in Little-Ease cramped no more!"
And their shrouded figures pacing with joy I could see
As you see the stage from the gallery. And they had no heed of
    me.

'And I lifted my head quite dazed from the churchyard wall
And I doubted not that it warned I should soon have my call.
But –' . . . Then in the ashes he emptied the dregs of his cup,
And onward he went, and the darkness swallowed him up.

The Second Visit

CLACK, clack, clack, went the mill-wheel as I came,
And she was on the bridge with the thin hand-rail,
And the miller at the door, and the ducks at mill-tail;
I come again years after, and all there seems the same.

    And so indeed it is: the apple-tree'd old house,
And the deep mill-pond, and the wet wheel clacking,
And a woman on the bridge, and white ducks quacking,
And the miller at the door, powdered pale from boots to brows.

But it's not the same miller whom long ago I knew,
Nor are they the same apples, nor the same drops that dash

Over the wet wheel, nor the ducks below that splash,
Nor the woman who to fond plaints replied, 'You know I do!'

In Front of the Landscape

PLUNGING and labouring on in a tide of visions,
    Dolorous and dear,
Forward I pushed my way as amid waste waters
    Stretching around,
Through whose eddies there glimmered the customed landscape
    Yonder and near

Blotted to feeble mist. And the coomb and the upland
    Coppice-crowned,
Ancient chalk-pit, milestone, rills in the grass-flat
    Stroked by the light,
Seemed but a ghost-like gauze, and no substantial
    Meadow or mound.

What were the infinite spectacles featuring foremost
    Under my sight,
Hindering me to discern my paced advancement
    Lengthening to miles;
What were the re-creations killing the daytime
    As by the night?

O they were speechful faces, gazing insistent,
    Some as with smiles,
Some as with slow-born tears that brinily trundled
    Over the wrecked
Cheeks that were fair in their flush-time, ash now with anguish,
    Harrowed by wiles.

Yes, I could see them, feel them, hear them, address them –
    Halo-bedecked –
And, alas, onwards, shaken by fierce unreason,
    Rigid in hate,
Smitten by years-long wryness born of misprision,
    Dreaded, suspect.

Then there would breast me shining sights, sweet seasons
     Further in date;
Instruments of strings with the tenderest passion
     Vibrant, beside
Lamps long extinguished, robes, cheeks, eyes with the earth's
     crust
     Now corporate.

Also there rose a headland of hoary aspect
     Gnawed by the tide,
Frilled by the nimb of the morning as two friends stood there
     Guilelessly glad –
Wherefore they knew not – touched by the fringe of an ecstasy
     Scantly descried.

Later images too did the day unfurl me,
     Shadowed and sad,
Clay cadavers of those who had shared in the dramas,
     Laid now at ease,
Passions all spent, chiefest the one of the broad brow
     Sepulture-clad.

So did beset me scenes, miscalled of the bygone,
     Over the leaze,
Past the clump, and down to where lay the beheld ones;
     – Yea, as the rhyme
Sung by the sea-swell, so in their pleading dumbness
     Captured me these.

For, their lost revisiting manifestations
     In their live time
Much had I slighted, caring not for their purport,
     Seeing behind
Things more coveted, reckoned the better worth calling
     Sweet, sad, sublime.

Thus do they now show hourly before the intenser
     Stare of the mind
As they were ghosts avenging their slights by my bypast
     Body-borne eyes,

Show, too, with fuller translation than rested upon them
    As living kind.

Hence wag the tongues of the passing people, saying
    In their surmise,
'Ah – whose is this dull form that perambulates, seeing nought
    Round him that looms
Whithersoever his footsteps turn in his farings,
    Save a few tombs?'

On an Invitation to the United States

I

MY ardours for emprize nigh lost
Since Life has bared its bones to me,
I shrink to seek a modern coast
Whose riper times have yet to be;
Where the new regions claim them free
From that long drip of human tears
Which peoples old in tragedy
Have left upon the centuried years.

II

For, wonning in these ancient lands,
Enchased and lettered as a tomb,
And scored with prints of perished hands,
And chronicled with dates of doom,
Though my own Being bear no bloom
I trace the lives such scenes enshrine,
Give past exemplars present room,
And their experience count as mine.

The Farm-Woman's Winter

I

IF seasons all were summers,
    And leaves would never fall,
And hopping casement-comers
    Were foodless not at all,

And fragile folk might be here
    That white winds bid depart;
Then one I used to see here
    Would warm my wasted heart!

II

One frail, who, bravely tilling
    Long hours in gripping gusts,
Was mastered by their chilling,
    And now his ploughshare rusts.
So savage winter catches
    The breath of limber things,
And what I love he snatches,
    And what I love not, brings.

Night-Time in Mid-Fall

IT is a storm-strid night, winds footing swift
    Through the blind profound;
  I know the happenings from their sound;
Leaves totter down still green, and spin and drift;
The tree-trunks rock to their roots, which wrench and lift
The loam where they run onward underground.

The streams are muddy and swollen; eels migrate
    To a new abode;
  Even cross, 'tis said, the turnpike-road;
(Men's feet have felt their crawl, home-coming late):
The westward fronts of towers are saturate,
Church-timbers crack, and witches ride abroad.

A Sheep Fair [16]

THE day arrives of the autumn fair,
    And torrents fall,
Though sheep in throngs are gathered there,
    Ten thousand all,
Sodden, with hurdles round them reared:

And, lot by lot, the pens are cleared,
And the auctioneer wrings out his beard,
And wipes his book, bedrenched and smeared,
And rakes the rain from his face with the edge of his hand,
    As torrents fall.

The wool of the ewes is like a sponge
    With the daylong rain:
Jammed tight, to turn, or lie, or lunge,
    They strive in vain.
Their horns are soft as finger-nails,
Their shepherds reek against the rails,
The tied dogs soak with tucked-in tails,
The buyers' hat-brims fill like pails,
Which spill small cascades when they shift their stand
    In the daylong rain.

POSTSCRIPT

Time has trailed lengthily since met
    At Pummery Fair
Those panting thousands in their wet
    And woolly wear:
And every flock long since has bled,
And all the dripping buyers have sped,
And the hoarse auctioneer is dead,
Who 'Going – going!' so often said,
As he consigned to doom each meek, mewed band
    At Pummery Fair.

Vagrant's Song[17]

(WITH AN OLD WESSEX REFRAIN)

I

WHEN a dark-eyed dawn
    Crawls forth, cloud-drawn,
And starlings doubt the night-time's close;
    And 'three months yet,'
    They seem to fret,

'Before we cease us slaves of snows,
    And sun returns
    To loose the burns,
And this wild woe called Winter goes!' –
    O a hollow tree
    Is as good for me
    As a house where the back-brand* glows!
Che-hane, mother; che-hane, mother,
    As a house where the back-brand glows!

II

    When autumn brings
    A whirr of wings
Among the evergreens around,
    And sundry thrills
    About their quills
Awe rooks, and misgivings abound,
    And the joyless pines
    In leaning lines
Protect from gales the lower ground,
    O a hollow tree
    Is as good for me
    As a house of a thousand pound!
Che-hane, mother; che-hane, mother,
    As a house of a thousand pound!

Shortening Days at the Homestead

THE first fire since the summer is lit, and is smoking into the
    room:
    The sun-rays thread it through, like woof-lines in a loom.
    Sparrows spurt from the hedge, whom misgivings appal
That winter did not leave last year for ever, after all.
    Like shock-headed urchins, spiny-haired,
    Stand pollard willows, their twigs just bared.

* 'back-brand' – the log which used to be laid at the back of a wood fire.

Who is this coming with pondering pace,
Black and ruddy, with white embossed,
His eyes being black, and ruddy his face,
And the marge of his hair like morning frost?
      It's the cider-maker,
      And appletree-shaker,
And behind him on wheels, in readiness,
His mill, and tubs, and vat, and press.

An Unkindly May

A SHEPHERD stands by a gate in a white smock-frock:
He holds the gate ajar, intently counting his flock.

The sour spring wind is blurting boisterous-wise,
And bears on it dirty clouds across the skies;
Plantation timbers creak like rusty cranes,
And pigeons and rooks, dishevelled by late rains,
Are like gaunt vultures, sodden and unkempt,
And song-birds do not end what they attempt:
The buds have tried to open, but quite failing
Have pinched themselves together in their quailing.
The sun frowns whitely in eye-trying flaps
Through passing cloud-holes, mimicking audible taps.
'Nature, you're not commendable to-day!'
I think. 'Better to-morrow!' she seems to say.

That shepherd still stands in that white smock-frock,
Unnoting all things save the counting his flock.

Throwing a Tree

NEW FOREST

THE two executioners stalk along over the knolls,
Bearing two axes with heavy heads shining and wide,
And a long limp two-handled saw toothed for cutting great
    boles,
And so they approach the proud tree that bears the death-mark
    on its side.

Jackets doffed they swing axes and chop away just above
ground,
And the chips fly about and lie white on the moss and fallen
leaves;
Till a broad deep gash in the bark is hewn all the way round,
And one of them tries to hook upward a rope, which at last he
achieves.

The saw then begins, till the top of the tall giant shivers:
The shivers are seen to grow greater each cut than before:
They edge out the saw, tug the rope; but the tree only
quivers,
And kneeling and sawing again, they step back to try pulling
once more.

Then, lastly, the living mast sways, further sways: with a
shout
Job and Ike rush aside. Reached the end of its long staying
powers
The tree crashes downward: it shakes all its neighbours
throughout,
And two hundred years' steady growth has been ended in less
than two hours.

The Jubilee of a Magazine[18]

(TO THE EDITOR)

YES; your up-dated modern page –
All flower-fresh, as it appears –
Can claim a time-tried lineage,

That reaches backward fifty years
(Which, if but short for sleepy squires,
Is much in magazines' careers).

– Here, on your cover, never tires
The sower, reaper, thresher, while
As through the seasons of our sires

Each wills to work in ancient style
With seedlip, sickle, share and flail,
Though modes have since moved many a mile!

The steel-roped plough now rips the vale,
With cog and tooth the sheaves are won,
Wired wheels drum out the wheat like hail;

But if we ask, what has been done
To unify the mortal lot
Since your bright leaves first saw the sun,

Beyond mechanic furtherance – what
Advance can rightness, candour, claim?
Truth bends abashed, and answers not.

Despite your volumes' gentle aim
To straighten visions wry and wrong,
Events jar onward much the same!

– Had custom tended to prolong,
As on your golden page engrained,
Old processes of blade and prong,

And best invention been retained
For high crusades to lessen tears
Throughout the race, the world had gained! . . .
But too much, this, for fifty years.

Great Things

SWEET cyder is a great thing,
    A great thing to me,
Spinning down to Weymouth town
    By Ridgway thirstily,
And maid and mistress summoning
    Who tend the hostelry:
O cyder is a great thing,
    A great thing to me!

88

The dance it is a great thing,
  A great thing to me,
With candles lit and partners fit
  For night-long revelry;
And going home when day-dawning
  Peeps pale upon the lea:
O dancing is a great thing,
  A great thing to me!

Love is, yea, a great thing,
  A great thing to me,
When, having drawn across the lawn
  In darkness silently,
A figure flits like one a-wing
  Out from the nearest tree:
O love is, yes, a great thing,
  A great thing to me!

Will these be always great things,
  Great things to me? . . .
Let it befall that One will call,
  'Soul, I have need of thee:'
What then? Joy-jaunts, impassioned flings,
  Love, and its ecstasy,
Will always have been great things,
  Great things to me!

Any Little Old Song

ANY little old song
  Will do for me,
Tell it of joys gone long,
  Or joys to be,
Or friendly faces best
  Loved to see.

Newest themes I want not
  On subtle strings,

And for thrillings pant not
That new song brings:
I only need the homeliest
Of heartstirrings.

Timing Her

(WRITTEN TO AN OLD FOLK-TUNE)

LALAGE'S coming:
Where is she now, O?
Turning to bow, O,
And smile, is she,
Just at parting,
Parting, parting,
As she is starting
To come to me?

Where is she now, O,
Now, and now, O,
Shadowing a bough, O,
Of hedge or tree
As she is rushing,
Rushing, rushing,
Gossamers brushing
To come to me?

Lalage's coming;
Where is she now, O;
Climbing the brow, O,
Of hills I see?
Yes, she is nearing,
Nearing, nearing,
Weather unfearing
To come to me.

Near is she now, O,
Now, and now, O;
Milk the rich cow, O,
Forward the tea;

Shake the down bed for her,
Linen sheets spread for her,
Drape round the head for her
Coming to me.

Lalage's coming,
She's nearer now, O,
End anyhow, O,
To-day's husbandry!
Would a gilt chair were mine,
Slippers of vair were mine,
Brushes for hair were mine
Of ivory!

What will she think, O,
She who's so comely,
Viewing how homely
A sort are we!
Nothing resplendent,
No prompt attendant,
Not one dependent
Pertaining to me!

Lalage's coming;
Where is she now, O?
Fain I'd avow, O,
Full honestly
Nought here's enough for her,
All is too rough for her,
Even my love for her
Poor in degree.

She's nearer now, O,
Still nearer now, O,
She 'tis, I vow, O,
Passing the lea.
Rush down to meet her there,
Call out and greet her there,
Never a sweeter there
Crossed to me!

Lalage's come; aye,
Come is she now, O! . . .
Does Heaven allow, O,
A meeting to be?
Yes, she is here now,
Here now, here now,
Nothing to fear now,
Here's Lalage!

The Night of the Dance

THE cold moon hangs to the sky by its horn,
    And centres its gaze on me;
The stars, like eyes in reverie,
Their westering as for a while forborne,
    Quiz downward curiously.

Old Robert draws the backbrand in,
    The green logs steam and spit;
The half-awakened sparrows flit
From the riddled thatch; and owls begin
    To whoo from the gable-slit.

Yes; far and nigh things seem to know
    Sweet scenes are impending here;
That all is prepared; that the hour is near
For welcomes, fellowships, and flow
    Of sally, song, and cheer;

That spigots are pulled and viols strung;
    That soon will arise the sound
Of measures trod to tunes renowned;
That She will return in Love's low tongue
    My vows as we wheel around.

Julie-Jane

SING; how 'a would sing!
How 'a would raise the tune
When we rode in the waggon from harvesting
    By the light o' the moon!

Dance; how 'a would dance!
If a fiddlestring did but sound
She would hold out her coats, give a slanting glance,
 And go round and round.

Laugh; how 'a would laugh!
Her peony lips would part
As if none such a place for a lover to quaff
 At the deeps of a heart.

Julie, O girl of joy,
Soon, soon that lover he came.
Ah, yes; and gave thee a baby-boy,
 But never his name . . .

– Tolling for her, as you guess;
And the baby too . . . 'Tis well.
You knew her in maidhood likewise? – Yes,
 That's her burial bell.

'I suppose,' with a laugh, she said,
'I should blush that I'm not a wife;
But how can it matter, so soon to be dead,
 What one does in life!'

When we sat making the mourning
By her death-bed side, said she,
'Dears, how can you keep from your lovers, adorning
 In honour of me!'

Bubbling and brightsome eyed!
But now – O never again.
She chose her bearers before she died
 From her fancy-men.

NOTE. – It is, or was, a common custom in Wessex, and probably other country places, to prepare the mourning beside the death-bed, the dying person sometimes assisting, who also selects his or her bearers on such occasions.

'Coats' (line 7), old name for petticoats.

Let Me Enjoy

I

LET me enjoy the earth no less
Because the all-enacting Might
That fashioned forth its loveliness
Had other aims than my delight.

II

About my path there flits a Fair,
Who throws me not a word or sign;
I'll charm me with her ignoring air,
And laud the lips not meant for mine.

III

From manuscripts of moving song
Inspired by scenes and dreams unknown
I'll pour out raptures that belong
To others, as they were my own.

IV

And some day hence, towards Paradise
And all its blest – if such should be –
I will lift glad, afar-off eyes,
Though it contain no place for me.

The Ballad-Singer

SING, Ballad-singer, raise a hearty tune;
Make me forget that there was ever a one
I walked with in the meek light of the moon
　　When the day's work was done.

Rhyme, Ballad-rhymer, start a country song;
Make me forget that she whom I loved well
Swore she would love me dearly, love me long,
　　Then – what I cannot tell!

Sing, Ballad-singer, from your little book;
Make me forget those heart-breaks, achings, fears;
Make me forget her name, her sweet sweet look –
     Make me forget her tears.

Former Beauties

THESE market-dames, mid-aged, with lips thin-drawn,
     And tissues sere,
Are they the ones we loved in years agone,
     And courted here?

Are these the muslined pink young things to whom
     We vowed and swore
In nooks on summer Sundays by the Froom,
     Or Budmouth shore?

Do they remember those gay tunes we trod
     Clasped on the green;
Aye; trod till moonlight set on the beaten sod
     A satin sheen?

They must forget, forget! They cannot know
     What once they were,
Or memory would transfigure them, and show
     Them always fair.

Seen by the Waits

THROUGH snowy woods and shady
     We went to play a tune
To the lonely manor-lady
     By the light of the Christmas moon.

We violed till, upward glancing
     To where a mirror leaned,
It showed her airily dancing,
     Deeming her movements screened;

Dancing alone in the room there,
    Thin-draped in her robe of night;
Her postures, glassed in the gloom there,
    Were a strange phantasmal sight.

She had learnt (we heard when homing)
    That her roving spouse was dead:
Why she had danced in the gloaming
    We thought, but never said.

Apostrophe to an Old Psalm Tune[19]

I MET you first – ah, when did I first meet you?
When I was full of wonder, and innocent,
Standing meek-eyed with those of choric bent,
    While dimming day grew dimmer
      In the pulpit-glimmer.

Much riper in years I met you – in a temple
Where summer sunset streamed upon our shapes,
And you spread over me like a gauze that drapes,
    And flapped from floor to rafters,
      Sweet as angels' laughters.

But you had been stripped of some of your old vesture
By Monk, or another. Now you wore no frill,
And at first you startled me. But I knew you still,
    Though I missed the minim's waver,
      And the dotted quaver.

I grew accustomed to you thus. And you hailed me
Through one who evoked you often. Then at last
Your raiser was borne off, and I mourned you had passed
    From my life with your late outsetter;
      Till I said, ''Tis better!'

But you waylaid me. I rose and went as a ghost goes,
And said, eyes-full: 'I'll never hear it again!
It is overmuch for scathed and memoried men
    When sitting among strange people
      Under their steeple.'

Now, a new stirrer of tones calls you up before me
And wakes your speech, as she of Endor did
(When sought by Saul who, in disguises hid,
    Fell down on the earth to hear it)
        Samuel's spirit.

So, your quired oracles beat till they make me tremble
As I discern your mien in the old attire,
Here in these turmoiled years of belligerent fire
    Living still on – and onward, maybe,
        Till Doom's great day be!

Sunday, 13 August 1916

A Merrymaking in Question

'I WILL get a new string for my fiddle,
    And call to the neighbours to come,
And partners shall dance down the middle
    Until the old pewter-wares hum:
    And we'll sip the mead, cyder, and rum!'

From the night came the oddest of answers:
    A hollow wind, like a bassoon,
And headstones all ranged up as dancers,
    And cypresses droning a croon,
    And gurgoyles that mouthed to the tune.

Reminiscences of a Dancing Man[20]

I

WHO now remembers Almack's balls –
    Willis's sometime named –
In those two smooth-floored upper halls
    For faded ones so famed?
Where as we trod to trilling sound
The fancied phantoms stood around,
    Or joined us in the maze,

Of the powdered Dears from Georgian years,
Whose dust lay in sightless sealed-up biers,
    The fairest of former days.

II

Who now remembers gay Cremorne,
    And all its jaunty jills,
And those wild whirling figures born
    Of Jullien's grand quadrilles?
With hats on head and morning coats
There footed to his prancing notes
    Our partner-girls and we;
And the gas-jets winked, and the lustres clinked,
And the platform throbbed as with arms enlinked
    We moved to the minstrelsy.

III

Who now recalls those crowded rooms
    Of old yclept 'The Argyle',
Where to the deep Drum-polka's booms
    We hopped in standard style?
Whither have danced those damsels now!
Is Death the partner who doth moue
    Their wormy chaps and bare?
Do their spectres spin like sparks within
The smoky halls of the Prince of Sin
    To a thunderous Jullien air?

An Ancient to Ancients

WHERE once we danced, where once we sang,
    Gentlemen,
The floors are sunken, cobwebs hang,
And cracks creep; worms have fed upon
The doors. Yea, sprightlier times were then
Than now, with harps and tabrets gone,
    Gentlemen!

Where once we rowed, where once we sailed,
　　　Gentlemen,
And damsels took the tiller, veiled
Against too strong a stare (God wot
Their fancy, then or anywhen!)
Upon that shore we are clean forgot,
　　　Gentlemen!

We have lost somewhat, afar and near,
　　　Gentlemen,
The thinning of our ranks each year
Affords a hint we are nigh undone,
That we shall not be ever again
The marked of many, loved of one,
　　　Gentlemen.

In dance the polka hit our wish,
　　　Gentlemen,
The paced quadrille, the spry schottische,
'Sir Roger'. – And in opera spheres
The 'Girl' (the famed 'Bohemian'),
And 'Trovatore', held the ears,
　　　Gentlemen.

This season's paintings do not please,
　　　Gentlemen,
Like Etty, Mulready, Maclise;
Throbbing romance has waned and waned,
No wizard wields the witching pen
Of Bulwer, Scott, Dumas, and Sand,
　　　Gentlemen.

The bower we shrined to Tennyson,
　　　Gentlemen,
Is roof-wrecked; damps there drip upon
Sagged seats, the creeper-nails are rust,
The spider is sole denizen;
Even she who voiced those rhymes is dust,
　　　Gentlemen!

We who met sunrise sanguine-souled,
      Gentlemen,
Are wearing weary. We are old;
These younger press; we feel our root
Is imminent to Aïdes' den, –
That evening shades are stretching out,
      Gentlemen!

And yet, though ours be failing frames,
      Gentlemen,
So were some others' history names,
Who trode their track light-limbed and fast
As these youth, and not alien
From enterprise, to their long last,
      Gentlemen.

Sophocles, Plato, Socrates,
      Gentlemen,
Pythagoras, Thucydides,
Herodotus, and Homer, – yea,
Clement, Augustin, Origen,
Burnt brightlier towards their setting-day,
      Gentlemen.

And ye, red-lipped and smooth-browed; list,
      Gentlemen;
Much is there waits you we have missed;
Much lore we leave you worth the knowing,
Much, much has lain outside our ken:
Nay, rush not: time serves: we are going,
      Gentlemen.

Music in a Snowy Street

THE weather is sharp,
But the girls are unmoved:
One wakes from a harp,
The next from a viol,
A strain that I loved
When life was no trial.

The tripletime beat
Bounds forth on the snow,
But the spry springing feet
Of a century ago,
And the arms that enlaced
As the couples embraced,
Are silent old bones
Under graying gravestones.

The snow-feathers sail
Across the harp-strings,
Whose throbbing threads wail
Like love-satiate things.
Each lyre's grimy mien,
With its rout-raising tune,
Against the new white
Of the flake-laden noon,
Is incongruous to sight,
Hinting years they have seen
Of revel at night
Ere these damsels became
Possessed of their frame.

O bygone whirls, heys,
Crotchets, quavers, the same
That were danced in the days
Of grim Bonaparte's fame,
Or even by the toes
Of the fair Antoinette, –
Yea, old notes like those
Here are living on yet! –
But of their fame and fashion
How little these know
Who strum without passion
For pence, in the snow!

Song to an Old Burden[21]

THE feet have left the wormholed flooring,
    That danced to the ancient air,
    The fiddler, all-ignoring,
Sleeps by the gray-grassed 'cello player:
Shall I then foot around around around,
    As once I footed there!

The voice is heard in the room no longer
    That trilled, none sweetlier,
    To gentle stops or stronger,
Where now the dust-draped cobwebs stir:
Shall I then sing again again again,
    As once I sang with her!

The eyes that beamed out rapid brightness
    Have longtime found their close,
    The cheeks have wanned to whiteness
That used to sort with summer rose:
Shall I then joy anew anew anew,
    As once I joyed in those!

O what's to me this tedious Maying,
    What's to me this June?
    O why should viols be playing
To catch and reel and rigadoon?
Shall I sing, dance around around around,
    When phantoms call the tune!

The Bride-Night Fire[22]

(A WESSEX TRADITION)

THEY had long met o' Zundays – her true love and she –
    And at junketings, maypoles, and flings;
But she bode wi' a thirtover uncle, and he
Swore by noon and by night that her goodman should be

thirtover, cross

Naibour Sweatley – a wight often weak at the knee
From taking o' sommat more cheerful than tea –
  Who tranted, and moved people's things.

She cried, 'O pray pity me!' Nought would he hear;
  Then with wild rainy eyes she obeyed.
She chid when her Love was for clinking off wi' her:
The pa'son was told, as the season drew near,
To throw over pu'pit the names of the pair
  As fitting one flesh to be made.

The wedding-day dawned and the morning drew on;
  The couple stood bridegroom and bride;
The evening was passed, and when midnight had gone
The feasters horned, 'God save the King,' and anon
  The pair took their homealong ride.

The lover Tim Tankens mourned heart-sick and leer
  To be thus of his darling deprived:
He roamed in the dark ath'art field, mound, and mere,
And, a'most without knowing it, found himself near
The house of the tranter, and now of his Dear,
  Where the lantern-light showed 'em arrived.

The bride sought her chamber so calm and so pale
  That a Northern had thought her resigned;
But to eyes that had seen her in tidetimes of weal,
Like the white cloud o' smoke, the red battlefield's vail,
  That look spak' of havoc behind.

The bridegroom yet laitered a beaker to drain,
  Then reeled to the linhay for more,
When the candle-snoff kindled some chaff from his grain –
Flames spread, and red vlankers wi' might and wi' main
  Around beams, thatch, and chimley-tun roar.

tranted, traded as carrier	*horned*, sang loudly
homealong, homeward	*leer*, empty-stomached
tidetimes, holidays	*linhay*, lean-to building
vlankers, fire-flakes	*chimley-tun*, chimney-stack

Young Tim away yond, rafted up by the light,
  Through brimbles and underwood tears,
Till he comes to the orchet, when crooping from sight
In the lewth of a codlin-tree, bivering wi' fright,
Wi' on'y her night-rail to cover her plight,
  His lonesome young Barbree appears.

Her cwold little figure half-naked he views
  Played about by the frolicsome breeze,
Her light-tripping totties, her ten little tooes,
All bare and besprinkled wi' Fall's chilly dews,
While her great gallied eyes through her hair hanging loose
  Shone as stars through a tardle o' trees.

She eyed him; and, as when a weir-hatch is drawn,
  Her tears, penned by terror afore,
With a rushing of sobs in a shower were strawn,
Till her power to pour 'em seemed wasted and gone
  From the heft o' misfortune she bore.

'O Tim, my *own* Tim I must call 'ee – I will!
  All the world has turned round on me so!
Can you help her who loved 'ee, though acting so ill?
Can you pity her misery – feel for her still?
When worse than her body so quivering and chill
  Is her heart in its winter o' woe!

'I think I mid almost ha' borne it,' she said,
  'Had my griefs one by one come to hand;
But O, to be slave to thik husbird, for bread,
And then, upon top o' that, driven to wed,
And then, upon top o' that, burnt out o' bed,
  Is more than my nater can stand!'

rafted, roused	*crooping*. squatting down
lewth, shelter	*bivering*, with chattering teeth
totties, feet	*Fall*, autumn
gallied, frightened	*tardle*, entanglement
heft, weight	*mid*, might
thik husbird, that rascal	

Like a lion 'ithin en Tim's spirit outsprung –
(Tim had a great soul when his feelings were wrung) –
   'Feel for 'ee, dear Barbree?' he cried;
And his warm working-jacket then straightway he flung
Round about her, and horsed her by jerks, till she clung
Like a chiel on a gipsy, her figure uphung
    By the sleeves that he tightly had tied.

Over piggeries, and mixens, and apples, and hay,
   They lumpered straight into the night;
And finding ere long where a halter-path lay,
Sighted Tim's house by dawn, on'y seen on their way
By a naibour or two who were up wi' the day,
    But who gathered no clue to the sight.

Then tender Tim Tankens he searched here and there
   For some garment to clothe her fair skin;
But though he had breeches and waistcosts to spare,
He had nothing quite seemly for Barbree to wear,
Who, half shrammed to death, stood and cried on a chair
    At the caddle she found herself in.

There was one thing to do, and that one thing he did,
   He lent her some clothes of his own,
And she took 'em perforce; and while swiftly she slid
Them upon her Tim turned to the winder, as bid,
Thinking, 'O that the picter my duty keeps hid
    To the sight o' my eyes mid be shown!'

In the tallet he stowed her; there huddied she lay,
   Shortening sleeves, legs, and tails to her limbs;
But most o' the time in a mortal bad way,
Well knowing that there'd be the divel to pay
If 'twere found that, instead o' the element's prey,
    She was living in lodgings at Tim's.

mixens, manure-heaps	*lumpered*, stumbled
halter-path, bridle-path	*shrammed*, numbed
caddle, quandary	*mid*, might
tallet, loft	*huddied*, hidden

'Where's the tranter?' said men and boys; 'where can he be?'
'Where's the tranter?' said Barbree alone.
'Where on e'th is the tranter?' said everybod-y:
They sifted the dust of his perished roof-tree,
    And all they could find was a bone.

Then the uncle cried, 'Lord, pray have mercy on me!'
    And in terror began to repent.
But before 'twas complete, and till sure she was free,
Barbree drew up her loft-ladder, tight turned her key –
Tim bringing up breakfast and dinner and tea –
    Till the news of her hiding got vent.

Then followed the custom-kept rout, shout, and flare
Of a skimmity-ride through the naibourhood, ere
    Folk had proof o' wold Sweatley's decay.
Whereupon decent people all stood in a stare,
Saying Tim and his lodger should risk it, and pair:
So he took her to church. An' some laughing lads there
Cried to Tim, 'After Sweatley!' She said, 'I declare
    I stand as a maiden to-day!'

Written 1866; printed 1875

The Dance at the Phoenix

To Jenny came a gentle youth
    From inland leazes lone,
His love was fresh as apple-blooth
    By Parrett, Yeo, or Tone.
And duly he entreated her
To be his tender minister,
    And take him for her own.

Now Jenny's life had hardly been
    A life of modesty;
And few in Casterbridge had seen
    More loves of sorts than she

skimmity-ride, satirical procession with effigies   *wold*, old

From scarcely sixteen years above;
Among them sundry troopers of
    The King's-Own Cavalry.

But each with charger, sword, and gun,
    Had bluffed the Biscay wave;
And Jenny prized her rural one
    For all the love he gave.
She vowed to be, if they were wed,
His honest wife in heart and head
    From bride-ale hour to grave.

Wedded they were. Her husband's trust
    In Jenny knew no bound,
And Jenny kept her pure and just,
    Till even malice found
No sin or sign of ill to be
In one who walked so decently
    The duteous helpmate's round.

Two sons were born, and bloomed to men,
    And roamed, and were as not:
Alone was Jenny left again
    As ere her mind had sought
A solace in domestic joys,
And ere the vanished pair of boys
    Were sent to sun her cot.

She numbered near on sixty years,
    And passed as elderly,
When, on a day, with flushing fears,
    She learnt from shouts of glee,
And shine of swords, and thump of drum,
Her early loves from war had come,
    The King's-Own Cavalry.

She turned aside, and bowed her head
    Anigh Saint Peter's door;
'Alas for chastened thoughts!' she said;
    'I'm faded now, and hoar,

And yet those notes – they thrill me through,
And those gay forms move me anew
    As they moved me of yore!' . . .

'Twas Christmas, and the Phoenix Inn
    Was lit with tapers tall,
For thirty of the trooper men
    Had vowed to give a ball
As 'Theirs' had done ('twas handed down)
When lying in the selfsame town
    Ere Buonaparte's fall.

That night the throbbing 'Soldier's Joy',
    The measured tread and sway
Of 'Fancy-Lad' and 'Maiden Coy',
    Reached Jenny as she lay
Beside her spouse; till springtide blood
Seemed scouring through her like a flood
    That whisked the years away.

She rose, arrayed, and decked her head
    Where the bleached hairs grew thin;
Upon her cap two bows of red
    She fixed with hasty pin;
Unheard descending to the street
She trod the flags with tune-led feet,
    And stood before the Inn.

Save for the dancers', not a sound
    Disturbed the icy air;
No watchman on his midnight round
    Or traveller was there;
But over All-Saints', high and bright,
Pulsed to the music Sirius white,
    The Wain by Bullstake Square.

She knocked, but found her further stride
    Checked by a sergeant tall:
'Gay Granny, whence come you?' he cried;
    'This is a private ball.'

– 'No one has more right here than me!
Ere you were born, man,' answered she,
    'I knew the regiment all!'

'Take not the lady's visit ill!'
    The steward said; 'for see,
We lack sufficient partners still,
    So, prithee, let her be!'
They seized and whirled her mid the maze,
And Jenny felt as in the days
    Of her immodesty.

Hour chased each hour, and night advanced;
    She sped as shod with wings;
Each time and every time she danced –
    Reels, jigs, poussettes, and flings:
They cheered her as she soared and swooped,
(She had learnt ere art in dancing drooped
    From hops to slothful swings).

The favourite Quick-step 'Speed the Plough' –
    (Cross hands, cast off, and wheel) –
'The Triumph', 'Sylph', 'The Row-dow-dow',
    Famed 'Major Malley's Reel',
'The Duke of York's', 'The Fairy Dance',
'The Bridge of Lodi' (brought from France),
    She beat out, toe and heel.

The 'Fall of Paris' clanged its close,
    And Peter's chime went four,
When Jenny, bosom-beating, rose
    To seek her silent door.
They tiptoed in escorting her,
Lest stroke of heel or clink of spur
    Should break her goodman's snore.

The fire that lately burnt fell slack
    When lone at last was she;
Her nine-and-fifty years came back;
    She sank upon her knee

Beside the durn, and like a dart
A something arrowed through her heart
    In shoots of agony.

Their footsteps died as she leant there,
    Lit by the morning star
Hanging above the moorland, where
    The aged elm-rows are;
As overnight, from Pummery Ridge
To Maembury Ring and Standfast Bridge
    No life stirred, near or far.

Though inner mischief worked amain,
    She reached her husband's side;
Where, toil-weary, as he had lain
    Beneath the patchwork pied
When forthward yestereve she crept,
And as unwitting, still he slept
    Who did in her confide.

A tear sprang as she turned and viewed
    His features free from guile;
She kissed him long, as when, just wooed,
    She chose his domicile.
She felt she would give more than life
To be the single-hearted wife
    That she had been erstwhile . . .

Time wore to six. Her husband rose
    And struck the steel and stone;
He glanced at Jenny, whose repose
    Seemed deeper than his own.
With dumb dismay, on closer sight,
He gathered sense that in the night,
    Or morn, her soul had flown.

When told that some too mighty strain
    For one so many-yeared
Had burst her bosom's master-vein,
    His doubts remained unstirred.

His Jenny had not left his side
Betwixt the eve and morning-tide:
   – The King's said not a word.

Well! times are not as times were then,
   Nor fair ones half so free;
And truly they were martial men,
   The King's-Own Cavalry.
And when they went from Casterbridge
And vanished over Mellstock Ridge,
   'Twas saddest morn to see.

News for Her Mother

I

One mile more is
Where your door is,
   Mother mine! –
Harvest's coming,
Mills are strumming,
   Apples fine,
And the cider made to-year will be as wine.

II

Yet, not viewing
What's a-doing
   Here around
Is it thrills me,
And so fills me
   That I bound
Like a ball or leaf or lamb along the ground.

III

Tremble not now
At your lot now,
   Silly soul!
Hosts have sped them

Quick to wed them,
Great and small,
Since the first two sighing half-hearts made a whole.

IV

Yet I wonder,
Will it sunder
Her from me?
Will she guess that
I said 'Yes,' – that
His I'd be,
Ere I thought she might not see him as I see!

V

Old brown gable,
Granary, stable,
Here you are!
O my mother,
Can another
Ever bar
Mine from thy heart, make thy nearness seem afar?

The Ruined Maid[23]

'O 'MELIA, my dear, this does everything crown!
Who could have supposed I should meet you in Town?
And whence such fair garments, such prosperi-ty?' –
'O didn't you know I'd been ruined?' said she.

– 'You left us in tatters, without shoes or socks,
Tired of digging potatoes, and spudding up docks;
And now you've gay bracelets and bright feathers three!' –
'Yes; that's how we dress when we're ruined,' said she.

– 'At home in the barton you said "thee" and "thou",
And "thik oon", and "theäs oon", and "t'other"; but now
Your talking quite fits 'ee for high compa-ny!' –
'Some polish is gained with one's ruin,' said she.

– 'Your hands were like paws then, your face blue and bleak
But now I'm bewitched by your delicate cheek,
And your little gloves fit as on any la-dy!' –
'We never do work when we're ruined,' said she.

– 'You used to call home-life a hag-ridden dream,
And you'd sigh, and you'd sock; but at present you seem
To know not of megrims or melancho-ly!' –
'True. One's pretty lively when ruined,' said she.

– 'I wish I had feathers, a fine sweeping gown,
And a delicate face, and could strut about Town!' –
'My dear – a raw country girl, such as you be,
Cannot quite expect that. You ain't ruined,' said she.

Westbourne Park Villas, 1866

The Woman I Met

A STRANGER, I threaded sunken-hearted
        A lamp-lit crowd,
And anon there passed me a soul departed,
        Who mutely bowed.
In my far-off youthful years I had met her,
Full-pulsed; but now, no more life's debtor,
        Onward she slid
    In a shroud that furs half-hid.

'Why do you trouble me, dead woman,
        Trouble me;
You whom I knew when warm and human?
        – How it be
That you quitted earth and are yet upon it
Is, to any who ponder on it,
        Past being read!'
    'Still, it is so,' she said.

'These were my haunts in my olden sprightly
        Hours of breath;
Here I went tempting frail youth nightly
        To their death;

113

But you deemed me chaste – me, a tinselled sinner!
How thought you one with pureness in her
      Could pace this street
    Eyeing some man to greet?

'Well; your very simplicity made me love you
      Mid such town dross,
Till I set not Heaven itself above you,
      Who grew my Cross;
For you'd only nod, despite how I sighed for you;
So you tortured me, who fain would have died for you!
    – What I suffered then
    Would have paid for the sins of ten!

'Thus went the days. I feared you despised me
      To fling me a nod
Each time, no more: till love chastised me
      As with a rod
That a fresh bland boy of no assurance
Should fire me with passion beyond endurance,
      While others all
    I hated, and loathed their call.

'I said: "It is his mother's spirit
      Hovering around
To shield him, maybe!" I used to fear it,
      As still I found
My beauty left no least impression,
And remnants of pride withheld confession
      Of my true trade
    By speaking; so I delayed.

'I said: "Perhaps with a costly flower
      He'll be beguiled."
I held it, in passing you one late hour,
      To your face: you smiled,
Keeping step with the throng; though you did not see there
A single one that rivalled me there! . . .
      Well: it's all past.
    I died in the Lock at last.'

So walked the dead and I together
                The quick among,
Elbowing our kind of every feather
                Slowly and long;
Yea, long and slowly. That a phantom should stalk there
With me seemed nothing strange, and talk there
                That winter night
        By flaming jets of light.

She showed me Juans who feared their call-time,
                Guessing their lot;
She showed me her sort that cursed their fall-time,
                And that did not.
Till suddenly murmured she: 'Now, tell me,
Why asked you never, ere death befell me,
                To have my love,
        Much as I dreamt thereof?'

I could not answer. And she, well weeting
                All in my heart,
Said: 'God your guardian kept our fleeting
                Forms apart!'
Sighing and drawing her furs around her
Over the shroud that tightly bound her,
                With wafts as from clay
        She turned and thinned away.

London, 1918

A Trampwoman's Tragedy

(182–)

I

FROM Wynyard's Gap the livelong day,
                The livelong day,
We beat afoot the northward way
                We had travelled times before.
The sun-blaze burning on our backs,

Our shoulders sticking to our packs,
By fosseway, fields, and turnpike tracks
    We skirted sad Sedge-Moor.

II

Full twenty miles we jaunted on,
    We jaunted on, –
My fancy-man, and jeering John,
    And Mother Lee, and I.
And, as the sun drew down to west,
We climbed the toilsome Poldon crest,
And saw, of landskip sights the best,
    The inn that beamed thereby.

III

For months we had padded side by side,
    Ay, side by side
Through the Great Forest, Blackmoor wide,
    And where the Parret ran.
We'd faced the gusts on Mendip ridge,
Had crossed the Yeo unhelped by bridge,
Been stung by every Marshwood midge,
    I and my fancy-man.

IV

Lone inns we loved, my man and I,
    My man and I;
'King's Stag', 'Windwhistle' high and dry,
    'The Horse' on Hintock Green,
The cosy house at Wynyard's Gap,
'The Hut' renowned on Bredy Knap,
And many another wayside tap
    Where folk might sit unseen.

V

Now as we trudged – O deadly day,
    O deadly day! –
I teased my fancy-man in play
    And wanton idleness.

I walked alongside jeering John,
I laid his hand my waist upon;
I would not bend my glances on
    My lover's dark distress.

VI

Thus Poldon top at last we won,
    At last we won,
And gained the inn at sink of sun
    Far-famed as 'Marshal's Elm'.
Beneath us figured tor and lea,
From Mendip to the western sea –
I doubt if finer sight there be
    Within this royal realm.

VII

Inside the settle all a-row –
    All four a-row
We sat, I next to John, to show
    That he had wooed and won.
And then he took me on his knee,
And swore it was his turn to be
My favoured mate, and Mother Lee
    Passed to my former one.

VIII

Then in a voice I had never heard,
    I had never heard,
My only Love to me: 'One word,
    My lady, if you please!
Whose is the child you are like to bear? –
His? After all my months o' care?'
God knows 'twas not! But, O despair!
    I nodded – still to tease.

IX

Then up he sprung, and with his knife –
    And with his knife

He let out jeering Johnny's life,
    Yes; there, at set of sun.
The slant ray through the window nigh
Gilded John's blood and glazing eye,
Ere scarcely Mother Lee and I
    Knew that the deed was done.

X

The taverns tell the gloomy tale,
    The gloomy tale,
How that at Ivel-chester jail
    My Love, my sweetheart swung;
Though stained till now by no misdeed
Save one horse ta'en in time o' need;
(Blue Jimmy stole right many a steed
    Ere his last fling he flung.)

XI

Thereaft I walked the world alone,
    Alone, alone!
On his death-day I gave my groan
    And dropt his dead-born child.
'Twas nigh the jail, beneath a tree,
None tending me; for Mother Lee
Had died at Glaston, leaving me
    Unfriended on the wild.

XII

And in the night as I lay weak,
    As I lay weak,
The leaves a-falling on my cheek,
    The red moon low declined.
The ghost of him I'd die to kiss
Rose up and said: 'Ah, tell me this!
Was the child mine, or was it his?
    Speak, that I rest may find!'

XIII

O doubt not but I told him then,
    I told him then,
That I had kept me from all men
    Since we joined lips and swore.
Whereat he smiled, and thinned away
As the wind stirred to call up day . . .
– 'Tis past! And here alone I stray
    Haunting the Western Moor.

NOTES. – 'Windwhistle' (Stanza IV). The highness and dryness of Wind-whistle Inn was impressed upon the writer two or three years ago, when, after climbing on a hot afternoon to the beautiful spot near which it stands and entering the inn for tea, he was informed by the landlady that none could be had, unless he would fetch water from a valley half a mile off, the house containing not a drop, owing to its situation. However, a tantalizing row of full barrels behind her back testified to a wetness of a certain sort, which was not at that time desired.

    'Marshal's Elm' (Stanza VI), so picturesquely situated, is no longer an inn, though the house, or part of it, still remains. It used to exhibit a fine old swinging sign.

    'Blue Jimmy' (Stanza X) was a notorious horse-stealer of Wessex in those days, who appropriated more than a hundred horses before he was caught, among others one belonging to a neighbour of the writer's grandfather. He was hanged at the now demolished Ivelchester or Ilchester jail above men-tioned – that building formerly of so many sinister associations in the minds of the local peasantry, and the continual haunt of fever, which at last led to its condemnation. Its site is now an innocent-looking green meadow.

April 1902

The Workbox

'SEE, here's the workbox, little wife,
    That I made of polished oak.'
He was a joiner, of village life;
    She came of borough folk.

He holds the present up to her
    As with a smile she nears
And answers to the profferer,
    ''Twill last all my sewing years!'

'I warrant it will. And longer too.
   'Tis a scantling that I got
Off poor John Wayward's coffin, who
   Died of they knew not what.

'The shingled pattern that seems to cease
   Against your box's rim
Continues right on in the piece
   That's underground with him.

'And while I worked it made me think
   Of timber's varied doom;
One inch where people eat and drink,
   The next inch in a tomb.

'But why do you look so white, my dear,
   And turn aside your face?
You knew not that good lad, I fear,
   Though he came from your native place?'

'How could I know that good young man,
   Though he came from my native town,
When he must have left far earlier than
   I was a woman grown?'

'Ah, no. I should have understood!
   It shocked you that I gave
To you one end of a piece of wood
   Whose other is in a grave?'

'Don't, dear, despise my intellect,
   Mere accidental things
Of that sort never have effect
   On my imaginings.'

Yet still her lips were limp and wan,
   Her face still held aside,
As if she had known not only John,
   But known of what he died.

At Tea

THE kettle descants in a cosy drone,
And the young wife looks in her husband's face,
And then at her guest's, and shows in her own
Her sense that she fills an envied place;
And the visiting lady is all abloom,
And says there was never so sweet a room.

And the happy young housewife does not know
That the woman beside her was first his choice,
Till the fates ordained it could not be so . . .
Betraying nothing in look or voice
The guest sits smiling and sips her tea,
And he throws her a stray glance yearningly.

In Church

'AND now to God the Father,' he ends,
And his voice thrills up to the topmost tiles:
Each listener chokes as he bows and bends,
And emotion pervades the crowded aisles.
Then the preacher glides to the vestry-door,
And shuts it, and thinks he is seen no more.

The door swings softly ajar meanwhile,
And a pupil of his in the Bible class,
Who adores him as one without gloss or guile,
Sees her idol stand with a satisfied smile
And re-enact at the vestry-glass
Each pulpit gesture in deft dumb-show
That had moved the congregation so.

By Her Aunt's Grave

'SIXPENCE a week,' says the girl to her lover,
'Aunt used to bring me, for she could confide
In me alone, she vowed. 'Twas to cover

The cost of her headstone when she died.
And that was a year ago last June;
I've not yet fixed it. But I must soon.'

'And where is the money now, my dear?'
'O, snug in my purse . . . Aunt was *so* slow
In saving it – eighty weeks, or near.' . . .
'Let's spend it,' he hints. 'For she won't know
There's a dance to-night at the Load of Hay.'
She passively nods. And they go that way.

In the Study

HE enters, and mute on the edge of a chair
Sits a thin-faced lady, a stranger there,
A type of decayed gentility;
And by some small signs he well can guess
That she comes to him almost breakfastless.
'I have called – I hope I do not err –
I am looking for a purchaser
Of some score volumes of the works
Of eminent divines I own, –
Left by my father – though it irks
My patience to offer them.' And she smiles
As if necessity were unknown;
'But the truth of it is that oftenwhiles
I have wished, as I am fond of art,
To make my rooms a little smart,
And these old books are so in the way.'
And lightly still she laughs to him,
As if to sell were a mere gay whim,
And that, to be frank, Life were indeed
To her not vinegar and gall,
But fresh and honey-like; and Need
No household skeleton at all.

In the Nuptial Chamber

'O THAT mastering tune!' And up in the bed
Like a lace-robed phantom springs the bride;
'And why?' asks the man she had that day wed,
With a start, as the band plays on outside.
'It's the townsfolk's cheery compliment
Because of our marriage, my Innocent.'

'O but you don't know! 'Tis the passionate air
To which my old Love waltzed with me,
And I swore as we spun that none should share
My home, my kisses, till death, save he!
And he dominates me and thrills me through,
And it's he I embrace while embracing you!'

At the Draper's

'I STOOD at the back of the shop, my dear,
    But you did not perceive me.
Well, when they deliver what you were shown
    I shall know nothing of it, believe me!'

And he coughed and coughed as she paled and said,
    'O, I didn't see you come in there –
Why couldn't you speak?' – 'Well, I didn't. I left
    That you should not notice I'd been there.

'You were viewing some lovely things. "*Soon required
    For a widow, of latest fashion;*"
And I knew 'twould upset you to meet the man
    Who had to be cold and ashen

And screwed in a box before they could dress you
    "In the last new note in mourning,"
As they defined it. So, not to distress you,
    I left you to your adorning.'

Her Second Husband Hears Her Story

'STILL, Dear, it is incredible to me
    That here, alone,
You should have sewed him up until he died,
And in this very bed. I do not see
How you could do it, seeing what might betide.'

'Well, he came home one midnight, liquored deep –
    Worse than I'd known –
And lay down heavily, and soundly slept:
Then, desperate driven, I thought of it, to keep
Him from me when he woke. Being an adept

'With needle and thimble, as he snored, click-click
    An hour I'd sewn,
Till, had he roused, he couldn't have moved from bed,
So tightly laced in sheet and quilt and tick
He lay. And in the morning he was dead.

'Ere people came I drew the stitches out,
    And thus 'twas shown
To be a stroke.' – 'It's a strange tale!' said he.
'And this same bed?' – 'Yes, here it came about.'
'Well, it sounds strange – told here and now to me.

'Did you intend his death by your tight lacing?'
    'O, that I cannot own.
I could not think of else that would avail
When he should wake up, and attempt embracing.' –
    'Well, it's a cool queer tale!'

The Memorial Brass: 186–

'WHY do you weep there, O sweet lady,
    Why do you weep before that brass? –
(I'm a mere student sketching the mediaeval)
    Is some late death lined there, alas? –
Your father's? . . . Well, all pay the debt that paid he!'

'Young man, O must I tell! – My husband's! And under
    His name I set mine, and my *death*! –
Its date left vacant till my heirs should fill it,
    Stating me faithful till my last breath.'
– 'Madam, that you are a widow wakes my wonder!'

'O wait! For last month I – remarried!
    And now I fear 'twas a deed amiss.
We've just come home. And I am sick and saddened
    At what the new one will say to this;
And will he think – think that I should have tarried?

'I may add, surely, – with no wish to harm him –
    That he's a temper – yes, I fear!
And when he comes to church next Sunday morning,
    And sees that written . . . O dear, O dear!'
– 'Madam, I swear your beauty will disarm him!'

Copying Architecture in an Old Minster

(WIMBORNE)

How smartly the quarters of the hour march by
    That the jack-o'-clock never forgets;
Ding-dong; and before I have traced a cusp's eye,
Or got the true twist of the ogee over,
    A double ding-dong ricochetts.

Just so did he clang here before I came,
    And so will he clang when I'm gone
Through the Minster's cavernous hollows – the same

Tale of hours never more to be will he deliver
    To the speechless midnight and dawn!

I grow to conceive it a call to ghosts,
    Whose mould lies below and around.
Yes; the next 'Come, come,' draws them out from their posts,
And they gather, and one shade appears, and another,
    As the eve-damps creep from the ground.

See – a Courtenay stands by his quatre-foiled tomb,
    And a Duke and his Duchess near;
And one Sir Edmund in columned gloom,
And a Saxon king by the presbytery chamber;
    And shapes unknown in the rear.

Maybe they have met for a parle on some plan
    To better ail-stricken mankind;
I catch their cheepings, though thinner than
The overhead creak of a passager's pinion
    When leaving land behind.

Or perhaps they speak to the yet unborn,
    And caution them not to come
To a world so ancient and trouble-torn,
Of foiled intents, vain lovingkindness,
    And ardours chilled and numb.

They waste to fog as I stir and stand,
    And move from the arched recess,
And pick up the drawing that slipped from my hand,
And feel for the pencil I dropped in the cranny
    In a moment's forgetfulness.

The Young Glass-Stainer

'THESE Gothic windows, how they wear me out
    With cusp and foil, and nothing straight or square,
Crude colours, leaden borders roundabout,
    And fitting in Peter here, and Matthew there!

'What a vocation! Here do I draw now
The abnormal, loving the Hellenic norm;
Martha I paint, and dream of Hera's brow,
Mary, and think of Aphrodite's form.'

Nov. 1893

Drawing Details in an Old Church

I HEAR the bell-rope sawing,
And the oil-less axle grind,
As I sit alone here drawing
What some Gothic brain designed;
And I catch the toll that follows
    From the lagging bell,
Ere it spreads to hills and hollows
    Where people dwell.

I ask not whom it tolls for,
Incurious who he be;
So, some morrow, when those knolls for
One unguessed, sound out for me,
A stranger, loitering under
    In nave or choir,
May think, too, 'Whose, I wonder?'
    But not inquire.

A Cathedral Façade at Midnight

ALONG the sculptures of the western wall
    I watched the moonlight creeping:
It moved as if it hardly moved at all,
    Inch by inch thinly peeping
Round on the pious figures of freestone, brought
And poised there when the Universe was wrought
To serve its centre, Earth, in mankind's thought.

The lunar look skimmed scantly toe, breast, arm,
    Then edged on slowly, slightly,
To shoulder, hand, face; till each austere form
    Was blanched its whole length brightly
Of prophet, king, queen, cardinal in state,
That dead men's tools had striven to simulate;
And the stiff images stood irradiate.

A frail moan from the martyred saints there set
    Mid others of the erection
Against the breeze, seemed sighings of regret
    At the ancient faith's rejection
Under the sure, unhasting, steady stress
Of Reason's movement, making meaningless
The coded creeds of old-time godliness.

The Old Workman

'Why are you so bent down before your time,
Old mason? Many have not left their prime
So far behind at your age, and can still
    Stand full upright at will.'

He pointed to the mansion-front hard by,
And to the stones of the quoin against the sky;
'Those upper blocks,' he said, 'that there you see,
    It was that ruined me.'

There stood in the air up to the parapet
Crowning the corner height, the stones as set
By him – ashlar whereon the gales might drum
    For centuries to come.

'I carried them up,' he said, 'by a ladder there;
The last was as big a load as I could bear;
But on I heaved; and something in my back
    Moved, as 'twere with a crack.

'So I got crookt. I never lost that sprain;
And those who live there, walled from wind and rain
By freestone that I lifted, do not know
      That my life's ache came so.

'They don't know me, or even know my name,
But good I think it, somehow, all the same
To have kept 'em safe from harm, and right and tight,
      Though it has broke me quite.

'Yes; that I fixed it firm up there I am proud,
Facing the hail and snow and sun and cloud,
And to stand storms for ages, beating round
      When I lie underground.'

A Man²⁴

(IN MEMORY OF H. OF M.)

I

IN Casterbridge there stood a noble pile,
Wrought with pilaster, bay, and balustrade
In tactful times when shrewd Eliza swayed. –
      On burgher, squire, and clown
It smiled the long street down for near a mile.

II

But evil days beset that domicile;
The stately beauties of its roof and wall
Passed into sordid hands. Condemned to fall
      Were cornice, quoin, and cove,
And all that art had wove in antique style.

III

Among the hired dismantlers entered there
One till the moment of his task untold.
When charged therewith he gazed, and answered bold:
      'Be needy I or no,
I will not help lay low a house so fair!

IV

'Hunger is hard. But since the terms be such –
No wage, or labour stained with the disgrace
Of wrecking what our age cannot replace
     To save its tasteless soul –
I'll do without your dole. Life is not much!'

V

Dismissed with sneers he backed his tools and went,
And wandered workless; for it seemed unwise
To close with one who dared to criticize
     And carp on points of taste:
Rude men should work where placed, and be content.

VI

Years whiled. He aged, sank, sickened; and was not:
And it was said, 'A man intractable
And curst is gone.' None sighed to hear his knell,
     None sought his churchyard-place;
His name, his rugged face, were soon forgot.

VII

The stones of that fair hall lie far and wide,
And but a few recall its ancient mould;
Yet when I pass the spot I long to hold
     As truth what fancy saith:
'His protest lives where deathless things abide!'

The Abbey-Mason[25]

INVENTOR OF THE 'PERPENDICULAR' STYLE OF GOTHIC ARCHITECTURE

(With Memories of John Hicks, Architect)

THE new-vamped Abbey shaped apace
In the fourteenth century of grace;

(The church which, at an after date,
Acquired cathedral rank and state.)

Panel and circumscribing wall
Of latest feature, trim and tall,

Rose roundabout the Norman core
In prouder pose than theretofore,

Encasing magically the old
With parpend ashlars manifold.

The trowels rang out, and tracery
Appeared where blanks had used to be.

Men toiled for pleasure more than pay,
And all went smoothly day by day,

Till, in due course, the transept part
Engrossed the master-mason's art.

– Home-coming thence he tossed and turned
Throughout the night till the new sun burned.

'What fearful visions have inspired
These gaingivings?' his wife inquired;

'As if your tools were in your hand
You have hammered, fitted, muttered, planned;

'You have thumped as you were working hard:
I might have found me bruised and scarred.

'What then's amiss? What eating care
Looms nigh, whereof I am unaware?'

He answered not, but churchward went,
Viewing his draughts with discontent;

And fumbled there the livelong day
Till, hollow-eyed, he came away.

– 'Twas said, 'The master-mason's ill!'
And all the abbey works stood still.

Quoth Abbot Wygmore: 'Why, O why
Distress yourself? You'll surely die!'

The mason answered, trouble-torn,
'This long-vogued style is quite outworn!

'The upper archmould nohow serves
To meet the lower tracery curves:

'The ogees bend too far away
To give the flexures interplay.

'This it is causes my distress . . .
So it will ever be unless

'New forms be found to supersede
The circle when occasions need.

'To carry it out I have tried and toiled,
And now perforce must own me foiled!

'Jeerers will say: "Here was a man
Who could not end what he began!"'

– So passed that day, the next, the next;
The abbot scanned the task, perplexed;

The townsmen mustered all their wit
To fathom how to compass it,

But no raw artistries availed
Where practice in the craft had failed . . .

– One night he tossed, all open-eyed,
And early left his helpmeet's side.

Scattering the rushes of the floor
He wandered from the chamber door

And sought the sizing pile, whereon
Struck dimly a cadaverous dawn

Through freezing rain, that drenched the board
Of diagram-lines he last had scored –

Chalked phantasies in vain begot
To knife the architectural knot –

In front of which he dully stood,
Regarding them in hopeless mood.

He closelier looked; then looked again:
The chalk-scratched draught-board faced the rain,

Whose icicled drops deformed the lines
Innumerous of his lame designs,

So that they streamed in small white threads
From the upper segments to the heads

Of arcs below, uniting them
Each by a stalactitic stem.

– At once, with eyes that struck out sparks,
He adds accessory cusping-marks,

Then laughs aloud. The thing was done
So long assayed from sun to sun . . .

– Now in his joy he grew aware
Of one behind him standing there,

And, turning, saw the abbot, who
The weather's whim was watching too.

Onward to Prime the abbot went,
Tacit upon the incident.

– Men now discerned as days revolved
The ogive riddle had been solved;

Templates were cut, fresh lines were chalked
Where lines had been defaced and balked,

And the work swelled and mounted higher,
Achievement distancing desire;

Here jambs with transoms fixed between,
Where never the like before had been –

There little mullions thinly sawn
Where meeting circles once were drawn.

'We knew,' men said, 'the thing would go
After his craft-wit got aglow,

'And, once fulfilled what he has designed,
We'll honour him and his great mind!'

When matters stood thus poised awhile,
And all surroundings shed a smile,

The master-mason on an eve
Homed to his wife and seemed to grieve . . .

– 'The abbot spoke to me to-day;
He hangs about the works alway.

'He knows the source as well as I
Of the new style men magnify.

'He said: "You pride yourself too much
On your creation. Is it such?

' "Surely the hand of God it is
That conjured so, and only His! –

' "Disclosing by the frost and rain
Forms your invention chased in vain;

' "Hence the devices deemed so great
You copied, and did not create."

'I feel the abbot's words are just,
And that all thanks renounce I must.

'Can a man welcome praise and pelf
For hatching art that hatched itself? . . .

'So, I shall own the deft design
Is Heaven's outshaping, and not mine.'

'What!' said she. 'Praise your works ensure
To throw away, and quite obscure

'Your beaming and beneficent star?
Better you leave things as they are!

'Why, think awhile. Had not your zest
In your loved craft curtailed your rest –

'Had you not gone there ere the day
The sun had melted all away!'

– But, though his good wife argued so,
The mason let the people know

That not unaided sprang the thought
Whereby the glorious fane was wrought,

But that by frost when dawn was dim
The method was disclosed to him.

'Yet,' said the townspeople thereat,
''Tis your own doing, even with that!'

But he – chafed, childlike, in extremes –
The temperament of men of dreams –

Aloofly scrupled to admit
That he did aught but borrow it,

And diffidently made request
That with the abbot all should rest.

– As none could doubt the abbot's word,
Or question what the church averred,

The mason was at length believed
Of no more count than he conceived,

And soon began to lose the fame
That late had gathered round his name . . .

– Time passed, and like a living thing
The pile went on embodying,

And workmen died, and young ones grew,
And the old mason sank from view

And Abbotts Wygmore and Staunton went
And Horton sped the embellishment.

But not till years had far progressed
Chanced it that, one day, much impressed,

Standing within the well-graced aisle,
He asked who first conceived the style;

And some decrepit sage detailed
How, when invention nought availed,

The cloud-cast waters in their whim
Came down, and gave the hint to him

Who struck each arc, and made each mould;
And how the abbot would not hold

As sole begetter him who applied
Forms the Almighty sent as guide;

And how the master lost renown,
And wore in death no artist's crown.

– Then Horton, who in inner thought
Had more perceptions than he taught,

Replied: 'Nay; art can but transmute;
Invention is not absolute;

'Things fail to spring from nought at call,
And art-beginnings most of all.

'He did but what all artists do,
Wait upon Nature for his cue.'

– 'Had you been here to tell them so,
Lord Abbot, sixty years ago,

'The mason, now long underground,
Doubtless a different fate had found.

'He passed into oblivion dim,
And none knew what became of him!

'His name? 'Twas of some common kind
And now has faded out of mind.'

The Abbott: 'It shall not be hid!
I'll trace it.' . . . But he never did.

– When longer yet dank death had wormed
The brain wherein the style had germed

From Gloucester church it flew afar –
The style called Perpendicular. –

To Winton and to Westminster
It ranged, and grew still beautifuller:

From Solway Frith to Dover Strand
Its fascinations starred the land,

Not only on cathedral walls
But upon courts and castle halls,

Till every edifice in the isle
Was patterned to no other style,

And till, long having played its part
The curtain fell on Gothic art.

– Well: when in Wessex on your rounds,
Take a brief step beyond its bounds,

And enter Gloucester: seek the quoin
Where choir and transept interjoin,

And, gazing at the forms there flung
Against the sky by one unsung –

The ogee arches transom-topped,
The tracery-stalks by spandrels stopped,

Petrified lacework – lightly lined
On ancient massiveness behind –

Muse that some minds so modest be
As to renounce fame's fairest fee,

(Like him who crystallized on this spot
His visionings, but lies forgot,

137

And many a mediaeval one
Whose symmetries salute the sun)

While others boom a baseless claim,
And upon nothing rear a name.

The Sunshade

AH – it's the skeleton of a lady's sunshade,
　　Here at my feet in the hard rock's chink,
　　Merely a naked sheaf of wires! –
　　Twenty years have gone with their livers and diers
　　Since it was silked in its white or pink.

Noonshine riddles the ribs of the sunshade,
　　No more a screen from the weakest ray;
　　Nothing to tell us the hue of its dyes,
　　Nothing but rusty bones as it lies
　　In its coffin of stone, unseen till to-day.

Where is the woman who carried that sunshade
　　Up and down this seaside place? –
　　Little thumb standing against its stem,
　　Thoughts perhaps bent on a love-stratagem,
　　Softening yet more the already soft face!

Is the fair woman who carried that sunshade
　　A skeleton just as her property is,
　　Laid in the chink that none may scan?
　　And does she regret – if regret dust can –
　　The vain things thought when she flourished this?

Swanage Cliffs

The Clock-Winder

　　IT is dark as a cave,
　　Or a vault in the nave
　　When the iron door
　　Is closed, and the floor
　　Of the church relaid
　　With trowel and spade.

138

But the parish-clerk
Cares not for the dark
As he winds in the tower
At a regular hour
The rheumatic clock
Whose dilatory knock
You can hear when praying
At the day's decaying,
Or at any lone while
From a pew in the aisle.

Up, up from the ground
Around and around
In the turret stair
He clambers, to where
The wheelwork is,
With its tick, click, whizz,
Reposefully measuring
Each day to its end
That mortal men spend
In sorrowing and pleasuring.
Nightly thus does he climb
To the trackway of Time.

Him I followed one night
To this place without light,
And, ere I spoke, heard
Him say, word by word,
At the end of his winding,
The darkness unminding: –

'So I wipe out one more,
My Dear, of the sore
Sad days that still be,
Like a drying Dead Sea,
Between you and me!'

Who she was no man knew:
He had long borne him blind
To all womankind;
And was ever one who
Kept his past out of view.

The Curate's Kindness

A WORKHOUSE IRONY

I

I THOUGHT they'd be strangers aroun' me,
    But she's to be there!
Let me jump out o' waggon and go back and drown me
    At Pummery or Ten-Hatches Weir.

II

I thought: 'Well, I've come to the Union –
    The workhouse at last –
After honest hard work all the week, and Communion
    O' Zundays, these fifty years past.

III

''Tis hard; but,' I thought, 'never mind it:
    There's gain in the end:
And when I get used to the place I shall find it
    A home, and may find there a friend.

IV

'Life there will be better than t'other,
    For peace is assured.
The men in one wing and their wives in another
    Is strictly the rule of the Board.'

V

Just then one young Pa'son arriving
    Steps up out of breath
To the side o' the waggon wherein we were driving
    To Union; and calls out and saith:

VI

'Old folks, that harsh order is altered,
    Be not sick of heart!
The Guardians they poohed and they pished and they paltered
    When urged not to keep you apart.

VII

' "It is wrong," I maintained, "to divide them,
    Near forty years wed."
"Very well, sir. We promise, then, they shall abide them
    In one wing together," they said.'

VIII

Then I sank – knew 'twas quite a foredone thing
    That misery should be
To the end! . . . To get freed of her there was the one thing
    Had made the change welcome to me.

IX

To go there was ending but badly;
    'Twas shame and 'twas pain;
'But anyhow,' thought I, 'thereby I shall gladly
    Get free of this forty years' chain.'

X

I thought they'd be strangers aroun' me,
    But she's to be there!
Let me jump out o' waggon and go back and drown me
    At Pummery or Ten-Hatches Weir.

At a Pause in a Country Dance

(MIDDLE OF LAST CENTURY)

THEY stood at the foot of the figure,
And panted: they'd danced it down through –
That 'Dashing White Serjeant' they loved so: -
A window, uncurtained, was nigh them
That end of the room. Thence in view

Outside it a valley updrew,
Where the frozen moon lit frozen snow:
At the furthermost reach of the valley
A light from a window shone low.
'They are inside that window,' said she,

As she looked. 'They sit up there for me;
And baby is sleeping there, too.'
He glanced. 'Yes,' he said. 'Never mind,
Let's foot our way up again; do!
And dance down the line as before.

'What's the world to us, meeting once more!'
'– Not much, when your husband full trusts you,
And thinks the child his that I bore!'
He was silent. The fiddlers six-eighted
With even more passionate vigour.

The pair swept again up the figure,
The child's cuckoo-father and she,
And the next couples threaded below,
And the twain wove their way to the top
Of 'The Dashing White Serjeant' they loved so,
Restarting: right, left, to and fro.

– From the homestead, seen yon, the small glow
Still adventured forth over the white,
Where the child slept, unknowing who sired it,
In the cradle of wicker tucked tight,
And its grandparents, nodding, admired it
In elbow-chairs through the slow night.

The Chapel-Organist [26]

(A.D. 185–)

I've been thinking it through, as I play here to-night, to play
never again,
By the light of that lowering sun peering in at the window-pane,

And over the back-street roofs, throwing shades from the boys of
   the chore
In the gallery, right upon me, sitting up to these keys once
   more . . .

How I used to hear tongues ask, as I sat here when I was new:
'Who is she playing the organ? She touches it mightily true!'
'She travels from Havenpool Town,' the deacon would softly
   speak,
'The stipend can hardly cover her fare hither twice in the week.'
(It fell far short of doing, indeed; but I never told,
For I have craved minstrelsy more than lovers, or beauty, or
   gold.)

'Twas so he answered at first, but the story grew different later:
'It cannot go on much longer, from what we hear of her now!'
At the meaning wheeze in the words the inquirer would shift his
   place
Till he could see round the curtain that screened me from people
   below.
'A handsome girl,' he would murmur, upstaring (and so I am).
'But – too much sex in her build; fine eyes, but eyelids too
   heavy;
A bosom too full for her age; in her lips too voluptuous a dye.'
(It may be. But who put it there? Assuredly it was not I.)

I went on playing and singing when this I had heard, and more,
Though tears half-blinded me; yes, I remained going on and on,
Just as I used me to chord and to sing at the selfsame time! . . .
For it's a contralto – my voice is; they'll hear it again here
   to-night
In the psalmody notes that I love far beyond every lower delight.

Well, the deacon, in fact, that day had learnt new tidings about
   me;
They troubled his mind not a little, for he was a worthy man.
(He trades as a chemist in High Street, and during the week he
   had sought
His fellow-deacon, who throve as a bookbinder over the way.)

'These are strange rumours,' he said. 'We must guard the good
name of the chapel.

If, sooth, she's of evil report, what else can we do but dismiss
her?'

'– But get such another to play here we cannot for double the
price!'

It settled the point for the time, and I triumphed awhile in their
strait,

And my much-beloved grand semibreves went living on, pending
my fate.

At length in the congregation more headshakes and murmurs
were rife,

And my dismissal was ruled, though I was not warned of it then.

But a day came when they declared it. The news entered me as a
sword;

I was broken; so pallid of face that they thought I should faint,
they said.

I rallied. 'O, rather than go, I will play you for nothing!' said I.

'Twas in much desperation I spoke it, for bring me to forfeit I
could not

Those melodies chorded so richly for which I had laboured and
lived.

They paused. And for nothing I played at the chapel through
Sundays again,

Upheld by that art which I loved more than blandishments
lavished of men.

But it fell that murmurs anew from the flock broke the pastor's
peace.

Some member had seen me at Havenpool, comrading close a
sea-captain.

(O yes; I was thereto constrained, lacking means for the fare to
and fro.)

Yet God knows, if aught He knows ever, I loved the Old-
Hundredth, Saint Stephen's,

Mount Zion, New Sabbath, Miles-Lane, Holy Rest, and Arabia,
and Eaton,

Above all embraces of body by wooers who sought me and
     won! . . .
Next week 'twas declared I was seen coming home with a swain
     ere the sun.

The deacons insisted then, strong; and forgiveness I did not
     implore.
I saw all was lost for me, quite, but I made a last bid in my
     throbs.
My bent, finding victual in lust, men's senses had libelled my soul,
But the soul should die game, if I knew it! I turned to my
     masters and said:
'I yield, Gentlemen, without parlance. But – let me just hymn
     you *once* more!
It's a little thing, Sirs, that I ask; and a passion is music with
     me!'
They saw that consent would cost nothing, and show as good
     grace, as knew I,
Though tremble I did, and feel sick, as I paused thereat, dumb
     for their words.
They gloomily nodded assent, saying, 'Yes, if you care to.
     Once more,
And only once more, understand.' To that with a bend I agreed.
– 'You've a fixed and a far-reaching look,' spoke one who had
     eyed me awhile.
'I've a fixed and a far-reaching plan, and my look only showed
     it,' I smile.

This evening of Sunday is come – the last of my functioning
     here.
'She plays as if she were possessed!' they exclaim, glancing
     upward and round.
'Such harmonies I never dreamt the old instrument capable of!'
Meantime the sun lowers and goes; shades deepen; the lights are
     turned up,
And the people voice out the last singing: tune Tallis: the
     Evening Hymn.
(I wonder Dissenters sing Ken: it shows them more liberal in
     spirit

At this little chapel down here than at certain new others I know.)

I sing as I play. Murmurs some one: 'No woman's throat richer
than hers!'

'True: in these parts,' think I. 'But, my man, never more will its
richness outspread.'

And I sing with them onward: 'The grave dread as little do I as
my bed.'

I lift up my feet from the pedals; and then, while my eyes are still
wet

From the symphonies born of my fingers, I do that whereon I am
set,

And draw from my 'full round bosom' (their words; how can *I*
help it heave?)

A bottle blue-coloured and fluted – a vinaigrette, they may
conceive –

And before the choir measures my meaning, reads aught in my
moves to and fro,

I drink from the phial at a draught, and they think it a pick-me-
up; so.

Then I gather my books as to leave, bend over the keys as to
pray.

When they come to me motionless, stooping, quick death will
have whisked me away.

'Sure, nobody meant her to poison herself in her haste, after all!'

The deacons will say as they carry me down and the night
shadows fall,

'Though the charges were true,' they will add. 'It's a case red as
scarlet withal!'

I have never once minced it. Lived chaste I have not. Heaven
knows it above! . . .

But past all the heavings of passion – it's music has been my
life-love! . . .

That tune did go well – this last playing! . . . I reckon they'll
bury me here . . .

Not a soul from the seaport my birthplace – will come, or bestow
me . . . a tear.

Honeymoon Time at an Inn[27]

AT the shiver of morning, a little before the false dawn,
    The moon was at the window-square,
  Deedily brooding in deformed decay –
  The curve hewn off her cheek as by an adze;
At the shiver of morning a little before the false dawn
    So the moon looked in there.

Her speechless eyeing reached across the chamber,
    Where lay two souls opprest,
  One a white lady sighing, 'Why am I sad!'
  To him who sighed back, 'Sad, my Love, am I!'
And speechlessly the old moon conned the chamber,
    And these two reft of rest.

While their large-pupilled vision swept the scene there,
    Nought seeming imminent,
  Something fell sheer, and crashed, and from the floor
  Lay glittering at the pair with a shattered gaze,
While their large-pupilled vision swept the scene there,
    And the many-eyed thing outleant.

With a start they saw that it was an old-time pier-glass
    Which had stood on the mantel near,
  Its silvering blemished, – yes, as if worn away
  By the eyes of the countless dead who had smirked at it
Ere these two ever knew that old-time pier-glass
    And its vague and vacant leer.

As he looked, his bride like a moth skimmed forth, and kneeling
    Quick, with quivering sighs,
  Gathered the pieces under the moon's sly ray,
  Unwitting as an automaton what she did;
Till he entreated, hasting to where she was kneeling,
    'Let it stay where it lies!'

'Long years of sorrow this means!' breathed the lady
    As they retired. 'Alas!'
    And she lifted one pale hand across her eyes.

'Don't trouble, Love; it's nothing,' the bridegroom said.
'Long years of sorrow for us!' murmured the lady,
   'Or ever this evil pass!'

And the Spirits Ironic laughed behind the wainscot,
   And the Spirits of Pity sighed.
  'It's good,' said the Spirits Ironic, 'to tickle their minds
With a portent of their wedlock's aftergrinds.'
And the Spirits of Pity sighed behind the wainscot,
   'It's a portent we cannot abide!

'More, what shall happen to prove the truth of the portent?'
   – 'Oh; in brief, they will fade till old,
And their loves grow numbed ere death, by the cark of care.'
  – 'But nought see we that asks for portents there? –
'Tis the lot of all.' – 'Well, no less true is a portent
   That it fits all mortal mould.'

The Contretemps

A FORWARD rush by the lamp in the gloom,
   And we clasped, and almost kissed;
But she was not the woman whom
I had promised to meet in the thawing brume
On that harbour-bridge; nor was I he of her tryst.

So loosening from me swift she said:
   'O why, why feign to be
The one I had meant! – to whom I have sped
To fly with, being so sorrily wed!'
  – 'Twas thus and thus that she upbraided me.

My assignation had struck upon
   Some others' like it, I found.
And her lover rose on the night anon;
And then her husband entered on
The lamplit, snowflaked, sloppiness around.

'Take her and welcome, man!' he cried:
   'I wash my hands of her.
I'll find me twice as good a bride!'
– All this to me, whom he had eyed,
Plainly, as his wife's planned deliverer.

And next the lover: 'Little I knew,
   Madam, you had a third!
Kissing here in my very view!'
– Husband and lover then withdrew.
I let them; and I told them not they erred.

Why not? Well, there faced she and I –
   Two strangers who'd kissed, or near,
Chancewise. To see stand weeping by
A woman once embraced, will try
The tension of a man the most austere.

So it began; and I was young,
   She pretty, by the lamp,
As flakes came waltzing down among
The waves of her clinging hair, that hung
Heavily on her temples, dark and damp.

And there alone still stood we two;
   She one cast off for me,
Or so it seemed: while night ondrew,
Forcing a parley what should do
We twain hearts caught in one catastrophe.

In stranded souls a common strait
   Wakes latencies unknown,
Whose impulse may precipitate
A life-long leap. The hour was late,
And there was the Jersey boat with its funnel agroan.

'Is wary walking worth much pother?'
   It grunted, as still it stayed.
'One pairing is as good as another
Where all is venture! Take each other,
And scrap the oaths that you have aforetime made.'

– Of the four involved there walks but one
   On earth at this late day.
And what of the chapter so begun?
In that odd complex what was done?
  Well; happiness comes in full to none:
Let peace lie on lulled lips: I will not say.

  Weymouth

The Torn Letter

I

I TORE your letter into strips
   No bigger than the airy feathers
   That ducks preen out in changing weathers
Upon the shifting ripple-tips.

II

In darkness on my bed alone
   I seemed to see you in a vision,
   And hear you say: 'Why this derision
Of one drawn to you, though unknown?'

III

Yes, eve's quick mood had run its course,
   The night had cooled my hasty madness;
   I suffered a regretful sadness
Which deepened into real remorse.

IV

I thought what pensive patient days
   A soul must know of grain so tender,
   How much of good must grace the sender
Of such sweet words in such bright phrase.

V

Uprising then, as things unpriced
    I sought each fragment, patched and mended;
    The midnight whitened ere I had ended
And gathered words I had sacrificed.

VI

But some, alas, of those I threw
    Were past my search, destroyed for ever:
    They were your name and place; and never
Did I regain those clues to you.

VII

I learnt I had missed, by rash unheed,
    My track; that, so the Will decided,
    In life, death, we should be divided,
And at the sense I ached indeed.

VIII

That ache for you, born long ago,
    Throbs on: I never could outgrow it.
    What a revenge, did you but know it!
But that, thank God, you do not know.

At Wynyard's Gap[28]

SHE (*on horseback*)

THE hounds pass here?

HE (*on horseback*)

                     They did an hour ago,
Just in full cry, and went down-wind, I saw,
Towards Pen Wood, where they may kill, and draw
A second time, and bear towards the Yeo.

SHE

How vexing! And I've crept along unthinking.

HE

Ah! – lost in dreams. Fancy to fancy linking!

SHE (*more softly*)

Not that, quite . . . Now, to settle what I'll do.

HE

Go home again. But have you seen the view
From the top there? Not? It's really worth your while. –
You must dismount, because there is a stile.

*They dismount, hitch their horses, and climb a few-score yards from
the road.*

There you see half South Wessex, – combe, and glen,
And down, to Lewsdon Hill and Pilsdon Pen.

SHE

Yes. It is fine. And I, though living out there
By Crewkerne, never knew it. (*She turns her head*) Well, I declare,
Look at the horses! – How shall I catch my mare?

The horses have got loose and scampered off.

Now that's your fault, through leading me up here!
You must have known 'twould happen –

HE

No, my dear!

SHE

I'm not your dear.

HE (*blandly*)

But you can't help being so,
If it comes to that. The fairest girl I've seen
Is of course dear – by her own fault, I mean.

SHE (*quickly*)

What house is that we see just down below?

HE

Oh – that's the inn called 'Wynyard's Gap'. – I'll go
While you wait here, and catch those brutes. Don't stir.

He goes. She waits.

SHE

What a handsome man. Not local, I'll aver.

He comes back.

HE

I met a farmer's labourer some way on;
He says he'll bring them to us here anon,
If possible before the day is dim.
Come down to the inn: there we can wait for him.

They descend slowly in that direction.

SHE

What a lonely inn. Why is there such a one?

HE

For us to wait at. Thus 'tis things are done.

SHE

Thus things are done? Well – what things do you mean?

HE

Romantic things. Meetings unknown, unseen.

SHE

But ours is accident, and needn't have been,
And isn't what I'd plan with a stranger, quite,
Particularly at this time – nearly night.

153

HE

Nor I. But still, the tavern's loneliness
Is favourable for lovers in distress,
When they've eloped, for instance, and are in fear
Of being pursued. No one would find them here.

He goes to speak to the labourer approaching; and returns.

He says the horses long have passed the combe,
And cannot be overtaken. They'll go home.

SHE

And what's to be done? And it's beginning to rain.
'Tis always so. One trouble brings a train!

HE

It seems to me that here we'd better stay
And rest us till some vehicle comes this way:
In fact, we might put up here till the morning:
The floods are high, and night-farers have warning.

SHE

Put up? Do you think so!

HE

         I incline to such,
My *dear* (do you mind?)

SHE

  Yes. – Well (*more softly*), I don't much,
If I seem like it. But I ought to tell you
One thing. I'm married. Being so, it's well you –

HE

Oh, so am I. (*A silence, he regarding her*) I note a charming thing –
You stand so stock-still that your ear-ring shakes
At each pulsation which the vein there makes.

SHE

Does it? Perhaps because it's flustering.
To be caught thus! (*In a murmur*) Why did we chance to meet
    here?

HE

God knows! Perhaps to taste a bitter-sweet here. –
Still, let us enter. Shelter we must get:
The night is darkening and is growing wet.
So, anyhow, you can treat me as a lover
Just for this once. To-morrow 'twill be over!

> *They reach the inn. The door is locked, and they
> discern a board marked 'To Let'. While they stand
> stultified a van is seen drawing near, with passengers.*

SHE

Ah, here's an end of it! The Crewkerne carrier.

HE

So cynic circumstance erects its barrier!

SHE (*mischievously*)

To your love-making, which would have grown stronger,
No doubt, if we had stayed on here much longer?

> *The carrier comes up. Her companion reluctantly hails him.*

HE

Yes . . . And in which you might have shown some ruth,
Had but the inn been open! – Well, forsooth,
I'm sorry it's not. Are you? Now, dear, the truth!

SHE (*with gentle evasiveness*)

I am – almost. But best 'tis thus to be.
For – dear one – there I've said it! – you can see
That both at one inn (though roomed separately,
Of course) – so lone, too – might have been unfit,
Perfect as 'tis for lovers, I admit.

HE (*after a sigh*)

Carrier! A lift for my wife, please.

SHE (*in quick undertones*)

Wife? But nay –

HE (*continuing*)

Her horse has thrown her and has gone astray:
See she gets safe to Crewkerne. I've to stay.

CARRIER

I will, sir! I'm for Crookhorn straight away.

HE (*to her, aloud*)

Right now, dear. I shall soon be home. Adieu! (*Kisses her*)

SHE (*whispering confusedly*)

You shouldn't! Pretending you are my husband, too!
I now must act the part of wife to you!

HE (*whispering*)

Yes, since I've kissed you, dear. You see it's done
To silence tongues as we're found here alone
At night, by gossipers, and seem as shown
Staying together!

SHE (*whispering*)

Then must I, too, kiss?

HE

Yes: a mere matter of form, you know,
To check all scandal. People will talk so!

SHE

I'd no idea it would reach to this!   (*Kisses him*)
What makes it worse is, I'm ashamed to say,
I've a young baby waiting me at home!

HE

Ah – there you beat me! – But, my dearest, play
The wife to the end, and don't give me away,
Despite the baby, since we've got so far,
And what we've acted feel we almost are!

SHE (*sighing*)

Yes. 'Tis so! And my conscience has gone dumb!
  (*Aloud*)
'Bye, dear, awhile! I'll sit up till you come.
  (*In a whisper*)
Which means Good-bye for ever, truly heard!
Upon to-night be silent!

HE
                    Never a word,
Till Pilsdon Pen by Marshwood wind is stirred!

He hands her up. Exeunt omnes.

The Rejected Member's Wife

WE shall see her no more
        On the balcony,
Smiling, while hurt, at the roar
        As of surging sea
From the stormy sturdy band
        Who have doomed her lord's cause,
Though she waves her little hand
        As it were applause.

Here will be candidates yet,
        And candidates' wives,
Fervid with zeal to set
        Their ideals on our lives:
Here will come market-men
        On the market-days,
Here will clash now and then
        More such party assays.

And the balcony will fill
        When such times are renewed,
And the throng in the street will thrill
        With to-day's mettled mood;
But she will no more stand
        In the sunshine there,
With that wave of her white-gloved hand,
        And that chestnut hair.

January 1906

Midnight on the Great Western

IN the third-class seat sat the journeying boy,
        And the roof-lamp's oily flame
Played down on his listless form and face,
Bewrapt past knowing to what he was going,
        Or whence he came.

In the band of his hat the journeying boy
        Had a ticket stuck; and a string
Around his neck bore the key of his box,
That twinkled gleams of the lamp's sad beams
        Like a living thing.

What past can be yours, O journeying boy
        Towards a world unknown,
Who calmly, as if uncurious quite
On all at stake, can undertake
        This plunge alone?

Knows your soul a sphere, O journeying boy,
        Our rude realms far above,
Whence with spacious vision you mark and mete
This region of sin that you find you in,
        But are not of?

In a Waiting-Room

ON a morning sick as the day of doom
    With the drizzling gray
    Of an English May,
There were few in the railway waiting-room.
About its walls were framed and varnished
Pictures of liners, fly-blown, tarnished.
The table bore a Testament
For travellers' reading, if suchwise bent.

    I read it on and on,
And, thronging the Gospel of Saint John,
Were figures – additions, multiplications –
    By some one scrawled, with sundry emendations;
    Not scoffingly designed,
    But with an absent mind, –
Plainly a bagman's counts of cost,
What he had profited, what lost;
And whilst I wondered if there could have been
    Any particle of a soul
    In that poor man at all,
    To cypher rates of wage
    Upon that printed page,
    There joined in the charmless scene
And stood over me and the scribbled book
    (To lend the hour's mean hue
    A smear of tragedy too)
A soldier and wife, with haggard look
Subdued to stone by strong endeavour;
    And then I heard
    From a casual word
They were parting as they believed for ever.

    But next there came
    Like the eastern flame
Of some high altar, children – a pair –
Who laughed at the fly-blown pictures there.

'Here are the lovely ships that we,
Mother, are by and by going to see!
When we get there it's 'most sure to be fine,
And the band will play, and the sun will shine!'

It rained on the skylight with a din
As we waited and still no train came in;
But the words of the child in the squalid room
Had spread a glory through the gloom.

The New Toy

SHE cannot leave it alone,
        The new toy;
She pats it, smooths it, rights it, to show it's her own,
As the other train-passengers muse on its temper and tone,
        Till she draws from it cries of annoy: –
She feigns to appear as if thinking it nothing so rare
        Or worthy of pride, to achieve
This wonder a child, though with reason the rest of them there
        May so be inclined to believe.

A Wife and Another

'WAR ends, and he's returning
        Early; yea,
The evening next to-morrow's!' –
        – This I say
To her, whom I suspiciously survey,

Holding my husband's letter
        To her view. –
She glanced at it but lightly,
        And I knew
That one from him that day had reached her too.

There was no time for scruple;
    Secretly
I filched her missive, conned it,
    Learnt that he
Would lodge with her ere he came home to me.

To reach the port before her,
    And, unscanned,
There wait to intercept them
    Soon I planned:
That, in her stead, *I* might before him stand.

So purposed, so effected;
    At the inn
Assigned, I found her hidden: –
    O that sin
Should bear what she bore when I entered in!

Her heavy lids grew laden
    With despairs,
Her lips made soundless movements
    Unawares,
While I peered at the chamber hired as theirs.

And as beside its doorway,
    Deadly hued,
One inside, one withoutside
    We two stood,
He came – my husband – as she knew he would.

No pleasurable triumph
    Was that sight!
The ghastly disappointment
    Broke them quite.
What love was theirs, to move them with such might!

'Madam, forgive me!' said she,
    Sorrow be it,
'A child – I soon shall bear him . . .
    Yes – I meant
To tell you – that he won me ere he went.'

Then, as it were, within me
Something snapped,
As if my soul had largened:
Conscience-capped,
I saw myself the snarer – them the trapped.

'My hate dies, and I promise,
Grace-beguiled,'
I said, 'to care for you, be
Reconciled;
And cherish, and take interest in the child.'

Without more words I pressed him
Through the door
Within which she stood, powerless
To say more,
And closed it on them, and downstairward bore.

'He joins his wife – my sister,'
I, below,
Remarked in going – lightly –
Even as though
All had come right, and we had arranged it so . . .

As I, my road retracing,
Left them free,
The night alone embracing
Childless me,
I held I had not stirred God wrothfully.

The Collector Cleans His Picture[29]

Fili hominis, ecce ego tollo a te desiderabile oculorum tuorum in plaga. –
EZECH., XXIV 16

How I remember cleaning that strange picture! . . .
I had been deep in duty for my sick neighbour –
His besides my own – over several Sundays,
Often, too, in the week; so with parish pressures,
Baptisms, burials, doctorings, conjugal counsel –

All the whatnots asked of a rural parson –
Faith, I was well-nigh broken, should have been fully
Saving for one small secret relaxation,
One that in mounting manhood had grown my hobby.

This was to delve at whiles for easel-lumber,
Stowed in the backmost slums of a soon-reached city,
Merely on chance to uncloak some worthy canvas,
Panel, or plaque, blacked blind by uncouth adventure,
Yet under all concealing a precious artfeat.
Such I had found not yet. My latest capture
Came from the rooms of a trader in ancient house-gear
Who had no scent of beauty or soul for brushcraft.
Only a tittle cost it – murked with grimefilms,
Gatherings of slow years, thick-varnished over,
Never a feature manifest of man's painting.

So, one Saturday, time ticking hard on midnight
Ere an hour subserved, I set me upon it.
Long with coiled-up sleeves I cleaned and yet cleaned,
Till a first fresh spot, a high light, looked forth,
Then another, like fair flesh, and another;
Then a curve, a nostril, and next a finger,
Tapering, shapely, significantly pointing slantwise.
'Flemish?' I said. 'Nay, Spanish . . . But, nay, Italian!'
– Then meseemed it the guise of the ranker Venus,
Named of some Astarte, of some Cotytto.
Down I knelt before it and kissed the panel,
Drunk with the lure of love's inhibited dreamings.

Till the dawn I rubbed, when there leered up at me
A hag, that had slowly emerged from under my hands there,
Pointing the slanted finger towards a bosom
Eaten away of a rot from the lusts of a lifetime . . .
– I could have ended myself at the lashing lesson!
Stunned I sat till roused by a clear-voiced bell-chime,
Fresh and sweet as the dew-fleece under my luthern.
It was the matin service calling to me
From the adjacent steeple.

The Enemy's Portrait

HE saw the portrait of his enemy, offered
At auction in a street he journeyed nigh,
That enemy, now late dead, who in his lifetime
Had injured deeply him the passer-by.
'To get that picture, pleased be God, I'll try,
And utterly destroy it; and no more
Shall be inflicted on man's mortal eye
A countenance so sinister and sore!'

And so he bought the painting. Driving homeward,
'The frame will come in useful,' he declared,
'The rest is fuel.' On his arrival, weary,
Asked what he bore with him, and how he fared,
He said he had bid for a picture, though he cared
For the frame only: on the morrow he
Would burn the canvas, which could well be spared,
Seeing that it portrayed his enemy.

Next day some other duty found him busy:
The foe was laid his face against the wall;
But on the next he set himself to loosen
The straining-strips. And then a casual call
Prevented his proceeding therewithal;
And thus the picture waited, day by day,
Its owner's pleasure, like a wretched thrall,
Until a month and more had slipped away.

And then upon a morn he found it shifted,
Hung in a corner by a servitor.
'Why did you take on you to hang that picture?
You know it was the frame I bought it for.'
'It stood in the way of every visitor,
And I just hitched it there.' – 'Well, it must go:
I don't commemorate men whom I abhor.
Remind me 'tis to do. The frame I'll stow.'

But things become forgotten. In the shadow
Of the dark corner hung it by its string,
And there it stayed – once noticed by its owner,
Who said, 'Ah me – I must destroy that thing!'
But when he died, there, none remembering,
It hung, till moved to prominence, as one sees;
And comers pause and say, examining,
'I thought they were the bitterest enemies?'

The Glimpse

SHE sped through the door
And, following in haste,
And stirred to the core,
I entered hot-faced;
But I could not find her,
No sign was behind her.
'Where is she?' I said:
– 'Who?' they asked that sat there;
'Not a soul's come in sight.'
– 'A maid with red hair.'
– 'Ah.' They paled. 'She is dead.
People see her at night,
But you are the first
On whom she has burst
In the keen common light.'

It was ages ago,
When I was quite strong:
I have waited since, – O,
I have waited so long!
– Yea, I set me to own
The house, where now lone
I dwell in void rooms
Booming hollow as tombs!
But I never come near her,
Though nightly I hear her.

And my cheek has grown thin
And my hair has grown gray
With this waiting therein;
But she still keeps away!

The Pedestrian

AN INCIDENT OF 1883

'SIR, will you let me give you a ride?
Nox venit, and the heath is wide.'
– My phaeton-lantern shone on one
    Young, fair, even fresh,
    But burdened with flesh:
A leathern satchel at his side,
His breathings short, his coat undone.

'Twas as if his corpulent figure slopped
With the shake of his walking when he stopped,
And, though the night's pinch grew acute,
    He wore but a thin
    Wind-thridded suit,
Yet well-shaped shoes for walking in,
Artistic beaver, cane gold-topped.

'Alas, my friend,' he said with a smile,
'I am daily bound to foot ten mile –
Wet, dry, or dark – before I rest.
    Six months to live
    My doctors give
Me as my prospect here, at best,
Unless I vamp my sturdiest!'

His voice was that of a man refined,
A man, one well could feel, of mind,
Quite winning in its musical ease;
    But in mould maligned
    By some disease;
And I asked again. But he shook his head;
Then, as if more were due, he said: –

'A student was I – of Schopenhauer,
Kant, Hegel, – and the fountained bower
Of the Muses, too, knew my regard:
    But ah – I fear me
    The grave gapes near me! . . .
Would I could this gross sheath discard,
And rise an ethereal shape, unmarred!'

How I remember him! – his short breath,
His aspect, marked for early death,
As he dropped into the night for ever;
    One caught in his prime
    Of high endeavour;
From all philosophies soon to sever
Through an unconscienced trick of Time!

Beyond the Last Lamp

(NEAR TOOTING COMMON)

I

WHILE rain, with eve in partnership,
Descended darkly, drip, drip, drip,
Beyond the last lone lamp I passed
    Walking slowly, whispering sadly,
    Two linked loiterers, wan, downcast:
Some heavy thought constrained each face,
And blinded them to time and place.

II

The pair seemed lovers, yet absorbed
In mental scenes no longer orbed
By love's young rays. Each countenance
    As it slowly, as it sadly
    Caught the lamplight's yellow glance,
Held in suspense a misery
At things which had been or might be.

III

When I retrod that watery way
Some hours beyond the droop of day,
Still I found pacing there the twain
    Just as slowly, just as sadly,
      Heedless of the night and rain.
One could but wonder who they were
And what wild woe detained them there.

IV

Though thirty years of blur and blot
Have slid since I beheld that spot,
And saw in curious converse there
    Moving slowly, moving sadly
      That mysterious tragic pair,
Its olden look may linger on –
All but the couple; they have gone.

V

Whither? Who knows, indeed . . . And yet
To me, when nights are weird and wet,
Without those comrades there at tryst
    Creeping slowly, creeping sadly,
      That lone lane does not exist.
There they seem brooding on their pain,
And will, while such a lane remain.

A Light Snow-Fall after Frost

ON the flat road a man at last appears:
    How much his whitening hairs
Owe to the settling snow's mute anchorage,
And how much to life's rough pilgrimage,
    One cannot certify.

    The frost is on the wane,
And cobwebs hanging close outside the pane

Pose as festoons of thick white worsted there,
Of their pale presence no eye being aware
    Till the rime made them plain.

    A second man comes by;
His ruddy beard brings fire to the pallid scene:
    His coat is faded green;
    Hence seems it that his mien
    Wears something of the dye
Of the berried holm-trees that he passes nigh.

The snow-feathers so gently swoop that though
    But half an hour ago
The road was brown, and now is starkly white,
A watcher would have failed defining quite
    When it transformed it so.

Near Surbiton

In the British Museum

'WHAT do you see in that time-touched stone,
    When nothing is there
But ashen blankness, although you give it
    A rigid stare?

'You look not quite as if you saw,
    But as if you heard,
Parting your lips, and treading softly
    As mouse or bird.

'It is only the base of a pillar, they'll tell you,
    That came to us
From a far old hill men used to name
    Areopagus.'

– 'I know no art, and I only view
    A stone from a wall,
But I am thinking that stone has echoed
    The voice of Paul,

'Paul as he stood and preached beside it
  Facing the crowd,
A small gaunt figure with wasted features,
  Calling out loud

'Words that in all their intimate accents
  Patterned upon
That marble front, and were wide reflected,
  And then were gone.

'I'm a labouring man, and know but little,
  Or nothing at all;
But I can't help thinking that stone once echoed
  The voice of Paul.'

At Madame Tussaud's in Victorian Years

'That same first fiddler who leads the orchestra to-night
 Here fiddled four decades of years ago;
He bears the same babe-like smile of self-centred delight,
Same trinket on watch-chain, same ring on the hand with the
  bow.

'But his face, if regarded, is woefully wanner, and drier,
 And his once dark beard has grown straggling and gray;
Yet a blissful existence he seems to have led with his lyre,
In a trance of his own, where no wearing or tearing had sway.

'Mid these wax figures, who nothing can do, it may seem
 That to do but a little thing counts a great deal;
To be watched by kings, councillors, queens, may be flattering to
  him –
With their glass eyes longing they too could wake notes that
  appeal.'

   •   •   •

Ah, but he played staunchly – that fiddler – whoever he was,
 With the innocent heart and the soul-touching string:

May he find the Fair Haven! For did he not smile with good
    cause?
Yes; gamuts that graced forty years'-flight were not a small
    thing!

Barthélémon at Vauxhall

François Hippolite Barthélémon, first-fiddler at Vauxhall Gardens, composed
what was probably the most popular morning hymn-tune ever written. It
was formerly sung, full-voiced, every Sunday in most churches, to Bishop
Ken's words, but is now seldom heard.

HE said: 'Awake my soul, and with the sun,' . . .
And paused upon the bridge, his eyes due east,
Where was emerging like a full-robed priest
The irradiate globe that vouched the dark as done.

It lit his face – the weary face of one
Who in the adjacent gardens charged his string,
Nightly, with many a tuneful tender thing,
Till stars were weak, and dancing hours outrun.

And then were threads of matin music spun
In trial tones as he pursued his way:
'This is a morn,' he murmured, 'well begun:
This strain to Ken will count when I am clay!'

And count it did; till, caught by echoing lyres,
It spread to galleried naves and mighty quires.

An East-End Curate

A SMALL blind street off East Commercial Road;
    Window, door; window, door;
    Every house like the one before,
Is where the curate, Mr Dowle, has found a pinched abode.
Spectacled, pale, moustache straw-coloured, and with a long thin
    face,
Day or dark his lodgings' narrow doorstep does he pace.

A bleached pianoforte, with its drawn silk plaitings faded,
Stands in his room, its keys much yellowed, cyphering, and
      abraded,
'Novello's Anthems' lie at hand, and also a few glees,
And 'Laws of Heaven for Earth' in a frame upon the wall one
      sees.

He goes through his neighbours' houses as his own, and none
      regards,
And opens their back-doors off-hand, to look for them in their
      yards:
A man is threatening his wife on the other side of the wall,
But the curate lets it pass as knowing the history of it all.

Freely within his hearing the children skip and laugh and say:
      'There's Mister Dow-well! There's Mister Dow-well!'
      in their play;
      And the long, pallid, devoted face notes not,
But stoops along abstractedly, for good, or in vain, Got wot!

No Buyers

A STREET SCENE

A LOAD of brushes and baskets and cradles and chairs
      Labours along the street in the rain:
With it a man, a woman, a pony with whiteybrown hairs. –
      The man foots in front of the horse with a shambling sway
      At a slower tread than a funeral train,
      While to a dirge-like tune he chants his wares,
Swinging a Turk's-head brush (in a drum-major's way
      When the bandsmen march and play).

A yard from the back of the man is the whiteybrown pony's nose:
He mirrors his master in every item of pace and pose:
      He stops when the man stops, without being told,
      And seems to be eased by a pause; too plainly he's old,
      Indeed, not strength enough shows

To steer the disjointed waggon straight,
Which wriggles left and right in a rambling line,
Deflected thus by its own warp and weight,
And pushing the pony with it in each incline.

The woman walks on the pavement verge,
Parallel to the man:
She wears an apron white and wide in span,
And carries a like Turk's-head, but more in nursing-wise:
Now and then she joins in his dirge,
But as if her thoughts were on distant things.
The rain clams her apron till it clings. –
So, step by step, they move with their merchandize,
And nobody buys.

'A Gentleman's Second-Hand Suit'

HERE it is hanging in the sun
By the pawn-shop door,
A dress-suit – all its revels done
Of heretofore.
Long drilled to the waltzer's swing and sway,
As its tokens show:
What it has seen, what it could say
If it did but know!

The sleeve bears still a print of powder
Rubbed from her arms
When she warmed up as the notes swelled louder
And livened her charms –
Or rather theirs, for beauties many
Leant there, no doubt,
Leaving these tell-tale traces when he
Spun them about.

Its cut seems rather in bygone style
On looking close,
So it mayn't have bent it for some while
To the dancing pose:

Anyhow, often within its clasp
    Fair partners hung,
Assenting to the wearer's grasp
    With soft sweet tongue.

Where is, alas, the gentleman
    Who wore this suit?
And where are his ladies? Tell none can:
    Gossip is mute.
Some of them may forget him quite
    Who smudged his sleeve,
Some think of a wild and whirling night
    With him, and grieve.

Last Look round St Martin's Fair [30]

THE sun is like an open furnace door,
Whose round revealed retort confines the roar
    Of fires beyond terrene;
The moon presents the lustre-lacking face
    Of a brass dial gone green,
    Whose hours no eye can trace.
The unsold heathcroppers are driven home
To the shades of the Great Forest whence they come
By men with long cord-waistcoats in brown monochrome.
The stars break out, and flicker in the breeze,
    It seems, that twitches the trees. –
    From its hot idol soon
The fickle unresting earth has turned to a fresh patroon –
    The cold, now brighter, moon.
The woman in red, at the nut-stall with the gun,
    Lights up, and still goes on:
She's redder in the flare-lamp than the sun
    Showed it ere it was gone.
Her hands are black with loading all the day,
And yet she treats her labour as 'twere play,
Tosses her ear-rings, and talks ribaldry

To the young men around as natural gaiety.
And not a weary work she'd readily stay,
And never again nut-shooting see,
Though crying, 'Fire away!'

The Harbour Bridge

FROM here, the quay, one looks above to mark
The bridge across the harbour, hanging dark
Against the day's-end sky, fair-green in glow
Over and under the middle archway's bow:
It draws its skeleton where the sun has set,
Yea, clear from cutwater to parapet;
On which mild glow, too, lines of rope and spar
    Trace themselves black as char.

Down here in shade we hear the painters shift
Against the bollards with a drowsy lift,
As moved by the incoming stealthy tide.
High up across the bridge the burghers glide
As cut black-paper portraits hastening on
In conversation none knows what upon:
Their sharp-edged lips move quickly word by word
    To speech that is not heard.

There trails the dreamful girl, who leans and stops,
There presses the practical woman to the shops,
There is a sailor, meeting his wife with a start,
And we, drawn nearer, judge they are keeping apart.
Both pause. She says: 'I've looked for you. I thought
We'd make it up.' Then no words can be caught.
At last: 'Won't you come home?' She moves still nigher:
    "'Tis comfortable, with a fire.'

'No,' he says gloomily. 'And, anyhow,
I can't give up the other woman now:
You should have talked like that in former days
When I was last home.' They go different ways.

And the west dims, and yellow lamplights shine:
And soon above, like lamps more opaline,
White stars ghost forth, that care not for men's wives,
    Or any other lives.

Weymouth

At the Aquatic Sports

WITH their backs to the sea two fiddlers stand
Facing the concourse on the strand,
    And a third man who sings.
The sports proceed; there are crab-catchings;
The people laugh as levity spreads;
Yet these three do not turn their heads
    To see whence the merriment springs.

They cease their music, but even then
They stand as before, do those three men,
    Though pausing, nought to do:
They never face to the seaward view
To enjoy the contests, add their cheer,
So wholly is their being here
    A business they pursue.

A Hurried Meeting

IT is August moonlight in the tall plantation,
Whose elms, by aged squirrels' footsteps worn,
    Outscreen the noon, and eve, and morn.
On the facing slope a faint irradiation
    From a mansion's marble front is borne,
        Mute in its woodland wreathing.
    Up here the night-jar whirrs forlorn,
And the trees seem to withhold their softest breathing.

176

To the moonshade slips a woman in muslin vesture:
Her naked neck the gossamer-web besmears,
   And she sweeps it away with a hasty gesture.
Again it touches her forehead, her neck, her ears,
      Her fingers, the backs of her hands.
      She sweeps it away again
      Impatiently, and then
She takes no notice; and listens, and sighs, and stands.

The night-hawk stops. A man shows in the obscure:
      They meet, and passively kiss,
And he says: 'Well, I've come quickly. About this –
      Is it really so? You are sure?'
   'I am sure. In February it will be.
   That such a thing should come to me!
We should have known. We should have left off meeting.
Love is a terrible thing: a sweet allure
      That ends in heart-outeating!'

   'But what shall we do, my Love, and how?'
   'You need not call me by that name now.'
Then he more coldly: 'What is your suggestion?'
'I've told my mother, and she sees a way,
Since of our marriage there can be no question.
We are crossing South – near about New Year's Day
      The event will happen there.
It is the only thing that we can dare
      To keep them unaware!'
      'Well, you can marry me.'
She shook her head. 'No: that can never be.

'"Twill be brought home as hers. She's forty-one,
When many a woman's bearing is not done,
      And well might have a son. –
We should have left off specious self-deceiving:
      I feared that such might come,
      And knowledge struck me numb.
Love is a terrible thing: witching when first begun,
      To end in grieving, grieving!'

And with one kiss again the couple parted:
Inferior clearly he; she haughty-hearted.
He watched her down the slope to return to her place,
The marble mansion of her ancient race,
And saw her brush the gossamers from her face
As she emerged from shade to the moonlight ray.
    And when she had gone away
  The night-jar seemed to imp, and say,
   'You should have taken warning:
Love is a terrible thing: sweet for a space,
  And then all mourning, mourning!'

A Last Journey

  'FATHER, you seem to have been sleeping fair?'
The child uncovered the dimity-curtained window-square
    And looked out at the dawn,
    And back at the dying man nigh gone,
    And propped up in his chair,
Whose breathing a robin's 'chink' took up in antiphon.

    The open fireplace spread
  Like a vast weary yawn above his head,
Its thin blue blower waved against his whitening crown,
    For he could not lie down:
  He raised him on his arms so emaciated: –

  'Yes; I've slept long, my child. But as for rest,
    Well, that I cannot say.
The whole night have I footed field and turnpike-way –
  A regular pilgrimage – as at my best
    And very briskest day!

  ''Twas first to Weatherb'ry, to see them there,
    And thence to King's-Stag, where
I joined in a jolly trip to Weydon-Priors Fair:
  I shot for nuts, bought gingerbreads, cream-cheese;
    And, not content with these,
I went to London: heard the watchmen cry the hours.

'I soon was off again, and found me in the bowers
    Of father's apple-trees,
And he shook the apples down: they fell in showers,
Whereon he turned, smiled strange at me, as ill at ease;
    And then you pulled the curtain; and, ah me,
    I found me back where I wished not to be!'

'Twas told the child next day: 'Your father's dead.'
    And, struck, she questioned, 'O,
That journey, then, did father really go? –
Buy nuts, and cakes, and travel at night till dawn was red,
    And tire himself with journeying, as he said,
    To see those old friends that he cared for so?'

The Children and Sir Nameless

SIR NAMELESS, once of Athelhall, declared:
'These wretched children romping in my park
Trample the herbage till the soil is bared,
And yap and yell from early morn till dark!
Go keep them harnessed to their set routines:
Thank God I've none to hasten my decay;
For green remembrance there are better means
Than offspring, who but wish their sires away.'

Sir Nameless of the mansion said anon:
'To be perpetuate for my mightiness
Sculpture must image me when I am gone.'
– He forthwith summoned carvers there express
To shape a figure stretching seven-odd feet
(For he was tall) in alabaster stone,
With shield, and crest, and casque, and sword complete:
When done a statelier work was never known.

Three hundred years hied; Church-restorers came,
And, no one of his lineage being traced,
They thought an effigy so large in frame
Best fitted for the floor. There it was placed,

Under the seats for schoolchildren. And they
Kicked out his name, and hobnailed off his nose;
And, as they yawn through sermon-time, they say,
'Who was this old stone man beneath our toes?'

Squire Hooper

HOOPER was ninety. One September dawn
 He sent a messenger
For his physician, who asked thereupon
 What ailed the sufferer
Which he might circumvent, and promptly bid begone.

'Doctor, I summoned you,' the squire replied –
 'Pooh-pooh me though you may –
To ask what's happened to me – burst inside,
 It seems – not much, I'd say –
But awkward with a house-full here for a shoot to-day.'

And he described the symptoms. With bent head
 The listener looked grave.
'H'm . . . *You're a dead man in six hours*,' he said. –
 'I speak out, since you are brave –
And best 'tis you should know, that last things may be sped.'

'Right,' said the squire. 'And now comes – what to do?
 One thing: on no account
Must I now spoil the sport I've asked them to –
 My guests are paramount –
They must scour scrub and stubble; and big bags bring as due.'

He downed to breakfast, and bespoke his guests: –
 'I find I have to go
An unexpected journey, and it rests
 With you, my friends, to show
The shoot can go off gaily, whether I'm there or no.'

Thus blandly spoke he; and to the fields they went,
   And Hooper up the stair.
They had a glorious day; and stiff and spent
   Returned as dusk drew near. –
'Gentlemen,' said the doctor, 'he's not back as meant,

To his deep regret!' – So they took leave, each guest
   Observing: 'I dare say
Business detains him in the town: 'tis best
   We should no longer stay
Just now. We'll come again anon;' and they went their way.

Meeting two men in the obscurity
   Shouldering a box a thin
Cloth-covering wrapt, one sportsman cried: 'Damn me,
   I thought them carrying in,
At first, a coffin; till I knew it could not be.'

Winter Night in Woodland[31]

(OLD TIME)

THE bark of a fox rings, sonorous and long: –
Three barks, and then silentness; 'wong, wong, wong!'
   In quality horn-like, yet melancholy,
   As from teachings of years; for an old one is he.
The hand of all men is against him, he knows; and yet, why?
That he knows not, – will never know, down to his death-halloo
   cry.

With clap-nets and lanterns off start the bird-baiters,
In trim to make raids on the roosts in the copse,
   Where they beat the boughs artfully, while their awaiters
   Grow heavy at home over divers warm drops.
The poachers, with swingels, and matches of brimstone, outcreep
To steal upon pheasants and drowse them a-perch and asleep.

Out there, on the verge, where a path wavers through,
Dark figures, filed singly, thrid quickly the view,
   Yet heavily laden: land-carriers are they
   In the hire of the smugglers from some nearest bay.

Each bears his two 'tubs', slung across, one in front, one behind,
To a further snug hiding, which none but themselves are to find.

And then, when the night has turned twelve the air brings
    From dim distance, a rhythm of voices and strings:
'Tis the quire, just afoot on their long yearly rounds,
    To rouse by worn carols each house in their bounds;
Robert Penny, the Dewys, Mail, Voss, and the rest; till anon
Tired and thirsty, but cheerful, they home to their beds in the
    dawn.

Friends Beyond [32]

WILLIAM DEWY, Tranter Reuben, Farmer Ledlow late at
    plough,
        Robert's kin, and John's, and Ned's,
And the Squire, and Lady Susan, lie in Mellstock churchyard
    now!

'Gone,' I call them, gone for good, that group of local hearts and
    heads;
        Yet at mothy curfew-tide,
And at midnight when the noon-heat breathes it back from walls
    and leads,

They've a way of whispering to me – fellow-wight who yet
    abide –
        In the muted, measured note
Of a ripple under archways, or a lone cave's stillicide:

'We have triumphed: this achievement turns the bane to
    antidote,
        Unsuccesses to success,
Many thought-worn eves and morrows to a morrow free of
    thought.

'No more need we corn and clothing, feel of old terrestrial stress;
        Chill detraction stirs no sigh;
Fear of death has even bygone us: death gave all that we possess.'

W.D. – 'Ye mid burn the old bass-viol that I set such value by.'
Squire. – 'You may hold the manse in fee,
    You may wed my spouse, may let my children's memory of
        me die.'

Lady S. – 'You may have my rich brocades, my laces; take each
        household key;
    Ransack coffer, desk, bureau;
    Quiz the few poor treasures hid there, con the letters kept by
        me.'

Far. – 'Ye mid zell my favourite heifer, ye mid let the charlock
        grow,
    Foul the grinterns, give up thrift.'
Far. Wife. – 'If ye break my best blue china, children, I shan't
    care or ho.'

All. – 'We've no wish to hear the tidings, how the people's
        fortunes shift;
    What your daily doings are;
    Who are wedded, born, divided; if your lives beat slow or
        swift.

'Curious not the least are we if our intents you make or mar,
        If you quire to our old tune,
If the City stage still passes, if the weirs still roar afar.'

– Thus, with very gods' composure, freed those crosses late and
        soon
        Which, in life, the Trine allow
(Why, none witteth), and ignoring all that haps beneath the
        moon,

William Dewy, Tranter Reuben, Farmer Ledlow late at plough,
        Robert's kin, and John's, and Ned's,
And the Squire, and Lady Susan, murmur mildly to me now.

The Rash Bride

AN EXPERIENCE OF THE MELLSTOCK QUIRE

I

WE Christmas-carolled down the Vale, and up the Vale, and round the Vale,
We played and sang that night as we were yearly wont to do –
A carol in a minor key, a carol in the major D,
Then at each house: 'Good wishes: many Christmas joys to you!'

II

Next, to the widow's John and I and all the rest drew on. And I
Discerned that John could hardly hold the tongue of him for joy.
The widow was a sweet young thing whom John was bent on marrying,
And quiring at her casement seemed romantic to the boy.

III

'She'll make reply, I trust,' said he, 'to our salute? She must!' said he,
'And then I will accost her gently – much to her surprise! –
For knowing not I am with you here, when I speak up and call her dear
A tenderness will fill her voice, a bashfulness her eyes.'

IV

So, by her window-square we stood; ay, with our lanterns there we stood,
And he along with us, – not singing, waiting for a sign;
And when we'd quired her carols three a light was lit and out looked she,
A shawl about her bedgown, and her colour red as wine.

V

And sweetly then she bowed her thanks, and smiled, and spoke aloud her thanks;

When lo, behind her back there, in the room, a man appeared.
I knew him – one from Woolcomb way – Giles Swetman – honest
    as the day,
But eager, hasty; and I felt that some strange trouble neared.

VI

'How comes he there? . . . Suppose,' said we, 'she's wed of late!
    Who knows?' said we.
– 'She married yester-morning – only mother yet has known
The secret o't!' shrilled one small boy. 'But now I've told, let's
    wish 'em joy!'
A heavy fall aroused us: John had gone down like a stone.

VII

We rushed to him and caught him round, and lifted him, and
    brought him round,
When, hearing something wrong had happened, oped the
    window she:
'Has one of you fallen ill?' she asked, 'by these night labours
    overtasked?'
None answered. That she'd done poor John a cruel turn felt we.

VIII

Till up spoke Michael: 'Fie, young dame! You've broke your
    promise, sly young dame,
By forming this new tie, young dame, and jilting John so true,
Who trudged to-night to sing to 'ee because he thought he'd
    bring to 'ee
Good wishes as your coming spouse. May ye such trifling rue!'

IX

Her man had said no word at all; but being behind had heard it
    all,
And now cried: 'Neighbours, on my soul I knew not 'twas like
    this!'
And then to her: 'If I had known you'd had in tow not me alone,
No wife should you have been of mine. It is a dear bought bliss!'

X

She changed death-white, and heaved a cry: we'd never heard so
grieved a cry
As came from her at this from him: heartbroken quite seemed
she;
And suddenly, as we looked on, she turned, and rushed; and she
was gone,
Whither, her husband, following after, knew not; nor knew we.

XI

We searched till dawn about the house; within the house,
without the house,
We searched among the laurel boughs that grew beneath the
wall,
And then among the crocks and things, and stores for winter
junketings,
In linhay, loft, and dairy; but we found her not at all.

XII

Then John rushed in: 'O friends,' he said, 'hear this, this, this!'
and bends his head:
'I've – searched round by the – *well*, and find the cover open
wide!
I am fearful that – I can't say what . . . Bring lanterns, and
some cords to knot.'
We did so, and we went and stood the deep dark hole beside.

XIII

And then they, ropes in hand, and I – ay, John, and all the band,
and I
Let down a lantern to the depths – some hundred feet and more;
It glimmered like a fog-dimmed star; and there, beside its light,
afar,
White drapery floated, and we knew the meaning that it bore.

XIV

The rest is naught . . . We buried her o' Sunday. Neighbours
carried her;

And Swetman – he who'd married her – now miserablest of men,
Walked mourning first; and then walked John; just quivering,
  but composed anon;
And we the quire formed round the grave, as was the custom
  then.

XV

Our old bass player, as I recall – his white hair blown – but why
  recall! –
His viol upstrapped, bent figure – doomed to follow her full
  soon –
Stood bowing, pale and tremulous; and next to him the rest of
  us . . .
We sang the Ninetieth Psalm to her – set to Saint Stephen's
  tune.

The Country Wedding

(A FIDDLER'S STORY)

LITTLE fogs were gathered in every hollow,
But the purple hillocks enjoyed fine weather
As we marched with our fiddles over the heather
– How it comes back! – to their wedding that day.

Our getting there brought our neighbours and all, O!
Till, two and two, the couples stood ready.
And her father said: 'Souls, for God's sake, be steady!'
And we strung up our fiddles, and sounded out 'A'.

The groomsman he stared, and said, 'You must follow!'
But we'd gone to fiddle in front of the party,
(Our feelings as friends being true and hearty)
And fiddle in front we did – all the way.

Yes, from their door by Mill-tail-Shallow,
And up Styles-Lane, and by Front-Street houses,
Where stood maids, bachelors, and spouses,
Who cheered the songs that we knew how to play.

I bowed the treble before her father,
Michael the tenor in front of the lady,
The bass-viol Reub – and right well played he! –
The serpent Jim; ay, to church and back.

I thought the bridegroom was flurried rather,
As we kept up the tune outside the chancel,
While they were swearing things none can cancel
Inside the walls to our drumstick's whack.

'Too gay!' she pleaded. 'Clouds may gather,
And sorrow come.' But she gave in, laughing,
And by supper-time when we'd got to the quaffing
Her fears were forgot, and her smiles weren't slack.

A grand wedding 'twas! And what would follow
We never thought. Or that we should have buried her
On the same day with the man that married her,
A day like the first, half hazy, half clear.

Yes: little fogs were in every hollow,
Though the purple hillocks enjoyed fine weather,
When we went to play 'em to church together,
And carried 'em there in an after year.

The Paphian Ball

ANOTHER CHRISTMAS EXPERIENCE OF THE MELLSTOCK QUIRE

WE went our Christmas rounds once more,
With quire and viols as theretofore.

Our path was near by Rushy-Pond,
Where Egdon-Heath outstretched beyond.

There stood a figure against the moon,
Tall, spare, and humming a weirdsome tune.

'You tire of Christian carols,' he said:
'Come and lute at a ball instead.

''Tis to your gain, for it ensures
That many guineas will be yours.

'A slight condition hangs on't, true,
But you will scarce say nay thereto:

'That you go blindfold; that anon
The place may not be gossiped on.'

They stood and argued with each other:
'Why sing from one house to another

'These ancient hymns in the freezing night,
And all for nought? 'Tis foolish, quite!'

' – 'Tis serving God, and shunning evil:
Might not elsedoing serve the devil?'

'But grand pay!' . . . They were lured by his call,
Agreeing to go blindfold all.

They walked, he guiding, some new track,
Doubting to find the pathway back.

In a strange hall they found them when
They were unblinded all again.

Gilded alcoves, great chandeliers,
Voluptuous paintings ranged in tiers,

In brief, a mansion large and rare,
With rows of dancers waiting there.

They tuned and played; the couples danced;
Half-naked women tripped, advanced,

With handsome partners footing fast,
Who swore strange oaths, and whirled them past.

And thus and thus the slow hours wore them:
While shone their guineas heaped before them.

Drowsy at length, in lieu of the dance
'*While Shepherds watched* . . .' they bowed by chance;

And in a moment, at a blink,
There flashed a change; ere they could think

The ball-room vanished and all its crew:
Only the well-known heath they view –

The spot of their crossing overnight,
When wheedled by the stranger's sleight.

There, east, the Christmas dawn hung red,
And dark Rainbarrow with its dead

Bulged like a supine negress' breast
Against Clyffe-Clump's faint far-off crest.

Yea; the rare mansion, gorgeous, bright,
The ladies, gallants, gone were quite.

The heaped-up guineas, too, were gone
With the gold table they were on.

'Why did not grasp we what was owed!'
Cried some, as homeward, shamed, they strode.

Now comes the marvel and the warning:
When they had dragged to church next morning,

With downcast heads and scarce a word,
They were astound at what they heard.

Praises from all came forth in showers
For how they'd cheered the midnight hours.

'We've heard you many times,' friends said,
'But like *that* never have you played!

'*Rejoice, ye tenants of the earth,*
And celebrate your Saviour's birth,

'Never so thrilled the darkness through,
Or more inspired us so to do!' . . .

– The man who used to tell this tale
Was the tenor-viol, Michael Mail;

Yes; Mail the tenor, now but earth! –
I give it for what it may be worth.

The Dead Quire

I

BESIDE the Mead of Memories,   .
Where Church-way mounts to Moaning Hill,
The sad man sighed his phantasies:
        He seems to sigh them still.

II

"'Twas the Birth-tide Eve, and the hamleteers
Made merry with ancient Mellstock zest,
But the Mellstock quire of former years
        Had entered into rest.

III

'Old Dewy lay by the gaunt yew tree,
And Reuben and Michael a pace behind,
And Bowman with his family
        By the wall that the ivies bind.

IV

'The singers had followed one by one,
Treble, and tenor, and thorough-bass;
And the worm that wasteth had begun
        To mine their mouldering place.

V

'For two-score years, ere Christ-day light,
Mellstock had throbbed to strains from these;
But now there echoed on the night
        No Christmas harmonies.

VI

'Three meadows off, at a dormered inn,
The youth had gathered in high carouse,
And, ranged on settles, some therein
        Had drunk them to a drowse.

VII

'Loud, lively, reckless, some had grown,
Each dandling on his jigging knee
Eliza, Dolly, Nance, or Joan –
  Livers in levity.

VIII

'The taper flames and hearthfire shine
Grew smoke-hazed to a lurid light,
And songs on subjects not divine
  Were warbled forth that night.

IX

'Yet many were sons and grandsons here
Of those who, on such eves gone by,
At that still hour had throated clear
  Their anthems to the sky.

X

'The clock belled midnight; and ere long
One shouted, "Now 'tis Christmas morn;
Here's to our women old and young,
  And to John Barleycorn!"

XI

They drink the toast and shout again:
The pewter-ware rings back the boom,
And for a breath-while follows then
  A silence in the room.

XII

'When nigh without, as in old days,
The ancient quire of voice and string
Seemed singing words of prayer and praise
  As they had used to sing:

XIII

'While shepherds watch'd their flocks by night, –
Thus swells the long familiar sound
In many a quaint symphonic flight –
    To, *Glory shone around.*

XIV

'The sons defined their fathers' tones,
The widow his whom she had wed,
And others in the minor moans
    The viols of the dead.

XV

'Something supernal has the sound
As verse by verse the strain proceeds,
And stilly staring on the ground
    Each roysterer holds and heeds.

XVI

'Towards its chorded closing bar
Plaintively, thinly, waned the hymn,
Yet lingered, like the notes afar
    Of banded seraphim.

XVII

'With brows abashed, and reverent tread,
The hearkeners sought the tavern door:
But nothing, save wan moonlight, spread
    The empty highway o'er.

XVIII

'While on their hearing fixed and tense
The aerial music seemed to sink,
As it were gently moving thence
    Along the river brink.

XIX

'Then did the Quick pursue the Dead
By crystal Froom that crinkles there;
And still the viewless quire ahead
    Voiced the old holy air.

XX

'By Bank-walk wicket, brightly bleached,
It passed, and 'twixt the hedges twain,
Dogged by the living; till it reached
    The bottom of Church Lane.

XXI

'There, at the turning, it was heard
Drawing to where the churchyard lay:
But when they followed thitherward
    It smalled, and died away.

XXII

'Each headstone of the quire, each mound,
Confronted them beneath the moon;
But no more floated therearound
    That ancient Birth-night tune.

XXIII

'There Dewy lay by the gaunt yew tree,
There Reuben and Michael, a pace behind,
And Bowman with his family
    By the wall that the ivies bind . . .

XXIV

'As from a dream each sobered son
Awoke, and musing reached his door:
'Twas said that of them all, not one
    Sat in a tavern more.'

XXV

– The sad man ceased; and ceased to heed
His listener, and crossed the leaze
From Moaning Hill towards the mead –
    The Mead of Memories.

1897

The Sailor's Mother

'O WHENCE do you come,
Figure in the night-fog that chills me numb?'

'I come to you across from my house up there,
And I don't mind the brine-mist clinging to me
    That blows from the quay,
For I heard him in my chamber, and thought you unaware.'

    'But what did you hear,
That brought you blindly knocking in this middle-watch so
    drear?'

'My sailor son's voice as 'twere calling at your door,
And I don't mind my bare feet clammy on the stones,
    And the blight to my bones,
For he only knows of *this* house I lived in before.'

    'Nobody's nigh,
Woman like a skeleton, with socket-sunk eye.'

'Ah – nobody's nigh! And my life is drearisome,
And this is the old home we loved in many a day
    Before he went away;
And the salt fog mops me. And nobody's come!'

From 'To Please His Wife'

In a Wood

SEE 'THE WOODLANDERS'

PALE beech and pine so blue,
    Set in one clay,
Bough to bough cannot you
    Live out your day?
When the rains skim and skip,
Why mar sweet comradeship,
Blighting with poison-drip
    Neighbourly spray?

Heart-halt and spirit-lame,
    City-opprest,
Unto this wood I came
    As to a nest;
Dreaming that sylvan peace
Offered the harrowed ease –
Nature a soft release
    From men's unrest.

But, having entered in,
    Great growths and small
Show them to men akin –
    Combatants all!
Sycamore shoulders oak,
Bines the slim sapling yoke,
Ivy-spun halters choke
    Elms stout and tall.

Touches from ash, O wych,
    Sting you like scorn!
You, too, brave hollies, twitch
    Sidelong from thorn.
Even the rank poplars bear
Lothly a rival's air,
Cankering in black despair
    If overborne.

Since, then, no grace I find
    Taught me of trees,
Turn I back to my kind,
    Worthy as these.
There at least smiles abound,
There discourse trills around,
There, now and then, are found
    Life-loyalties.

1887 : 1896

The Pine Planters [33]

(MARTY SOUTH'S REVERIE)

I

WE work here together
    In blast and breeze;
He fills the earth in,
    I hold the trees.

He does not notice
    That what I do
Keeps me from moving
    And chills me through.

He has seen one fairer
    I feel by his eye,
Which skims me as though
    I were not by.

And since she passed here
    He scarce has known
But that the woodland
    Holds him alone.

I have worked here with him
    Since morning shine,
He busy with his thoughts
    And I with mine.

I have helped him so many,
    So many days,
But never win any
    Small word of praise!

Shall I not sigh to him
    That I work on
Glad to be nigh to him
    Though hope is gone?

Nay, though he never
    Knew love like mine,
I'll bear it ever
    And make no sign!

II

From the bundle at hand here
    I take each tree,
And set it to stand, here
    Always to be;
When, in a second,
    As if from fear
Of Life unreckoned
    Beginning here,
It starts a sighing
    Through day and night,
Though while there lying
    'Twas voiceless quite.

It will sigh in the morning,
    Will sigh at noon,
At the winter's warning,
    In wafts of June;
Grieving that never
    Kind Fate decreed
It should for ever
    Remain a seed,

And shun the welter
    Of things without,
Unneeding shelter
    From storm and drought.

Thus, all unknowing
    For whom or what
We set it growing
    In this bleak spot,
It still will grieve here
    Throughout its time,
Unable to leave here,
    Or change its clime;
Or tell the story
    Of us to-day
When, halt and hoary,
    We pass away.

Tess's Lament

I

I WOULD that folk forgot me quite,
            Forgot me quite!
I would that I could shrink from sight,
    And no more see the sun.
Would it were time to say farewell,
To claim my nook, to need my knell,
Time for them all to stand and tell
    Of my day's work as done.

II

Ah! dairy where I lived so long,
            I lived so long;
Where I would rise up staunch and strong,
    And lie down hopefully.
'Twas there within the chimney-seat
He watched me to the clock's slow beat –
Loved me, and learnt to call me Sweet,
    And whispered words to me.

199

III

And now he's gone; and now he's gone; . . .
     And now he's gone!
The flowers we potted perhaps are thrown
  To rot upon the farm.
And where we had our supper-fire
May now grow nettle, dock, and briar,
And all the place be mould and mire
  So cozy once and warm.

IV

And it was I who did it all,
     Who did it all;
'Twas I who made the blow to fall
  On him who thought no guile.
Well, it is finished – past, and he
Has left me to my misery,
And I must take my Cross on me
  For wronging him awhile.

V

How gay we looked that day we wed,
     That day we wed!
'May joy be with ye!' they all said
  A-standing by the durn.
I wonder what they say o' us now,
And if they know my lot; and how
She feels who milks my favourite cow,
  And takes my place at churn!

VI

It wears me out to think of it,
     To think of it;
I cannot bear my fate as writ,
  I'd have my life unbe;

Would turn my memory to a blot,
Make every relic of me rot,
My doings be as they were not,
        And gone all trace of me!

Genoa and the Mediterranean

(MARCH 1887)

O EPIC-FAMED, god-haunted Central Sea,
Heave careless of the deep wrong done to thee
When from Torino's track I saw thy face first flash on me.

And multimarbled Genova the Proud,
Gleam all unconscious how, wide-lipped, up-browed,
I first beheld thee clad – not as the Beauty but the Dowd.

Out from a deep-delved way my vision lit
On housebacks pink, green, ochreous – where a slit
Shoreward 'twixt row and row revealed the classic blue through
        it.

And thereacross waved fishwives' high-hung smocks,
Chrome kerchiefs, scarlet hose, darned underfrocks;
Often since when my dreams of thee, O Queen, that frippery
        mocks:

Whereat I grieve, Superba! . . . Afterhours
Within Palazzo Doria's orange bowers
Went far to mend these marrings of thy soul-subliming powers.

But, Queen, such squalid undress none should see,
Those dream-endangering eyewounds no more be
Where lovers first behold thy form in pilgrimage to thee.

Shelley's Skylark

(THE NEIGHBOURHOOD OF LEGHORN: MARCH 1887)

SOMEWHERE afield here something lies
In Earth's oblivious eyeless trust
That moved a poet to prophecies –
A pinch of unseen, unguarded dust:

The dust of the lark that Shelley heard,
And made immortal through times to be; –
Though it only lived like another bird,
And knew not its immortality:

Lived its meek life; then, one day, fell –
A little ball of feather and bone;
And how it perished, when piped farewell,
And where it wastes, are alike unknown.

Maybe it rests in the loam I view,
Maybe it throbs in a myrtle's green,
Maybe it sleeps in the coming hue
Of a grape on the slopes of yon inland scene.

Go find it, faeries, go and find
That tiny pinch of priceless dust,
And bring a casket silver-lined,
And framed of gold that gems encrust;

And we will lay it safe therein,
And consecrate it to endless time;
For it inspired a bard to win
Ecstatic heights in thought and rhyme.

The Bridge of Lodi*

(SPRING 1887)

I

WHEN of tender mind and body,
    I was moved by minstrelsy,
And that air 'The Bridge of Lodi'
    Brought a strange delight to me.

II

In the battle-breathing jingle
    Of its forward-footing tune
I could see the armies mingle,
    And the columns crushed and hewn

*Pronounce 'Loddy'.

III

On that far-famed spot by Lodi
    Where Napoleon clove his way
To his fame, when like a god he
    Bent the nations to his sway.

IV

Hence the tune came capering to me
    While I traced the Rhone and Po;
Nor could Milan's Marvel woo me
    From the spot englamoured so.

V

And to-day, sunlit and smiling,
    Here I stand upon the scene,
With its saffron walls, dun tiling,
    And its meads of maiden green,

VI

Even as when the trackway thundered
    With the charge of grenadiers,
And the blood of forty hundred
    Splashed its parapets and piers . . .

VII

Any ancient crone I'd toady
    Like a lass in young-eyed prime,
Could she tell some tale of Lodi
    At that moving mighty time.

VIII

So, I ask the wives of Lodi
    For traditions of that day;
But, alas! not anybody
    Seems to know of such a fray.

IX

And they heed but transitory
    Marketings in cheese and meat,
Till I judge that Lodi's story
    Is extinct in Lodi's street.

X

Yet while here and there they thrid them
    In their zest to sell and buy,
Let me sit me down amid them
    And behold those thousands die . . .

XI

– Not a creature cares in Lodi
    How Napoleon swept each arch,
Or where up and downward trod he,
    Or for his outmatching march!

XII

So that wherefore should I be here,
    Watching Adda lip the lea,
When the whole romance to see here
    Is the dream I bring with me?

XIII

And why sing 'The Bridge of Lodi'
    As I sit thereon and swing,
When none shows by smile or nod he
    Guesses why or what I sing? . . .

XIV

Since all Lodi, low and head ones,
    Seem to pass that story by,
It may be the Lodi-bred ones
    Rate it truly, and not I.

XV

Once engrossing Bridge of Lodi,
    Is thy claim to glory gone?
Must I pipe a palinody,
    Or be silent thereupon?

XVI

And if here, from strand to steeple,
    Be no stone to fame the fight,
Must I say the Lodi people
    Are but viewing war aright? . . .

XVII

Nay; I'll sing 'The Bridge of Lodi' –
    That long-loved, romantic thing,
Though none show by smile or nod he
    Guesses why and what I sing!

In the Old Theatre, Fiesole

(APRIL 1887)

I TRACED the Circus whose gray stones incline
Where Rome and dim Etruria interjoin,
Till came a child who showed an ancient coin
That bore the image of a Constantine.

She lightly passed; nor did she once opine
How, better than all books, she had raised for me
In swift perspective Europe's history
Through the vast years of Caesar's sceptred line.

For in my distant plot of English loam
'Twas but to delve, and straightway there to find
Coins of like impress. As with one half blind
Whom common simples cure, her act flashed home
In that mute moment to my opened mind
The power, the pride, the reach of perished Rome.

Rome: On the Palatine

(APRIL 1887)

WE walked where Victor Jove was shrined awhile,
And passed to Livia's rich red mural show,
Whence, thridding cave and Criptoportico,
We gained Caligula's dissolving pile.

And each ranked ruin tended to beguile
The outer sense, and shape itself as though
It wore its marble gleams, its pristine glow
Of scenic frieze and pompous peristyle.

When lo, swift hands, on strings nigh overhead,
Began to melodize a waltz by Strauss:
It stirred me as I stood, in Caesar's house,
Raised the old routs Imperial lyres had led,

And blended pulsing life with lives long done,
Till Time seemed fiction, Past and Present one.

Rome: Building a New Street in the Ancient Quarter

(APRIL 1887)

THESE umbered cliffs and gnarls of masonry
Outskeleton Time's central city, Rome;
Whereof each arch, entablature, and dome
Lies bare in all its gaunt anatomy.

And cracking frieze and rotten metope
Express, as though they were an open tome
Top-lined with caustic monitory gnome;
'Dunces, Learn here to spell Humanity!'

And yet within these ruins' very shade
The singing workmen shape and set and join

206

Their frail new mansion's stuccoed cove and quoin
With no apparent sense that years abrade,
Though each rent wall their feeble works invade
Once shamed all such in power of pier and groin.

Rome: The Vatican: Sala delle Muse

(1887)

I SAT in the Muses' Hall at the mid of the day,
And it seemed to grow still, and the people to pass away,
And the chiselled shapes to combine in a haze of sun,
Till beside a Carrara column there gleamed forth One.

She looked not this nor that of those beings divine,
But each and the whole – an essence of all the Nine;
With tentative foot she neared to my halting-place,
A pensive smile on her sweet, small, marvellous face.

'Regarded so long, we render thee sad?' said she.
'Not you,' sighed I, 'but my own inconstancy!
I worship each and each; in the morning one,
And then, alas! another at sink of sun.

'To-day my soul clasps Form; but where is my troth
Of yesternight with Tune: can one cleave to both?'
– 'Be not perturbed,' said she. 'Though apart in fame,
As I and my sisters are one, those, too, are the same.'

– 'But my love goes further – to Story, and Dance, and Hymn,
The lover of all in a sun-sweep is fool to whim –
Is swayed like a river-weed as the ripples run!'
– 'Nay, wooer, thou sway'st not. These are but phases of one;

'And that one is I; and I am projected from thee,
One that out of thy brain and heart thou causest to be –
Extern to thee nothing. Grieve not, nor thyself becall,
Woo where thou wilt; and rejoice thou canst love at all!'

Rome: At the Pyramid of Cestius near the Graves of Shelley and Keats

(1887)

WHO, then, was Cestius,
And what is he to me? –
Amid thick thoughts and memories multitudinous
One thought alone brings he.

I can recall no word
Of anything he did;
For me he is a man who died and was interred
To leave a pyramid

Whose purpose was exprest
Not with its first design,
Nor till, far down in Time, beside it found their rest
Two countrymen of mine.

Cestius in life, maybe,
Slew, breathed out threatening;
I know not. This I know: in death all silently
He does a finer thing,

In beckoning pilgrim feet
With marble finger high
To where, by shadowy wall and history-haunted street,
Those matchless singers lie . . .

– Say, then, he lived and died
That stones which bear his name
Should mark, through Time, where two immortal Shades abide;
It is an ample fame.

Lausanne : In Gibbon's Old Garden : *11–12 p.m.*

27 JUNE 1897

(The 110th anniversary of the completion of the 'Decline and Fall'
at the same hour and place)

A SPIRIT seems to pass,
Formal in pose, but grave withal and grand:
He contemplates a volume in his hand,
And far lamps fleck him through the thin acacias.

Anon the book is closed,
With 'It is finished!' And at the alley's end
He turns, and when on me his glances bend
As from the Past comes speech – small, muted, yet composed.

'How fares the Truth now? – Ill?
– Do pens but slily further her advance?
May not one speed her but in phrase askance?
Do scribes aver the Comic to be Reverend still?

'Still rule those minds on earth
At whom sage Milton's wormwood words were hurled:
"Truth like a bastard comes into the world
Never without ill-fame to him who gives her birth" ?'

The Last Signal[34]

(11 OCT. 1886)

A MEMORY OF WILLIAM BARNES

SILENTLY I footed by an uphill road
That led from my abode to a spot yew-boughed;
Yellowly the sun sloped low down to westward,
And dark was the east with cloud.

Then, amid the shadow of that livid sad east,
Where the light was least, and a gate stood wide,
Something flashed the fire of the sun that was facing it,
Like a brief blaze on that side.

Looking hard and harder I knew what it meant –
The sudden shine sent from the livid east scene;
It meant the west mirrored by the coffin of my friend there,
    Turning to the road from his green,

To take his last journey forth – he who in his prime
Trudged so many a time from that gate athwart the land!
Thus a farewell to me he signalled on his grave-way,
    As with a wave of his hand.

Winterborne-Came Path

The Schreckhorn

(WITH THOUGHTS OF LESLIE STEPHEN)

(JUNE 1897)

ALOOF, as if a thing of mood and whim;
Now that its spare and desolate figure gleams
Upon my nearing vision, less it seems
A looming Alp-height than a guise of him
Who scaled its horn with ventured life and limb,
Drawn on by vague imaginings, maybe,
Of semblance to his personality
In its quaint glooms, keen lights, and rugged trim.

At his last change, when Life's dull coils unwind,
Will he, in old love, hitherward escape,
And the eternal essence of his mind
Enter this silent adamantine shape,
And his low voicing haunt its slipping snows
When dawn that calls the climber dyes them rose?

George Meredith

(1828–1909)

FORTY years aback, when much had place
That since has perished out of mind,
I heard that voice and saw that face.

He spoke as one afoot will wind
A morning horn ere men awake;
His note was trenchant, turning kind.

He was of those whose wit can shake
And riddle to the very core
The counterfeits that Time will break . . .

Of late, when we two met once more,
The luminous countenance and rare
Shone just as forty years before.

So that, when now all tongues declare
His shape unseen by his green hill,
I scarce believe he sits not there.

No matter. Further and further still
Through the world's vaporous vitiate air
His words wing on – as live words will.

May 1909

A Singer Asleep

(ALGERNON CHARLES SWINBURNE, 1837–1909)

I

IN this fair niche above the unslumbering sea,
That sentrys up and down all night, all day,
From cove to promontory, from ness to bay,
The Fates have fitly bidden that he should be
        Pillowed eternally.

II

– It was as though a garland of red roses
Had fallen about the hood of some smug nun
When irresponsibly dropped as from the sun,
In fulth of numbers freaked with musical closes,
Upon Victoria's formal middle time
        His leaves of rhythm and rhyme.

III

O that far morning of a summer day
When, down a terraced street whose pavements lay
Glassing the sunshine into my bent eyes,
I walked and read with a quick glad surprise
  New words, in classic guise, –

IV

The passionate pages of his earlier years,
Fraught with hot sighs, sad laughters, kisses, tears;
Fresh-fluted notes, yet from a minstrel who
Blew them not naïvely, but as one who knew
  Full well why thus he blew.

V

I still can hear the brabble and the roar
At those thy tunes, O still one, now passed through
That fitful fire of tongues then entered new!
Their power is spent like spindrift on this shore;
  Thine swells yet more and more.

VI

– His singing-mistress verily was no other
Than she the Lesbian, she the music-mother
Of all the tribe that feel in melodies;
Who leapt, love-anguished, from the Leucadian steep
Into the rambling world-encircling deep
  Which hides her where none sees.

VII

And one can hold in thought that nightly here
His phantom may draw down to the water's brim,
And hers come up to meet it, as a dim
Lone shine upon the heaving hydrosphere,
And mariners wonder as they traverse near,
  Unknowing of her and him.

VIII

One dreams him sighing to her spectral form:
'O teacher, where lies hid thy burning line;
Where are those songs, O poetess divine
Whose very orts are love incarnadine?'
And her smile back: 'Disciple true and warm,
Sufficient now are thine.' . . .

IX

So here, beneath the waking constellations,
Where the waves peal their everlasting strains,
And their dull subterrene reverberations
Shake him when storms make mountains of their plains –
Him once their peer in sad improvisations,
And deft as wind to cleave their frothy manes –
I leave him, while the daylight gleam declines
Upon the capes and chines.

Bonchurch, 1910

To Shakespeare

AFTER THREE HUNDRED YEARS

BRIGHT baffling Soul, least capturable of themes,
Thou, who display'dst a life of commonplace,
Leaving no intimate word or personal trace
Of high design outside the artistry
Of thy penned dreams,
Still shalt remain at heart unread eternally.

Through human orbits thy discourse to-day,
Despite thy formal pilgrimage, throbs on
In harmonies that cow Oblivion,
And, like the wind, with all-uncared effect
Maintain a sway
Not fore-desired, in tracks unchosen and unchecked.

And yet, at thy last breath, with mindless note
The borough clocks but samely tongued the hour,
The Avon just as always glassed the tower,
Thy age was published on thy passing-bell
    But in due rote
With other dwellers' deaths accorded a like knell.

And at the strokes some townsman (met, maybe,
And thereon queried by some squire's good dame
Driving in shopward) may have given thy name,
With, 'Yes, a worthy man and well-to-do;
    Though, as for me,
I knew him but by just a neighbour's nod, 'tis true.

'I' faith, few knew him much here, save by word,
He having elsewhere led his busier life;
Though to be sure he left with us his wife.'
– 'Ah, one of the tradesmen's sons, I now recall . . .
    Witty, I've heard . . .
We did not know him . . . Well, good-day. Death comes to all.'

So, like a strange bright bird we sometimes find
To mingle with the barn-door brood awhile,
Then vanish from their homely domicile –
Into man's poesy, we wot not whence,
    Flew thy strange mind,
Lodged there a radiant guest, and sped for ever thence.

1916

At Lulworth Cove a Century Back

HAD I but lived a hundred years ago
I might have gone, as I have gone this year,
By Warmwell Cross on to a Cove I know,
And Time have placed his finger on me there:

'*You see that man?*' – I might have looked, and said,
'O yes: I see him. One that boat has brought
Which dropped down Channel round Saint Alban's Head.
So commonplace a youth calls not my thought.'

214

'*You see that man?*' – 'Why yes; I told you; yes:
Of an idling town-sort; thin; hair brown in hue;
And as the evening light scants less and less
He looks up at a star, as many do.'

'*You see that man?*' – 'Nay, leave me!' then I plead,
'I have fifteen miles to vamp across the lea,
And it grows dark, and I am weary-kneed:
I have said the third time; yes, that man I see!'

'Good. That man goes to Rome – to death, despair;
And no one notes him now but you and I:
A hundred years, and the world will follow him there,
And bend with reverence where his ashes lie.'

September 1920

NOTE. – In September 1820 Keats, on his way to Rome, landed one day on
the Dorset coast, and composed the sonnet, 'Bright Star! would I were
steadfast as thou art.' The spot of his landing is judged to have been Lulworth
Cove.

An August Midnight

I

A SHADED lamp and a waving blind,
And the beat of a clock from a distant floor:
On this scene enter – winged, horned, and spined –
A longlegs, a moth, and a dumbledore;
While 'mid my page there idly stands
A sleepy fly, that rubs its hands . . .

II

Thus meet we five, in this still place,
At this point of time, at this point in space.
– My guests besmear my new-penned line,
Or bang at the lamp and fall supine.
'God's humblest, they!' I muse. Yet why?
They know Earth-secrets that know not I.

Max Gate, 1899

The Caged Thrush Freed and Home Again

(VILLANELLE)

'MEN know but little more than we,
Who count us least of things terrene,
How happy days are made to be!

'Of such strange tidings what think ye,
O birds in brown that peck and preen?
Men know but little more than we!

'When I was borne from yonder tree
In bonds to them, I hoped to glean
How happy days are made to be,

'And want and wailing turned to glee;
Alas, despite their mighty mien
Men know but little more than we!

'They cannot change the Frost's decree,
They cannot keep the skies serene;
How happy days are made to be

'Eludes great Man's sagacity
No less than ours, O tribes in treen!
Men know but little more than we
How happy days are made to be.'

At Day-Close in November

THE ten hours' light is abating,
      And a late bird wings across,
Where the pines, like waltzers waiting,
      Give their black heads a toss.

Beech leaves, that yellow the noon-time,
      Float past like specks in the eye;
I set every tree in my June time,
      And now they obscure the sky.

And the children who ramble through here
    Conceive that there never has been
A time when no tall trees grew here,
    That none will in time be seen.

Birds at Winter Nightfall

(TRIOLET)

AROUND the house the flakes fly faster,
And all the berries now are gone
From holly and cotonea-aster
Around the house. The flakes fly! – faster
Shutting indoors that crumb-outcaster
We used to see upon the lawn
Around the house. The flakes fly faster,
And all the berries now are gone!

Max Gate

Winter in Durnover Field

SCENE. – *A wide stretch of fallow ground recently sown with wheat, and frozen to iron hardness. Three large birds walking about thereon, and wistfully eyeing the surface. Wind keen from north-east : sky a dull grey.*

(TRIOLET)

Rook. – Throughout the field I find no grain;
    The cruel frost encrusts the cornland!
Starling. – Aye: patient pecking now is vain
      Throughout the field, I find . . .
Rook. –   No grain!
Pigeon. – Nor will be, comrade, till it rain,
      Or genial thawings loose the lorn land
      Throughout the field.
Rook. –   I find no grain:
    The cruel frost encrusts the cornland!

The Reminder

WHILE I watch the Christmas blaze
Paint the room with ruddy rays,
Something makes my vision glide
To the frosty scene outside.

There, to reach a rotting berry,
Toils a thrush, – constrained to very
Dregs of food by sharp distress,
Taking such with thankfulness.

Why, O starving bird, when I
One day's joy would justify,
And put misery out of view,
Do you make me notice you!

The Darkling Thrush

I LEANT upon a coppice gate
    When Frost was spectre-gray,
And Winter's dregs made desolate
    The weakening eye of day.
The tangled bine-stems scored the sky
    Like strings of broken lyres,
And all mankind that haunted nigh
    Had sought their household fires.

The land's sharp features seemed to be
    The Century's corpse outleant,
His crypt the cloudy canopy,
    The wind his death-lament.
The ancient pulse of germ and birth
    Was shrunken hard and dry,
And every spirit upon earth
    Seemed fervourless as I.

At once a voice arose among
    The bleak twigs overhead
In a full-hearted evensong
    Of joy illimited;
An aged thrush, frail, gaunt, and small,
    In blast-beruffled plume,
Had chosen thus to fling his soul
    Upon the growing gloom.

So little cause for carolings
    Of such ecstatic sound
Was written on terrestrial things
    Afar or nigh around,
That I could think there trembled through
    His happy good-night air
Some blessed Hope, whereof he knew
    And I was unaware.

    31 December 1900

The Rambler

I DO not see the hills around,
Nor mark the tints the copses wear;
I do not note the grassy ground
And constellated daisies there.

I hear not the contralto note
Of cuckoos hid on either hand,
The whirr that shakes the nighthawk's throat
When eve's brown awning hoods the land.

Some say each songster, tree, and mead –
All eloquent of love divine –
Receives their constant careful heed:
Such keen appraisement is not mine.

The tones around me that I hear,
The aspects, meanings, shapes I see,
Are those far back ones missed when near,
And now perceived too late by me!

The Year's Awakening

How do you know that the pilgrim track
Along the belting zodiac
Swept by the sun in his seeming rounds
Is traced by now to the Fishes' bounds
And into the Ram, when weeks of cloud
Have wrapt the sky in a clammy shroud,
And never as yet a tinct of spring
Has shown in the Earth's apparelling;
    O vespering bird, how do you know,
      How do you know?

How do you know, deep underground,
Hid in your bed from sight and sound,
Without a turn in temperature,
With weather life can scarce endure,
That light has won a fraction's strength,
And day put on some moments' length,
Whereof in merest rote will come,
Weeks hence, mild airs that do not numb;
    O crocus root, how do you know,
      How do you know?

February 1910

The Blinded Bird

So zestfully canst thou sing?
And all this indignity,
With God's consent, on thee!
Blinded ere yet a-wing
By the red-hot needle thou,
I stand and wonder how
So zestfully thou canst sing!

Resenting not such wrong,
Thy grievous pain forgot,
Eternal dark thy lot,

Groping thy whole life long,
After that stab of fire;
Enjailed in pitiless wire;
Resenting not such wrong!

Who hath charity? This bird.
Who suffereth long and is kind,
Is not provoked, though blind
And alive ensepulchred?
Who hopeth, endureth all things?
Who thinketh no evil, but sings?
Who is divine? This bird.

The Caged Goldfinch

WITHIN a churchyard, on a recent grave,
      I saw a little cage
That jailed a goldfinch. All was silence save
      Its hops from stage to stage.

There was inquiry in its wistful eye,
      And once it tried to sing;
Of him or her who placed it there, and why,
      No one knew anything.

A Backward Spring

THE trees are afraid to put forth buds,
And there is timidity in the grass;
The plots lie gray where gouged by spuds,
      And whether next week will pass
Free of sly sour winds is the fret of each bush
      Of barberry waiting to bloom.

Yet the snowdrop's face betrays no gloom,
And the primrose pants in its heedless push,
Though the myrtle asks if it's worth the fight
      This year with frost and rime
      To venture one more time

On delicate leaves and buttons of white
From the selfsame bough as at last year's prime,
And never to ruminate on or remember
What happened to it in mid-December.

April 1917

Weathers

I

THIS is the weather the cuckoo likes,
    And so do I;
When showers betumble the chestnut spikes,
    And nestlings fly:
And the little brown nightingale bills his best,
And they sit outside at 'The Travellers' Rest',
And maids come forth sprig-muslin drest,
And citizens dream of the south and west,
    And so do I.

II

This is the weather the shepherd shuns,
    And so do I;
When beeches drip in browns and duns,
    And thresh, and ply;
And hill-hid tides throb, throe on throe,
And meadow rivulets overflow,
And drops on gate-bars hang in a row,
And rooks in families homeward go,
    And so do I.

If It's Ever Spring Again

(SONG)

IF it's ever spring again,
    Spring again,
I shall go where went I when
Down the moor-cock splashed, and hen,

Seeing me not, amid their flounder,
Standing with my arm around her;
If it's ever spring again,
        Spring again,
I shall go where went I then.

If it's ever summer-time,
        Summer-time,
With the hay crop at the prime,
And the cuckoos – two – in rhyme,
As they used to be, or seemed to,
We shall do as long we've dreamed to,
If it's ever summer-time,
        Summer-time,
With the hay, and bees achime.

Summer Schemes

WHEN friendly summer calls again,
        Calls again
Her little fifers to these hills,
We'll go – we two – to that arched fane
Of leafage where they prime their bills
Before they start to flood the plain
With quavers, minims, shakes, and trills.
        ' – We'll go,' I sing; but who shall say
        What may not chance before that day!

And we shall see the waters spring,
        Waters spring
From chinks the scrubby copses crown;
And we shall trace their oncreeping
To where the cascade tumbles down
And sends the bobbing growths aswing,
And ferns not quite but almost drown.
        ' – We shall,' I say; but who may sing
        Of what another moon will bring!

A Wet August

NINE drops of water bead the jessamine,
And nine-and-ninety smear the stones and tiles:
– 'Twas not so in that August – full-rayed, fine –
When we lived out-of-doors, sang songs, strode miles.

Or was there then no noted radiancy
Of summer? Were dun clouds, a dribbling bough,
Gilt over by the light I bore in me,
And was the waste world just the same as now?

It can have been so: yea, that threatenings
Of coming down-drip on the sunless gray,
By the then golden chances seen in things
Were wrought more bright than brightest skies to-day.

1920

A Bird-Scene at a Rural Dwelling

WHEN the inmate stirs, the birds retire discreetly
From the window-ledge, whereon they whistled sweetly
   And on the step of the door,
   In the misty morning hoar;
  But now the dweller is up they flee
  To the crooked neighbouring codlin-tree;
And when he comes fully forth they seek the garden,
And call from the lofty costard, as pleading pardon
   For shouting so near before
   In their joy at being alive: –
Meanwhile the hammering clock within goes five.

I know a domicile of brown and green,
Where for a hundred summers there have been
Just such enactments, just such daybreaks seen.

Snow in the Suburbs

EVERY branch big with it,
    Bent every twig with it;
  Every fork like a white web-foot;
  Every street and pavement mute:
Some flakes have lost their way, and grope back upward, when
Meeting those meandering down they turn and descend again.
    The palings are glued together like a wall,
  And there is no waft of wind with the fleecy fall.

    A sparrow enters the tree,
    Whereon immediately
  A snow-lump thrice his own slight size
  Descends on him and showers his head and eyes,
      And overturns him,
      And near inurns him,
    And lights on a nether twig, when its brush
Starts off a volley of other lodging lumps with a rush.

    The steps are a blanched slope,
    Up which, with feeble hope,
  A black cat comes, wide-eyed and thin;
    And we take him in.

Last Words to a Dumb Friend

PET was never mourned as you,
Purrer of the spotless hue,
Plumy tail, and wistful gaze
While you humoured our queer ways,
Or outshrilled your morning call
Up the stairs and through the hall –
Foot suspended in its fall –
While, expectant, you would stand
Arched, to meet the stroking hand;
Till your way you chose to wend
Yonder, to your tragic end.

Never another pet for me!
Let your place all vacant be;
Better blankness day by day
Than companion torn away.
Better bid his memory fade,
Better blot each mark he made,
Selfishly escape distress
By contrived forgetfulness,
Than preserve his prints to make
Every morn and eve an ache.

From the chair whereon he sat
Sweep his fur, nor wince thereat;
Rake his little pathways out
Mid the bushes roundabout;
Smooth away his talons' mark
From the claw-worn pine-tree bark,
Where he climbed as dusk embrowned,
Waiting us who loitered round.

Strange it is this speechless thing,
Subject to our mastering,
Subject for his life and food
To our gift, and time, and mood;
Timid pensioner of us Powers,
His existence ruled by ours,
Should – by crossing at a breath
Into safe and shielded death,
By the merely taking hence
Of his insignificance –
Loom as largened to the sense,
Shape as part, above man's will,
Of the Imperturbable.

As a prisoner, flight debarred,
Exercising in a yard,
Still retain I, troubled, shaken,
Mean estate, by him forsaken;

And this home, which scarcely took
Impress from his little look,
By his faring to the Dim
Grows all eloquent of him.

Housemate, I can think you still
Bounding to the window-sill,
Over which I vaguely see
Your small mound beneath the tree,
Showing in the autumn shade
That you moulder where you played.

2 October 1904

Proud Songsters

THE thrushes sing as the sun is going,
And the finches whistle in ones and pairs,
And as it gets dark loud nightingales
    In bushes
Pipe, as they can when April wears,
   As if all Time were theirs.

These are brand-new birds of twelve-months' growing,
Which a year ago, or less than twain,
No finches were, nor nightingales,
    Nor thrushes,
But only particles of grain,
   And earth, and air, and rain.

Afternoon Service at Mellstock

(CIRCA 1850)

ON afternoons of drowsy calm
  We stood in the panelled pew,
Singing one-voiced a Tate-and-Brady psalm
  To the tune of 'Cambridge New'.

We watched the elms, we watched the rooks,
    The clouds upon the breeze,
Between the whiles of glancing at our books,
    And swaying like the trees.

So mindless were those outpourings! –
    Though I am not aware
That I have gained by subtle thought on things
    Since we stood psalming there.

The Impercipient

(AT A CATHEDRAL SERVICE)

THAT with this bright believing band
    I have no claim to be,
That faiths by which my comrades stand
    Seem fantasies to me,
And mirage-mists their Shining Land,
    Is a strange destiny.

Why thus my soul should be consigned
    To infelicity,
Why always I must feel as blind
    To sights my brethren see,
Why joys they've found I cannot find,
    Abides a mystery.

Since heart of mine knows not that ease
    Which they know; since it be
That He who breathes All's Well to these
    Breathes no All's-Well to me,
My lack might move their sympathies
    And Christian charity!

I am like a gazer who should mark
    An inland company
Standing upfingered, with, 'Hark! hark!
    The glorious distant sea!'
And feel, 'Alas, 'tis but yon dark
    And wind-swept pine to me!'

Yet I would bear my shortcomings
    With meet tranquillity,
But for the charge that blessed things
    I'd liefer not have be.
O, doth a bird deprived of wings
    Go earth-bound wilfully!

    .   .   .

Enough. As yet disquiet clings
    About us. Rest shall we.

The Voice of Things

FORTY Augusts – aye, and several more – ago,
    When I paced the headlands loosed from dull employ,
The waves huzza'd like a multitude below
    In the sway of an all-including joy
        Without cloy.

Blankly I walked there a double decade after,
    When thwarts had flung their toils in front of me,
And I heard the waters wagging in a long ironic laughter
    At the lot of men, and all the vapoury
        Things that be.

Wheeling change has set me again standing where
    Once I heard the waves huzza at Lammas-tide;
But they supplicate now – like a congregation there
    Who murmur the Confession – I outside,
        Prayer denied.

The Oxen

CHRISTMAS EVE, and twelve of the clock.
    'Now they are all on their knees,'
An elder said as we sat in a flock
    By the embers in hearthside ease.

229

We pictured the meek mild creatures where
    They dwelt in their strawy pen,
Nor did it occur to one of us there
    To doubt they were kneeling then.

So fair a fancy few would weave
    In these years! Yet, I feel,
If someone said on Christmas Eve,
    'Come; see the oxen kneel

'In the lonely barton by yonder coomb
    Our childhood used to know,'
I should go with him in the gloom,
    Hoping it might be so.

1915

God's Funeral[35]

I

I saw a slowly-stepping train –
Lined on the brows, scoop-eyed and bent and hoar –
Following in files across a twilit plain
A strange and mystic form the foremost bore.

II

And by contagious throbs of thought
Or latent knowledge that within me lay
And had already stirred me, I was wrought
To consciousness of sorrow even as they.

III

The fore-borne shape, to my blurred eyes,
At first seemed man-like, and anon to change
To an amorphous cloud of marvellous size,
At times endowed with wings of glorious range.

IV

And this phantasmal variousness
Ever possessed it as they drew along:
Yet throughout all it symboled none the less
Potency vast and loving-kindness strong.

V

Almost before I knew I bent
Towards the moving columns without a word;
They, growing in bulk and numbers as they went,
Struck out sick thoughts that could be overheard: –

VI

'O man-projected Figure, of late
Imaged as we, thy knell who shall survive?
Whence came it we were tempted to create
One whom we can no longer keep alive?

VII

'Framing him jealous, fierce, at first,
We gave him justice as the ages rolled,
Will to bless those by circumstance accurst,
And longsuffering, and mercies manifold.

VIII

'And, tricked by our own early dream
And need of solace, we grew self-deceived,
Our making soon our maker did we deem,
And what we had imagined we believed.

IX

'Till, in Time's stayless stealthy swing,
Uncompromising rude reality
Mangled the Monarch of our fashioning,
Who quavered, sank; and now has ceased to be.

X

'So, toward our myth's oblivion,
Darkling, and languid-lipped, we creep and grope
Sadlier than those who wept in Babylon,
Whose Zion was a still abiding hope.

XI

'How sweet it was in years far hied
To start the wheels of day with trustful prayer,
To lie down liegely at the eventide
    And feel a blest assurance he was there!

XII

'And who or what shall fill his place?
Whither will wanderers turn distracted eyes
For some fixed star to stimulate their pace
Towards the goal of their enterprise?' . . .

XIII

Some in the background then I saw,
Sweet women, youths, men, all incredulous,
Who chimed: 'This is a counterfeit of straw,
This requiem mockery! Still he lives to us!'

XIV

I could not buoy their faith: and yet
Many I had known: with all I sympathized;
And though struck speechless, I did not forget
That what was mourned for, I, too, long had prized.

XV

Still, how to bear such loss I deemed
The insistent question for each animate mind,
And gazing, to my growing sight there seemed
A pale yet positive gleam low down behind,

XVI

Whereof, to lift the general night,
A certain few who stood aloof had said,
'See you upon the horizon that small light –
Swelling somewhat?' Each mourner shook his head.

XVII

And they composed a crowd of whom
Some were right good, and many nigh the best . . .
Thus dazed and puzzled 'twixt the gleam and gloom
Mechanically I followed with the rest.

1908–10

Aquae Sulis

THE chimes called midnight, just at interlune,
And the daytime parle on the Roman investigations
Was shut to silence, save for the husky tune
The bubbling waters played near the excavations.

And a warm air came up from underground,
And the flutter of a filmy shape unsepulchred,
That collected itself, and waited, and looked around:
Nothing was seen, but utterances could be heard:

Those of the Goddess whose shrine was beneath the pile
Of the God with the baldachined altar overhead:
'And what did you win by raising this nave and aisle
Close on the site of the temple I tenanted?

'The notes of your organ have thrilled down out of view
To the earth-clogged wrecks of my edifice many a year,
Though stately and shining once – ay, long ere you
Had set up crucifix and candle here.

'Your priests have trampled the dust of mine without rueing,
Despising the joys of man whom I so much loved,

233

Though my springs boil on by your Gothic arcades and pewing,
And sculptures crude . . . Would Jove they could be removed!'

'Repress, O lady proud, your traditional ires;
You know not by what a frail thread we equally hang;
It is said we are images both – twitched by people's desires;
And that I, as you, fail like a song men yesterday sang!'

'What – a Jumping-jack you, and myself but a poor Jumping-jill,
Now worm-eaten, times agone twitched at Humanity's bid?
O I cannot endure it! – But, chance to us whatso there will,
Let us kiss and be friends! Come, agree you?' – None heard if he
    did . . .

And the olden dark hid the cavities late laid bare,
And all was suspended and soundless as before,
Except for a gossamery noise fading off in the air,
And the boiling voice of the waters' medicinal pour.

Bath

In the Servants' Quarters

'MAN, you too, aren't you, one of these rough followers of the
        criminal?
All hanging hereabout to gather how he's going to bear
Examination in the hall.' She flung disdainful glances on
The shabby figure standing at the fire with others there,
        Who warmed them by its flare.

'No indeed, my skipping maiden: I know nothing of the trial
        here,
Or criminal, if so he be. – I chanced to come this way,
And the fire shone out into the dawn, and morning airs are cold
        now;
I, too, was drawn in part by charms I see before me play,
        That I see not every day.'

'Ha, ha!' then laughed the constables who also stood to warm
        themselves,

234

The while another maiden scrutinized his features hard,
As the blaze threw into contrast every line and knot that wrinkled
        them,
Exclaiming, 'Why, last night when he was brought in by the
        guard,
        You were with him in the yard!'

'Nay, nay, you teasing wench, I say! You know you speak
        mistakenly.
Cannot a tired pedestrian who has legged it long and far
Here on his way from northern parts, engrossed in humble
        marketings,
Come in and rest awhile, although judicial doings are
        Afoot by morning star?'

'O, come, come!' laughed the constables. 'Why, man, you speak
        the dialect
He uses in his answers; you can hear him up the stairs.
So own it. We sha'n't hurt ye. There he's speaking now! His
        syllables
Are those you sound yourself when you are talking unawares,
        As this pretty girl declares.'

'And you shudder when his chain clinks!' she rejoined. 'O yes, I
        noticed it.
And you winced, too, when those cuffs they gave him echoed to
        us here.
They'll soon be coming down, and you may then have to defend
        yourself
Unless you hold your tongue, or go away and keep you clear
        When he's led to judgement near!'

'No! I'll be damned in hell if I know anything about the man!
No single thing about him more than everybody knows!
Must not I even warm my hands but I am charged with
        blasphemies?' . . .
– His face convulses as the morning cock that moment crows,
        And he droops, and turns, and goes.

Panthera

(For other forms of this legend – first met with in the second century – see Origen contra Celsum; the Talmud; Sepher Toldoth Jeschu; quoted fragments of lost Apocryphal gospels; Strauss, Haeckel; etc.)

YEA, as I sit here, crutched, and cricked, and bent,
I think of Panthera, who underwent
Much from insidious aches in his decline;
But his aches were not radical like mine;
They were the twinges of old wounds – the feel
Of the hand he had lost, shorn by barbarian steel,
Which came back, so he said, at a change in the air,
Fingers and all, as if it still were there.
My pains are otherwise: upclosing cramps
And stiffened tendons from this country's damps,
Where Panthera was never commandant. –
The Fates sent him by way of the Levant.

He had been blithe in his young manhood's time,
And as centurion carried well his prime.
In Ethiop, Araby, climes fair and fell,
He had seen service and had borne him well.
Nought shook him then: he was serene as brave;
Yet later knew some shocks, and would grow grave
When pondering them; shocks less of corporal kind
Than phantom-like, that disarranged his mind;
And it was in the way of warning me
(By much his junior) against levity
That he recounted them; and one in chief
Panthera loved to set in bold relief.

This was a tragedy of his Eastern days,
Personal in touch – though I have sometimes thought
That touch a possible delusion – wrought
Of half-conviction carried to a craze –
His mind at last being stressed by ails and age: –
Yet his good faith thereon I well could wage.

236

I had said it long had been a wish with me
That I might leave a scion – some small tree
As channel for my sap, if not my name –
Ay, offspring even of no legitimate claim,
In whose advance I secretly could joy.
Thereat he warmed.
                        'Cancel such wishes, boy!
A son may be a comfort or a curse,
A seer, a doer, a coward, a fool; yea, worse –
A criminal . . . That I could testify!' . . .
'Panthera has no guilty son!' cried I
All unbelieving. 'Friend, you do not know,'
He darkly dropt: 'True, I've none now to show,
For *the law took him*. Ay, in sooth, Jove shaped it so!'

'This noon is not unlike,' he again began,
'The noon these pricking memories print on me –
Yea, that day, when the sun grew copper-red,
And I served in Judaea . . . 'Twas a date
Of rest for arms. The *Pax Romana* ruled,
To the chagrin of frontier legionaries!
Palestine was annexed – though sullen yet, –
I, being in age some two-score years and ten,
And having the garrison in Jerusalem
Part in my hands as acting officer
Under the Governor. A tedious time
I found it, of routine, amid a folk
Restless, contentless, and irascible. –
Quelling some riot, sentrying court and hall,
Sending men forth on public meeting-days
To maintain order, were my duties there.

'Then came a morn in spring, and the cheerful sun
Whitened the city and the hills around,
And every mountain-road that clambered them,
Tincturing the greyness of the olives warm,
And the rank cacti round the valley's sides.
The day was one whereon death-penalties
Were put in force, and here and there were set

The soldiery for order, as I said,
Since one of the condemned had raised some heat,
And crowds surged passionately to see him slain.
I, mounted on a Cappadocian horse,
With some half-company of auxiliaries,
Had captained the procession through the streets
When it came streaming from the judgment-hall
After the verdicts of the Governor.
It drew to the great gate of the northern way
That bears towards Damascus; and to a knoll
Upon the common, just beyond the walls –
Whence could be swept a wide horizon round
Over the housetops to the remotest heights.
Here was the public execution-ground
For city crimes, called then and doubtless now
Golgotha, Kranion, or Calvaria.

'The usual dooms were duly meted out;
Some three or four were stript, transfixed, and nailed,
And no great stir occurred. A day of wont
It was to me, so far, and would have slid
Clean from my memory at its squalid close
But for an incident that followed these.

'Among the tag-rag rabble of either sex
That hung around the wretches as they writhed,
Till thrust back by our spears, one held my eye –
A weeping woman, whose strained countenance,
Sharpened against a looming livid cloud,
Was mocked by the crude rays of afternoon –
The mother of one of those who suffered there
I had heard her called when spoken roughly to
By my ranged men for pressing forward so.
It stole upon me hers was a face I knew;
Yet when, or how, I had known it, for a while
Eluded me. And then at once it came.

'Some thirty years or more before that noon
I was sub-captain of a company
Drawn from the legion of Calabria,

That marched up from Judaea north to Tyre.
We had pierced the old flat country of Jezreel,
The great Esdraelon Plain and fighting-floor
Of Jew with Canaanite, and with the host
Of Pharaoh-Necho, king of Egypt, met
While crossing there to strike the Assyrian pride.
We left behind Gilboa; passed by Nain;
Till bulging Tabor rose, embossed to the top
With arbute, terebinth, and locust growths.

'Encumbering me were sundry sick, so fallen
Through drinking from a swamp beside the way;
But we pressed on, till, bearing over a ridge,
We dipt into a world of pleasantness –
A vale, the fairest I had gazed upon –
Which lapped a village on its furthest slopes
Called Nazareth, brimmed round by uplands nigh.
In the midst thereof a fountain bubbled, where,
Lime-dry from marching, our glad halt we made
To rest our sick ones, and refresh us all.

'Here a day onward, towards the eventide,
Our men were piping to a Pyrrhic dance
Trod by their comrades, when the young women came
To fill their pitchers, as their custom was.
I proffered help to one – a slim girl, coy
Even as a fawn, meek, and as innocent.
Her long blue gown, the string of silver coins
That hung down by her banded beautiful hair,
Symboled in full immaculate modesty.

'Well, I was young, and hot, and readily stirred
To quick desire. 'Twas tedious timing out
The convalescence of the soldiery;
And I beguiled the long and empty days
By blissful yieldance to her sweet allure,
Who had no arts, but what out-arted all,
The tremulous tender charm of trustfulness.
We met, and met, and under the winking stars

That passed which peoples earth – true union, yea,
To the pure eye of her simplicity.

'Meanwhile the sick found health; and we pricked on.
I made her no rash promise of return,
As some do use; I was sincere in that;
I said we sundered never to meet again –
And yet I spoke untruth unknowingly! –
For meet again we did. Now, guess you aught?
The weeping mother on Calvaria
Was she I had known – albeit that time and tears
Had wasted rudely her once flowerlike form,
And her soft eyes, now swollen with sorrowing.

'Though I betrayed some qualms, she marked me not;
And I was scarce of mood to comrade her
And close the silence of so wide a time
To claim a malefactor as my son –
(For so I guessed him). And inquiry made
Brought rumour how at Nazareth long before
An old man wedded her for pity's sake
On finding she had grown pregnant, none knew how,
Cared for her child, and loved her till he died.

'Well; there it ended; save that then I learnt
That he – the man whose ardent blood was mine –
Had waked sedition long among the Jews,
And hurled insulting parlance at their god,
Whose temple bulked upon the adjoining hill,
Vowing that he would raze it, that himself
Was god as great as he whom they adored,
And by descent, moreover, was their king;
With sundry other incitements to misrule.

'The impalements done, and done the soldiers' game
Of raffling for the clothes, a legionary,
Longinus, pierced the young man with his lance
At signs from me, moved by his agonies
Through naysaying the drug they had offered him.
It brought the end. And when he had breathed his last

The woman went. I saw her never again . . .
Now glares my moody meaning on you, friend? –
That when you talk of offspring as sheer joy
So trustingly, you blink contingencies.
Fors Fortuna! He who goes fathering
Gives frightful hostages to hazardry!'

Thus Panthera's tale. 'Twas one he seldom told,
But yet it got abroad. He would unfold,
At other times, a story of less gloom,
Though his was not a heart where jests had room.
He would regret discovery of the truth
Was made too late to influence to ruth
The Procurator who had condemned his son –
Or rather him so deemed. For there was none
To prove that Panthera erred not: and indeed,
When vagueness of identity I would plead,
Panther himself would sometimes own as much –
Yet lothly. But, assuming fact was such,
That the said woman did not recognize
Her lover's face, is matter for surprise.
However, there's his tale, fantasy or otherwise.

Thereafter shone not men of Panthera's kind:
The indolent heads at home were ill-inclined
To press campaigning that would hoist the star
Of their lieutenants valorous afar.
Jealousies kept him irked abroad, controlled
And stinted by an Empire no more bold.
Yet in some actions southward he had share –
In Mauretania and Numidia; there
With eagle eye, and sword and steed and spur,
Quelling uprisings promptly. Some small stir
In Parthia next engaged him, until maimed,
As I have said; and cynic Time proclaimed
His noble spirit broken. What a waste
Of such a Roman! – one in youth-time graced
With indescribable charm, so I have heard,
Yea, magnetism impossible to word

When faltering as I saw him. What a fame,
O Son of Saturn, had adorned his name,
Might the Three so have urged Thee! – Hour by hour
His own disorders hampered Panthera's power
To brood upon the fate of those he had known,
Even of that one he always called his own –
Either in morbid dream or memory . . .
He died at no great age, untroublously,
An exit rare for ardent soldiers such as he.

The Wood Fire

(A FRAGMENT)

'THIS is a brightsome blaze you've lit, good friend, to-night!'
' – Aye, it has been the bleakest spring I have felt for years,
And nought compares with cloven logs to keep alight:
I buy them bargain-cheap of the executioners,
As I dwell near; and they wanted the crosses out of sight
By Passover, not to affront the eyes of visitors.

'Yes, they're from the crucifixions last week-ending
At Kranion. We can sometimes use the poles again,
But they get split by the nails, and 'tis quicker work than
    mending
To knock together new; though the uprights now and then
Serve twice when they're let stand. But if a feast's impending,
As lately, you've to tidy up for the comers' ken.

'Though only three were impaled, you may know it didn't pass
    off
So quietly as was wont? That Galilee carpenter's son
Who boasted he was king, incensed the rabble to scoff:
I heard the noise from my garden. This piece is the one he was
    on . . .
Yes, it blazes up well if lit with a few dry chips and shroff;
And it's worthless for much else, what with cuts and stains
    thereon.'

The Mother Mourns[36]

WHEN mid-autumn's moan shook the night-time,
    And sedges were horny,
And summer's green wonderwork faltered
    On leaze and in lane,

I fared Yell'ham-Firs way, where dimly
    Came wheeling around me
Those phantoms obscure and insistent
    That shadows unchain.

Till airs from the needle-thicks brought me
    A low lamentation,
As though from a tree-god disheartened,
    Perplexed, or in pain.

And, heeding, it awed me to gather
    That Nature herself there
Was breathing in aëry accents,
    With dirge-like refrain,

Weary plaint that Mankind, in these late days,
    Had grieved her by holding
Her ancient high fame of perfection
    In doubt and disdain . . .

– 'I had not proposed me a Creature
    (She soughed) so excelling
All else of my kingdom in compass
    And brightness of brain

'As to read my defects with a god-glance,
    Uncover each vestige
Of old inadvertence, annunciate
    Each flaw and each stain!

'My purpose went not to develop
    Such insight in Earthland;
Such potent appraisements affront me,
    And sadden my reign!

'Why loosened I olden control here
    To mechanize skywards,
Undeeming great scope could outshape in
    A globe of such grain?

'Man's mountings of mindsight I checked not,
    Till range of his vision
Now tops my intent, and finds blemish
    Throughout my domain.

'He holds as inept his own soul-shell –
    My deftest achievement –
Contemns me for fitful inventions
    Ill-timed and inane:

'No more sees my sun as a Sanct-shape,
    My moon as the Night-queen,
My stars as august and sublime ones
    That influences rain:

'Reckons gross and ignoble my teaching,
    Immoral my story,
My love-lights a lure that my species
    May gather and gain.

'"Give me," he has said, "but the matter
    And means the gods lot her,
My brain could evolve a creation
    More seemly, more sane."

– 'If ever a naughtiness seized me
    To woo adulation
From creatures more keen than those crude ones
    That first formed my train –

'If inly a moment I murmured,
    "The simple praise sweetly,
But sweetlier the sage" – and did rashly
    Man's vision unrein,

'I rue it! . . . His guileless forerunners,
    Whose brains I could blandish,
To measure the deeps of my mysteries
    Applied them in vain.

'From then my waste aimings and futile
    I subtly could cover;
"Every best thing," said they, "to best purpose
    Her powers preordain." –

'No more such! . . . My species are dwindling,
    My forests grow barren,
My popinjays fail from their tappings,
    My larks from their strain.

'My leopardine beauties are rarer,
    My tusky ones vanish,
My children have aped mine own slaughters
    To quicken my wane.

'Let me grow, then, but mildews and mandrakes,
    And slimy distortions,
Let nevermore things good and lovely
    To me appertain;

'For Reason is rank in my temples,
    And Vision unruly,
And chivalrous laud of my cunning
    Is heard not again!'

A Commonplace Day

THE day is turning ghost,
And scuttles from the kalendar in fits and furtively,
    To join the anonymous host
Of those that throng oblivion; ceding his place, maybe,
    To one of like degree.

I part the fire-gnawed logs,
Rake forth the embers, spoil the busy flames, and lay the ends
  Upon the shining dogs;
Further and further from the nooks the twilight's stride extends,
  And beamless black impends.

Nothing of tiniest worth
Have I wrought, pondered, planned; no one thing asking blame
  or praise,
  Since the pale corpse-like birth
Of this diurnal unit, bearing blanks in all its rays –
  Dullest of dull-hued Days!

Wanly upon the panes
The rain slides, as have slid since morn my colourless thoughts;
  and yet
  Here, while Day's presence wanes,
And over him the sepulchre-lid is slowly lowered and set,
  He wakens my regret.

Regret – though nothing dear
That I wot of, was toward in the wide world at his prime,
  Or bloomed elsewhere than here,
To die with his decease, and leave a memory sweet, sublime,
  Or mark him out in Time . . .

– Yet, maybe, in some soul,
In some spot undiscerned on sea or land, some impulse rose,
  Or some intent upstole
Of that enkindling ardency from whose maturer glows
  The world's amendment flows;

But which, benumbed at birth
By momentary chance or wile, has missed its hope to be
  Embodied on the earth;
And undervoicings of this loss to man's futurity
  May wake regret in me.

The Respectable Burgher

ON 'THE HIGHER CRITICISM'

SINCE Reverend Doctors now declare
That clerks and people must prepare
To doubt if Adam ever were;
To hold the flood a local scare;
To argue, though the stolid stare,
That everything had happened ere
The prophets to its happening sware;
That David was no giant-slayer,
Nor one to call a God-obeyer
In certain details we could spare,
But rather was a debonair
Shrewd bandit, skilled as banjo-player:
That Solomon sang the fleshly Fair,
And gave the Church no thought whate'er,
That Esther with her royal wear,
And Mordecai, the son of Jair,
And Joshua's triumphs, Job's despair,
And Balaam's ass's bitter blare;
Nebuchadnezzar's furnace-flare,
And Daniel and the den affair,
And other stories rich and rare,
Were writ to make old doctrine wear
Something of a romantic air:
That the Nain widow's only heir,
And Lazarus with cadaverous glare
(As done in oils by Piombo's care)
Did not return from Sheol's lair:
That Jael set a fiendish snare,
That Pontius Pilate acted square,
That never a sword cut Malchus' ear;
And (but for shame I must forbear)
That —— —— did not reappear! . . .
– Since thus they hint, nor turn a hair,

247

All churchgoing will I forswear,
And sit on Sundays in my chair,
And read that moderate man Voltaire.

A Refusal[37]

SAID the grave Dean of Westminster:
Mine is the best minster
Seen in Great Britain,
As many have written:
So therefore I cannot
Rule here if I ban not
Such liberty-taking
As movements for making
Its grayness environ
The memory of Byron,
Which some are demanding
Who think them of standing,
But in my own viewing
Require some subduing
For tendering suggestions
On Abbey-wall questions
That must interfere here
With my proper sphere here,
And bring to disaster
This fane and its master,
Whose dict is but Christian
Though nicknamed Philistian.

A lax Christian charity –
No mental clarity
Ruling its movements
For fabric improvements –
Demands admonition
And strict supervision
When bent on enshrining
Rapscallions, and signing

Their names on God's stonework,
As if like His own work
Were their lucubrations:
And passed is my patience
That such a creed-scorner
(Not mentioning horner)
Should claim Poets' Corner.

'Tis urged that some sinners
Arc here for worms' dinners
Already in person;
That he could not worsen
The walls by a name mere
With men of such fame here.
Yet nay; they but leaven
The others in heaven
In just true proportion,
While more mean distortion.
I will next be expected
That I get erected
To Shelley a tablet
In some niche or gablet.
Then – what makes my skin burn,
Yea, forehead to chin burn –
That I ensconce Swinburne!

August 1924

Epitaph on a Pessimist

I'M Smith of Stoke, aged sixty-odd,
  I've lived without a dame
From youth-time on; and would to God
  My dad had done the same.

From the French and Greek

Liddell and Scott

ON THE COMPLETION OF THEIR LEXICON

(Written after the death of Liddell in 1898. Scott had died some ten years earlier.)

'WELL, though it seems
Beyond our dreams,'
Said Liddell to Scott,
'We've really got
To the very end,
All inked and penned
Blotless and fair
Without turning a hair,
This sultry summer day, A.D.
Eighteen hundred and forty-three.

'I've often, I own,
Belched many a moan
At undertaking it,
And dreamt forsaking it.
– Yes, on to Pi,
When the end loomed nigh,
And friends said: "You've as good as done,"
I almost wished we'd not begun.
Even now, if people only knew
My sinkings, as we slowly drew
Along through Kappa, Lambda, Mu,
They'd be concerned at my misgiving,
And how I mused on a College living
Right down to Sigma,
But feared a stigma
If I succumbed, and left old Donnegan
For weary freshmen's eyes to con again:
And how I often, often wondered
What could have led me to have blundered
So far away from sound theology
To dialects and etymology;

Words, accents not to be breathed by men
Of any country ever again!'
      'My heart most failed,
      Indeed, quite quailed,'
      Said Scott to Liddell,
      'Long ere the middle! . . .
      'Twas one wet dawn
      When, slippers on,
      And a cold in the head anew,
      Gazing at Delta
      I turned and felt a
      Wish for bed anew,
      And to let supersedings
      Of Passow's readings
      In dialects go.
      "That German has read
      More than we!" I said;
Yea, several times did I feel so! . . .

'O that first morning, smiling bland,
With sheets of foolscap, quills in hand,
To write $\dot{\alpha}\dot{\alpha}\tau os$ and $\dot{\alpha}\alpha\gamma\acute{\eta}s$,
Followed by fifteen hundred pages,
      What nerve was ours
      So to back our powers,
Assured that we should reach $\dot{\omega}\dot{\omega}\delta\eta s$
While there was breath left in our bodies!'

Liddell replied: 'Well, that's past now;
The job's done, thank God, anyhow.'

      'And yet it's not,'
      Considered Scott,
      'For we've to get
      Subscribers yet
      We must remember;
      Yes; by September.'

'O Lord; dismiss that. We'll succeed.
Dinner is my immediate need.
I feel as hollow as a fiddle,
Working so many hours,' said Liddell.

A Private Man on Public Men

WHEN my contemporaries were driving
Their coach through Life with strain and striving,
And raking riches into heaps,
And ably pleading in the Courts
With smart rejoinders and retorts,
Or where the Senate nightly keeps
Its vigils, till their fames were fanned
By rumour's tongue throughout the land,
I lived in quiet, screened, unknown,
Pondering upon some stick or stone,
Or news of some rare book or bird
Latterly bought, or seen, or heard,
Not wishing ever to set eyes on
The surging crowd beyond the horizon,
Tasting years of moderate gladness
Mellowed by sundry days of sadness,
Shut from the noise of the world without,
Hearing but dimly its rush and rout,
Unenvying those amid its roar,
Little endowed, not wanting more.

Mute Opinion

I

I TRAVERSED a dominion
Whose spokesmen spake out strong
Their purpose and opinion
Through pulpit, press, and song.

I scarce had means to note there
A large-eyed few, and dumb,
Who thought not as those thought there
That stirred the heat and hum.

II

When, grown a Shade, beholding
That land in lifetime trode,
To learn if its unfolding
Fulfilled its clamoured code,
I saw, in web unbroken,
Its history outwrought
Not as the loud had spoken,
But as the mute had thought.

Embarcation

(SOUTHAMPTON DOCKS: OCTOBER 1899)

HERE, where Vespasian's legions struck the sands,
And Cerdic with his Saxons entered in,
And Henry's army leapt afloat to win
Convincing triumphs over neighbour lands,

Vaster battalions press for further strands,
To argue in the selfsame bloody mode
Which this late age of thought, and pact, and code,
Still fails to mend. – Now deckward tramp the bands,

Yellow as autumn leaves, alive as spring;
And as each host draws out upon the sea
Beyond which lies the tragical To-Be,
None dubious of the cause, none murmuring,

Wives, sisters, parents, wave white hands and smile,
As if they knew not that they weep the while.

Departure

(SOUTHAMPTON DOCKS: OCTOBER 1899)

WHILE the far farewell music thins and fails,
And the broad bottoms rip the bearing brine –
All smalling slowly to the gray sea-line –
And each significant red smoke-shaft pales,

Keen sense of severance everywhere prevails,
Which shapes the late long tramp of mounting men
To seeming words that ask and ask again:
'How long, O striving Teutons, Slavs, and Gaels

Must your wroth reasonings trade on lives like these,
That are as puppets in a playing hand? –
When shall the saner softer polities
Whereof we dream, have sway in each proud land
And patriotism, grown Godlike, scorn to stand
Bondslave to realms, but circle earth and seas?'

The Colonel's Soliloquy

(SOUTHAMPTON DOCKS: OCTOBER 1899)

'THE quay recedes. Hurrah! Ahead we go! . . .
It's true I've been accustomed now to home,
And joints get rusty, and one's limbs may grow
        More fit to rest than roam.

'But I can stand as yet fair stress and strain;
There's not a little steel beneath the rust;
My years mount somewhat, but here's to't again!
        And if I fall, I must.

'God knows that for myself I have scanty care;
Past scrimmages have proved as much to all;
In Eastern lands and South I have had my share
        Both of the blade and ball.

'And where those villains ripped me in the flitch
With their old iron in my early time,
I'm apt at change of wind to feel a twitch,
    Or at a change of clime.

'And what my mirror shows me in the morning
Has more of blotch and wrinkle than of bloom;
My eyes, too, heretofore all glasses scorning,
    Have just a touch of rheum . . .

'Now sounds "The Girl I've left behind me", – Ah,
The years, the ardours, wakened by that tune!
Time was when, with the crowd's farewell "Hurrah!"
    'Twould lift me to the moon.

'But now it's late to leave behind me one
Who if, poor soul, her man goes underground,
Will not recover as she might have done
    In days when hopes abound.

'She's waving from the wharfside, palely grieving,
As down we draw . . . Her tears make little show,
Yet now she suffers more than at my leaving
    Some twenty years ago!

'I pray those left at home will care for her;
I shall come back; I have before; though when
The Girl you leave behind you is a grandmother,
    Things may not be as then.'

The Going of the Battery

WIVES' LAMENT

(2 NOVEMBER 1899)

I

O IT was sad enough, weak enough, mad enough –
Light in their loving as soldiers can be –
First to risk choosing them, leave alone losing them
Now, in far battle, beyond the South Sea! . . .

II

– Rain came down drenchingly; but we unblenchingly
Trudged on beside them through mirk and through mire,
They stepping steadily – only too readily! –
Scarce as if stepping brought parting-time nigher.

III

Great guns were gleaming there, living things seeming there,
Cloaked in their tar-cloths, upmouthed to the night;
Wheels wet and yellow from axle to felloe,
Throats blank of sound, but prophetic to sight.

IV

Gas-glimmers drearily, blearily, eerily
Lit our pale faces outstretched for one kiss,
While we stood prest to them, with a last quest to them
Not to court perils that honour could miss.

V

Sharp were those sighs of ours, blinded these eyes of ours,
When at last moved away under the arch
All we loved. Aid for them each woman prayed for them,
Treading back slowly the track of their march.

VI

Some one said: 'Nevermore will they come: evermore
Are they now lost to us.' O it was wrong!
Though may be hard their ways, some Hand will guard their
    ways,
Bear them through safely, in brief time or long.

VII

– Yet, voices haunting us, daunting us, taunting us,
Hint in the night-time when life beats are low
Other and graver things . . . Hold we to braver things,
Wait we, in trust, what Time's fulness shall show.

Drummer Hodge

I

THEY throw in Drummer Hodge, to rest
    Uncoffined – just as found:
His landmark is a kopje-crest
    That breaks the veldt around;
And foreign constellations west
    Each night above his mound.

II

Young Hodge the Drummer never knew –
    Fresh from his Wessex home –
The meaning of the broad Karoo,
    The Bush, the dusty loam,
And why uprose to nightly view
    Strange stars amid the gloam.

III

Yet portion of that unknown plain
    Will Hodge for ever be;
His homely Northern breast and brain
    Grow to some Southern tree,
And strange-eyed constellations reign
    His stars eternally.

A Wife in London

(DECEMBER 1899)

I

SHE sits in the tawny vapour
    That the Thames-side lanes have uprolled,
    Behind whose webby fold on fold
Like a waning taper
    The street-lamp glimmers cold.

A messenger's knock cracks smartly,
　　Flashed news is in her hand
　　Of meaning it dazes to understand
Though shaped so shortly:
　　He – has fallen – in the far South Land . . .

II

'Tis the morrow; the fog hangs thicker,
　　The postman nears and goes:
　　A letter is brought whose lines disclose
By the firelight flicker
　　His hand, whom the worm now knows:

Fresh – firm – penned in highest feather –
　　Page-full of his hoped return,
　　And of home-planned jaunts by brake and burn
In the summer weather,
　　And of new love that they would learn.

The Man He Killed

　　'HAD he and I but met
　　　　By some old ancient inn,
　　We should have sat us down to wet
　　　　Right many a nipperkin!

　　'But ranged as infantry,
　　　　And staring face to face,
　　I shot at him as he at me,
　　　　And killed him in his place.

　　'I shot him dead because –
　　　　Because he was my foe,
　　Just so: my foe of course he was;
　　　　That's clear enough; although

　　'He thought he'd 'list, perhaps,
　　　　Off-hand like – just as I –
　　Was out of work – had sold his traps –
　　　　No other reason why.

'Yes; quaint and curious war is!
You shoot a fellow down
You'd treat if met where any bar is,
Or help to half-a-crown.'

1902

The Sergeant's Song

(1803)

WHEN Lawyers strive to heal a breach,
And Parsons practise what they preach;
Then Boney he'll come pouncing down,
And march his men on London town!
 Rollicum-rorum, tol-lol-lorum,
 Rollicum-rorum, tol-lol-lay!

When Justices hold equal scales,
And Rogues are only found in jails;
Then Boney he'll come pouncing down,
And march his men on London town!
 Rollicum-rorum, &c.

When Rich Men find their wealth a curse,
And fill therewith the Poor Man's purse;
Then Boney he'll come pouncing down,
And march his men on London town!
 Rollicum-rorum, &c.

When Husbands with their Wives agree,
And Maids won't wed from modesty;
Then Boney he'll come pouncing down,
And march his men on London town!
 Rollicum-rorum, tol-tol-lorum,
 Rollicum-rorum, tol-lol-lay!

1878
Published in 'The Trumpet-Major' 1880

The Night of Trafalgar

(BOATMAN'S SONG)

I

IN the wild October night-time, when the wind raved round the
land,
And the Back-sea met the Front-sea, and our doors were
blocked with sand,
And we heard the drub of Dead-man's Bay, where bones of
thousands are,
We knew not what the day had done for us at Trafalgár.
Had done,
Had done,
For us at Trafalgár!

II

'Pull hard, and make the Nothe, or down we go!' one says, says
he.
We pulled; and bedtime brought the storm; but snug at home
slept we.
Yet all the while our gallants after fighting through the day,
Were beating up and down the dark, sou'-west of Cadiz Bay.
The dark,
The dark,
Sou'-west of Cadiz Bay!

III

The victors and the vanquished then the storm it tossed and tore,
As hard they strove, those worn-out men, upon that surly shore;

Dead Nelson and his half-dead crew, his foes from near and far,
Were rolled together on the deep that night at Trafalgár!
                              The deep,
                              The deep,
                    That night at Trafalgár!

From *The Dynasts*, Part I, Act V, Scene vii.

Albuera

The dawn of a mid-May day in the same spring shows the village of Albuera
with the country around it, as viewed from the summit of a line of hills on
which the English and their allies are ranged under Beresford. The landscape
swept by the eye includes to the right foreground a hill loftier than any, and
somewhat detached from the range. The green slopes behind and around this
hill are untrodden – though in a few hours to be the sanguinary scene of the
most murderous struggle of the whole war.

The village itself lies to the left foreground, with its stream flowing behind
it from the distance on the right. A creeping brook at the bottom of the heights
held by the English joins the stream by the village. Behind the stream some of
the French forces are visible. Away behind these stretches a great wood
several miles in area, out of which the Albuera stream emerges, and behind
the furthest verge of the wood the morning sky lightens momently. The birds
in the wood, unaware that this day is to be different from every other day they
have known there, are heard singing their overtures with their usual serenity

DUMB SHOW

As objects grow more distinct it can be perceived that some strategic disposi-
tions of the night are being completed by the French forces, which the
evening before lay in the woodland to the front of the English army. They
have emerged during the darkness, and large sections of them – infantry,
cuirassiers, and artillery – have crept round to BERESFORD'S right without his
suspecting the movement, where they lie hidden by the great hill aforesaid,
though not more than half-a-mile from his right wing.

SPIRIT OF THE YEARS

A hot ado goes forward here to-day,
If I may read the Immanent Intent
    From signs and tokens blent
With weird unrest along the firmament
Of causal coils in passionate display.
– Look narrowly, and what you witness say.

SPIRIT OF THE PITIES

I see red smears upon the sickly dawn,
And seeming drops of gore. On earth below
Are men – unnatured and mechanic-drawn –
Mixt nationalities in row and row,
   Wheeling them to and fro
In moves dissociate from their souls' demand,
For dynasts' ends tha few even understand!

SPIRIT OF THE YEARS

Speak more materially, and less in dream.

SPIRIT OF RUMOUR

I'll do it . . . The stir of strife grows well defined
Around the hamlet and the church thereby:
Till, from the wood, the ponderous columns wind,
Guided by Godinot, with Werlé nigh.
They bear upon the vill. But the gruff guns
   Of Dickson's Portuguese
Punch spectral vistas through the maze of these! . . .
More Frenchmen press, and roaring antiphons
Of cannonry contuse the roofs and walls and trees.

SPIRIT OF THE PITIES

Wrecked are the ancient bridge, the green spring plot,
The blooming fruit-tree, the fair flower-knot!

SPIRIT OF RUMOUR

Yet the true mischief to the English might
Is meant to fall not there. Look to the right,
And read the shaping scheme by yon hill-side,
Where cannon, foot, and brisk dragoons you see,
With Werlé and Latour-Maubourg to guide,
Waiting to breast the hill-brow bloodily.

BERESFORD now becomes aware of this project on his flank, and sends orders
to throw back his right to face the attack. The order is not obeyed. Almost at
the same moment the French rush is made, the Spanish and Portuguese allies
of the Eng sh are beaten back, and the hill is won. But two English divisions
bear from the centre of their front and plod desperately up the hill to retake it.

SPIRIT SINISTER

Now he among us who may wish to be
A skilled practitioner in slaughtery,
Should watch this hour's fruition yonder there,
And he will know, if knowing ever were,
How mortals may be freed their fleshly cells,
And quaint red doors set ope in sweating fells,
By methods swift and slow and foul and fair!

The English, who have plunged up the hill, are caught in a heavy mist, that hides from them an advance in their rear of the lancers and hussars of the enemy. The lines of the Buffs, the Sixty-sixth, and those of the Forty-eighth, who were with them, in a chaos of smoke, steel, sweat, curses, and blood, are beheld melting down like wax from an erect position to confused heaps. Their forms lie rigid, or twitch and turn, as they are trampled over by the hoofs of the enemy's horse. Those that have not fallen are taken.

SPIRIT OF THE PITIES

It works as you, uncanny Phantom, wist! . . .
Whose is that towering form
   That tears across the mist
To where the shocks are sorest? – his with arm
Outstretched, and grimy face, and bloodshot eye,
Like one who, having done his deeds, will die?

SPIRIT OF RUMOUR

He is one Beresford, who heads the fight
   For England here to-day.

SPIRIT OF THE PITIES

              He calls the sight
Despite itself! – parries yon lancer's thrust,
And with his own sword renders dust to dust!

The ghastly climax of the strife is reached; the combatants are seen to be firing grape and canister at speaking distance, and discharging musketry in each other's faces when so close that their complexions may be recognized. Hot corpses, their mouths blackened by cartridge-biting, and surrounded by cast-away knapsacks, firelocks, hats, stocks, flint-boxes, and priming-horns, together with red and blue rags of clothing, gaiters, epaulettes, limbs, and viscera, accumulate on the slopes, increasing from twos and threes to half-dozens, and from half-dozens to heaps, which steam with their own warmth as the spring rain falls gently upon them.

The critical instant has come, and the English break. But a comparatively fresh division, with fusileers, is brought into the turmoil by HARDINGE and COLE, and these make one last strain to save the day, and their names and lives. The fusileers mount the incline, and issuing from the smoke and mist startle the enemy by their arrival on a spot deemed won.

SEMICHORUS I OF THE PITIES (*aerial music*)

They come, beset by riddling hail;
They sway like sedges in a gale;
They fail, and win, and win, and fail. Albuera!

SEMICHORUS II

They gain the ground there, yard by yard,
Their brows and hair and lashes charred,
Their blackened teeth set firm and hard.

SEMICHORUS I

Their mad assailants rave and reel,
And face, as men who scorn to feel,
The close-lined, three-edged prongs of steel.

SEMICHORUS II

Till faintness follows closing-in,
When, faltering headlong down, they spin
Like leaves. But those pay well who win Albuera.

SEMICHORUS I

Out of six thousand souls that sware
To hold the mount, or pass elsewhere,
But eighteen hundred muster there.

SEMICHORUS II

Pale Colonels, Captains, ranksmen lie,
Facing the earth or facing sky; –
They strove to live, they stretch to die.

SEMICHORUS I

Friends, foemen, mingle; heap and heap. –
Hide their hacked bones, Earth! – deep, deep, deep,
Where harmless worms caress and creep.

CHORUS

Hide their hacked bones, Earth! – deep, deep, deep,
Where harmless worms caress and creep. –
What man can grieve? what woman weep?
Better than waking is to sleep! Albuera!

The night comes on, and darkness covers the battle-field.

From *The Dynasts*, Part 2, Act VI, Scene iv.

The Road from Smolensko into Lithuania

The season is far advanced towards winter. The point of observation is high amongst the clouds, which, opening and shutting fitfully to the wind, reveal the earth as a confused expanse merely.

SPIRIT OF THE PITIES

Where are we? And why are we where we are?

SHADE OF THE EARTH

Above a wild waste garden-plot of mine
Nigh bare in this late age, and now grown chill,
Lithuania called by some. I gather not
Why we haunt here, where I can work no charm
Either upon the ground or over it.

SPIRIT OF THE YEARS

The wherefore will unfold. The rolling brume
That parts, and joins, and parts again below us
In ragged restlessness, unscreens by fits
The quality of the scene.

SPIRIT OF THE PITIES

                    I notice now
Primeval woods, pine, birch – the skinny growths
That can sustain life well where earth affords
But sustenance elsewhere yclept starvation.

SPIRIT OF THE YEARS

And what see you on the far land-verge there,
Labouring from eastward towards our longitude?

SPIRIT OF THE PITIES

An object like a dun-piled caterpillar,
Shuffling its length in painful heaves along,
Hitherward ... Yea, what is this Thing we see
Which, moving as a single monster might,
Is yet not one but many?

SPIRIT OF THE YEARS

                    Even the Army
Which once was called the Grand; now in retreat
From Moscow's muteness, urged by That within it;
Together with its train of followers –
Men, matrons, babes, in brabbling multitudes.

SPIRIT OF THE PITIES

And why such flight?

SPIRIT OF THE YEARS

                    Recording Angels, say.

RECORDING ANGEL I (in minor plain-song)

The host has turned from Moscow where it lay,
And Israel-like, moved by some master-sway,
Is made to wander on and waste away!

ANGEL II

By track of Tarutino first it flits;
Thence swerving, strikes at old Jaroslawitz;
The which, accurst by slaughtering swords, it quits.

ANGEL I

Harassed, it treads the trail by which it came,
To Borodino, field of bloodshot fame,
Whence stare unburied horrors beyond name!

ANGEL II

And so and thus it nears Smolensko's walls,
And, stayed its hunger, starts anew its crawls,
Till floats down one white morsel, which appals.

What has floated down from the sky upon the Army is a flake of snow. Then come another and another, till natural features, hitherto varied with the tints of autumn, are confounded, and all is phantasmal grey and white.

The caterpillar shape still creeps laboriously nearer, but instead of increasing in size by the rules of perspective, it gets more attenuated, and there are left upon the ground behind it minute parts of itself, which are speedily flaked over, and remain as white pimples by the wayside.

SPIRIT OF THE YEARS

These atoms that drop off are snuffed-out souls
Who are enghosted by the caressing snow.

Pines rise mournfully on each side of the nearing object; ravens in flocks advance with it overhead, waiting to pick out the eyes of strays who fall. The snowstorm increases, descending in tufts which can hardly be shaken off. The sky seems to join itself to the land. The marching figures drop rapidly, and almost immediately become white grave-mounds.

Endowed with enlarged powers of audition as of vision, we are struck by the mournful taciturnity that prevails. Nature is mute. Save for the incessant flogging of the wind-broken and lacerated horses there are no sounds.

With growing nearness more is revealed. In the glades of the forest, parallel to the French columns, columns of Russians are seen to be moving. And when the French presently reach Krasnoye they are surrounded by packs of cloaked Cossacks, bearing lances like huge needles a dozen feet long. The fore-part of the French army gets through the town; the rear is assaulted by infantry and artillery.

SPIRIT OF THE PITIES

The strange, one-eyed, white-shakoed, scarred old man,
Ruthlessly heading every onset made,
I seem to recognize.

SPIRIT OF THE YEARS

Kutúzof he:
The ceaselessly-attacked one, Michael Ney;
A pair as stout as thou, Earth, ever hast twinned!
Kutúzof, ten years younger, would extirp
The invaders, and our drama finish here,
With Bonaparte a captive or a corpse.
But he is old; death even has beckoned him;
And thus the so near-seeming happens not.

NAPOLÉON himself can be discerned amid the rest, marching on foot through the snowflakes, in a fur coat and with a stout staff in his hand. Further back NEY is visible with the remains of the rear.

There is something behind the regular columns like an articulated tail, and as they draw on, it shows itself to be a disorderly rabble of followers of both sexes. So the whole miscellany arrives at the foreground, where it is checked by a large river across the track. The soldiers themselves, like the rabble, are in motley raiment, some wearing rugs for warmth, some quilts and curtains, some even petticoats and other women's clothing. Many are delirious from hunger and cold.

But they set about doing what is a necessity for the least hope of salvation, and throw a bridge across the stream.

The point of vision descends to earth, close to the scene of action.

From *The Dynasts*, Part 3, Act 1, Scene ix.

The Bridge of the Beresina

The bridge is over the Beresina at Studzianka. On each side of the river are swampy meadows, now hard with frost, while further back are dense forests. Ice floats down the deep black stream in large cakes.

DUMB SHOW

The French sappers are working up to their shoulders in the water at the building of the bridge. Those so immersed work till, stiffened with ice to immobility, they die from the chill, when others succeed them.

Cavalry meanwhile attempt to swim their horses across, and some infantry try to wade through the stream.

Another bridge is begun hard by, the construction of which advances with greater speed; and it becomes fit for the passage of carriages and artillery.

NAPOLÉON is seen to come across to the homeward bank, which is the foreground of the scene. A good portion of the army also, under DAVOUT, NEY, and OUDINOT, lands by degrees on this side. But VICTOR'S corps is yet on the left or Moscow side of the stream, moving towards the bridge, and PARTONNEAUX with the rear-guard, who has not yet crossed, is at Borissow, some way below, where there is an old permanent bridge partly broken.

Enter with speed from the distance the Russians under TCHAPLITZ. More under TCHICHAGOFF enter the scene down the river on the left or further bank, and cross by the old bridge of Borissow. But they are too far from the new crossing to intercept the French as yet.

PLATOFF with his Cossacks next appears on the stage which is to be such a tragic one. He comes from the forest and approaches the left bank likewise. So also does WITTGENSTEIN, who strikes in between the uncrossed VICTOR and PARTONNEAUX. PLATOFF thereupon descends on the latter, who surrenders with the rear-guard; and thus seven thousand more are cut off from the already emaciated Grand Army.

TCHAPLITZ, of TCHICHAGOFF'S division, has meanwhile got round by the old bridge at Borissow to the French side of the new one, and attacks OUDINOT; but he is repulsed with the strength of despair. The French lose a further five thousand in this.

We now look across the river at VICTOR and his division, not yet over, and still defending the new bridges. WITTGENSTEIN descends upon him; but he holds his ground.

The determined Russians set up a battery of twelve cannon, so as to command the two new bridges, with the confused crowd of soldiers, carriages, and baggage, pressing to cross. The battery discharges into the surging multitude. More Russians come up, and, forming a semicircle round the bridges and the mass of French, fire yet more hotly on them with round shot and canister. As it gets dark the flashes light up the strained faces of the fugitives. Under the discharge and the weight of traffic, the bridge for the artillery gives way, and the throngs upon it roll shrieking into the stream and are drowned.

SEMICHORUS I OF THE PITIES (*aerial music*)

So loudly swell their shrieks as to be heard above the roar of guns
    and the wailful wind,
Giving in one brief cry their last wild word on that mock life
    through which they have harlequined!

SEMICHORUS II

To the other bridge the living heap betakes itself, the weak
    pushed over by the strong;
They loop together by their clutch like snakes; in knots they are
    submerged and borne along.

CHORUS

Then women are seen in the waterflow – limply bearing their
    infants between wizened white arms stretching above;
Yea, motherhood, sheerly sublime in her last despairing, and
    lighting her darkest declension with limitless love.

Meanwhile TCHICHAGOFF has come up with his twenty-seven thousand
men, and falls on OUDINOT, NEY, and 'the Sacred Squadron'. Altogether
we see forty or fifty thousand assailing eighteen thousand half-naked, badly
armed wretches, emaciated with hunger and encumbered with several
thousands of sick, wounded, and stragglers.

    VICTOR and his rear-guard, who have protected the bridges all day, come
over themselves at last. No sooner have they done so than the final bridge is
set on fire. Those who are upon it burn or drown; those who are on the fur-
ther side have lost their last chance, and perish either in attempting to wade
the stream or at the hands of the Russians.

SEMICHORUS I OF THE PITIES (*aerial music*)

What will be seen in the morning light?
What will be learnt when the spring breaks bright,
And the frost unlocks to the sun's soft sight?

SEMICHORUS II

Death in a thousand motley forms;
Charred corpses hooking each other's arms
In the sleep that defies all war's alarms!

CHORUS

Pale cysts of souls in every stage,
Still bent to embraces of love or rage, –
Souls passed to where History pens no page.

The flames of the burning bridge go out as it consumes to the water's edge,
and darkness mantles all, nothing continuing but the purl of the river and the
clickings of floating ice.

From *The Dynasts*, Part 3, Act I, Scene x.

Budmouth Dears [38]

(HUSSAR'S SONG)

I

WHEN we lay where Budmouth Beach is,
   O, the girls were fresh as peaches,
With their tall and tossing figures and their eyes of blue and
      brown!
   And our hearts would ache with longing
   As we paced from our sing-songing,
With a smart *Clink! Clink!* up the Esplanade and down.

II

   They distracted and delayed us
   By the pleasant pranks they played us,
And what marvel, then, if troopers, even of regiments of
      renown,
   On whom flashed those eyes divine, O,
   Should forget the countersign, O,
As we tore *Clink! Clink!* back to camp above the town.

III

   Do they miss us much, I wonder,
   Now that war has swept us sunder,
And we roam from where the faces smile to where the faces
      frown?
   And no more behold the features
   Of the fair fantastic creatures,
And no more *Clink! Clink!* past the parlours of the town?

IV

   Shall we once again there meet them?
   Falter fond attempts to greet them?
Will the gay sling-jacket* glow again beside the muslin gown? –

*Hussars, it may be remembered, used to wear a pelisse, dolman, or
'sling-jacket' (as the men called it), which hung loosely over the shoulder.
The writer is able to recall the picturesque effect of this uniform.

Will they archly quiz and con us
With a sideway glance upon us,
While our spurs *Clink! Clink!* up the Esplanade and down?

From *The Dynasts*, Part 3, Act II, Scene i.

The Road to Waterloo

The view is now from Quatre-Bras backward along the road by which the English arrived. Diminishing in a straight line from the foreground to the centre of the distance it passes over Mont Saint-Jean and through Waterloo to Brussels.

It is now tinged by a moving mass of English and Allied infantry, in retreat to a new position at Mont Saint-Jean. The sun shines brilliantly upon the foreground as yet, but towards Waterloo and the Forest of Soignes on the north horizon it is overcast with black clouds which are steadily advancing up the sky.

To mask the retreat the English outposts retain their position on the battle-field in the face of NEY'S troops, and keep up a desultory firing: the cavalry for the same reason remain, being drawn up in lines beside the intersecting Namur road.

Enter WELLINGTON, UXBRIDGE (who is in charge of the cavalry), MÜFFLING, VIVIAN, and others. They look through their field-glasses towards Frasnes, NEY'S position since his retreat of yesternight, and also towards NAPOLÉON'S at Ligny.

WELLINGTON

The noonday sun, striking so strongly there,
Makes mirrors of their arms. That they advance
Their growing radiance shows. Those gleams by Marbais
Suggest fixed bayonets.

UXBRIDGE

Vivian's glass reveals
That they are cuirassiers. Ney's troops, too, near
At last, methinks, along this other road.

WELLINGTON

One thing is sure: that here the whole French force
Schemes to unite and sharply follow us.
It formulates our fence. The cavalry

Must linger here no longer; but recede
To Mont Saint-Jean, as rearguard of the foot.
From the intelligence that Gordon brings
'Tis pretty clear old Blücher had to take
A damned good drubbing yesterday at Ligny,
And has been bent hard back! So that, for us,
Bound to the plighted plan, there is no choice
But to do like . . . No doubt they'll say at home
That we've been well thrashed too. It can't be helped,
They must! . . . (He looks round at the sky.) A heavy
 rainfall threatens us,
To make it all the worse!

The speaker and his staff ride off along the Brussels road in the rear of the infantry, and UXBRIDGE begins the retreat of the cavalry.

  CAPTAIN MERCER enters with a light battery.

   MERCER (excitedly)
      Look back, my lord;
Is it not Bonaparte himself we see
Upon the road I have come by?

   UXBRIDGE (looking through glass)
       Yes, by God;
His face as clear-cut as the edge of a cloud
The sun behind shows up! His suite and all!
Fire – fire! And aim you well.

   The battery hastily makes ready and fires.

          No! It won't do.
He brings on mounted ordnance of his Guard,
So we're in danger here. Then limber up,
And off as soon as may be.

The English artillery and cavalry retreat at full speed, just as the weather bursts, with flashes of lightning and drops of rain. They all clatter off along the Brussels road, UXBRIDGE and his aides galloping beside the column; till no British are left at Quatre-Bras except the slain.

 The focus of the scene follows the retreating English army, the highway and its margins panoramically gliding past the vision of the spectator. The phantoms chant monotonously while the retreat goes on.

CHORUS OF RUMOURS (*aerial music*)
Day's nether hours advance; storm supervenes
In heaviness unparalleled, that screens
With water-woven gauzes, vapour-bred,
The creeping clumps of half-obliterate red –
Severely harassed past each round and ridge
By the inimical lance. They gain the bridge
And village of Genappe, in equal fence
With weather and the enemy's violence.
– Cannon upon the foul and flooded road,
Cavalry in the cornfields mire-bestrowed,
With frothy horses floundering to their knees,
Make wayfaring a moil of miseries!
Till Britishry and Bonapartists lose
Their clashing colours for the tawny hues
That twilight sets on all its stealing tinct imbues.

The rising ground of Mont Saint-Jean, in front of Waterloo, is gained by the English vanguard and main masses of foot, and by degrees they are joined by the cavalry and artillery. The French are but little later in taking up their position amid the cornfields around La Belle Alliance.

Fires begin to shine up from the English bivouacs. Camp kettles are slung, and the men pile arms and stand round the blaze to dry themselves. The French opposite lie down like dead men in the dripping green wheat and rye, without supper and without fire.

By and by the English army also lies down, the men huddling together on the ploughed mud in their wet blankets, while some sleep sitting round the dying fires.

CHORUS OF THE YEARS (*aerial music*)
The eyelids of eve fall together at last,
And the forms so foreign to field and tree
Lie down as though native, and slumber fast!

CHORUS OF THE PITIES
Sore are the thrills of misgiving we see
In the artless champaign at this harlequinade,
Distracting a vigil where calm should be!

The green seems opprest, and the Plain afraid
Of a Something to come, whereof these are the proofs, –
Neither earthquake, nor storm, nor eclipse's shade!

CHORUS OF THE YEARS

Yea, the coneys are scared by the thud of hoofs,
And their white scuts flash at their vanishing heels,
And swallows abandon the hamlet-roofs.

The mole's tunnelled chambers are crushed by wheels,
The lark's eggs scattered, their owners fled;
And the hedgehog's household the sapper unseals.

The snail draws in at the terrible tread,
But in vain; he is crushed by the felloe-rim;
The worm asks what can be overhead,

And wriggles deep from a scene so grim,
And guesses him safe; for he does not know
What a foul red flood will be soaking him!

Beaten about by the heel and toe
Are butterflies, sick of the day's long rheum,
To die of a worse than the weather-foe.

Trodden and bruised to a miry tomb
Are ears that have greened but will never be gold,
And flowers in the bud that will never bloom.

CHORUS OF THE PITIES

So the season's intent, ere its fruit unfold,
Is frustrate, and mangled, and made succumb,
Like a youth of promise struck stark and cold! ...

And what of these who to-night have come?

CHORUS OF THE YEARS

The young sleep sound; but the weather awakes
In the veterans, pains from the past that numb;

Old stabs of Ind, old Peninsular aches,
Old Friedland chills, haunt their moist mud bed,
Cramps from Austerlitz; till their slumber breaks.

CHORUS OF SINISTER SPIRITS

And each soul shivers as sinks his head
On the loam he's to lease with the other dead
From to-morrow's mist-fall till Time be sped!

The fires of the English go out, and silence prevails, save for the soft hiss of
the rain that falls impartially on both the sleeping armies.

From *The Dynasts*, Part 3, Act VI, Scene viii.

The Convergence of the Twain

(LINES ON THE LOSS OF THE 'TITANIC')

I

IN a solitude of the sea
Deep from human vanity,
And the Pride of Life that planned her, stilly couches she.

II

Steel chambers, late the pyres
Of her salamandrine fires,
Cold currents thrid, and turn to rhythmic tidal lyres.

III

Over the mirrors meant
To glass the opulent
The sea-worm crawls – grotesque, slimed, dumb, indifferent.

IV

Jewels in joy designed
To ravish the sensuous mind
Lie lightless, all their sparkles bleared and black and blind.

V

Dim moon-eyed fishes near
Gaze at the gilded gear
And query: 'What does this vaingloriousness down here?' . . .

VI

Well: while was fashioning
This creature of cleaving wing,
The Immanent Will that stirs and urges everything

277

VII

Prepared a sinister mate
For her – so gaily great –
A Shape of Ice, for the time far and dissociate.

VIII

And as the smart ship grew
In stature, grace, and hue,
In shadowy silent distance grew the Iceberg too.

IX

Alien they seemed to be:
No mortal eye could see
The intimate welding of their later history,

X

Or sign that they were bent
By paths coincident
On being anon twin halves of one august event,

XI

Till the Spinner of the Years
Said 'Now!' And each one hears,
And consummation comes, and jars two hemispheres.

Channel Firing

THAT night your great guns, unawares,
Shook all our coffins as we lay,
And broke the chancel window-squares,
We thought it was the Judgment-day

And sat upright. While drearisome
Arose the howl of wakened hounds:
The mouse let fall the altar-crumb,
The worms drew back into the mounds,

The glebe cow drooled. Till God called, 'No;
It's gunnery practice out at sea
Just as before you went below;
The world is as it used to be:

'All nations striving strong to make
Red war yet redder. Mad as hatters
They do no more for Christés sake
Than you who are helpless in such matters.

'That this is not the judgment-hour
For some of them's a blessed thing,
For if it were they'd have to scour
Hell's floor for so much threatening . . .

'Ha, ha. It will be warmer when
I blow the trumpet (if indeed
I ever do; for you are men,
And rest eternal sorely need).'

So down we lay again. 'I wonder,
Will the world ever saner be,'
Said one, 'than when He sent us under
In our indifferent century!'

And many a skeleton shook his head.
'Instead of preaching forty year,'
My neighbour Parson Thirdly said,
'I wish I had stuck to pipes and beer.'

Again the guns disturbed the hour,
Roaring their readiness to avenge,
As far inland as Stourton Tower,
And Camelot, and starlit Stonehenge.

April 1914

Men Who March Away
(SONG OF THE SOLDIERS)

WHAT of the faith and fire within us
    Men who march away
    Ere the barn-cocks say
    Night is growing gray,
Leaving all that here can win us;
What of the faith and fire within us
    Men who march away?

Is it a purblind prank, O think you,
    Friend with the musing eye,
    Who watch us stepping by
    With doubt and dolorous sigh?
Can much pondering so hoodwink you!
Is it a purblind prank, O think you,
    Friend with the musing eye?

Nay. We well see what we are doing,
    Though some may not see –
    Dalliers as they be –
    England's need are we;
Her distress would leave us rueing:
Nay. We well see what we are doing,
    Though some may not see!

In our heart of hearts believing
    Victory crowns the just,
    And that braggarts must
    Surely bite the dust,
Press we to the field ungrieving,
In our heart of hearts believing
    Victory crowns the just.

Hence the faith and fire within us
    Men who march away
    Ere the barn-cocks say
    Night is growing gray,

Leaving all that here can win us;
Hence the faith and fire within us
Men who march away.

5 September 1914

His Country

I JOURNEYED from my native spot
    Across the south sea shine,
And found that people in hall and cot
Laboured and suffered each his lot
    Even as I did mine.

He travels southward and looks around;

Thus noting them in meads and marts
    It did not seem to me
That my dear country with its hearts,
Minds, yearnings, worse and better parts
    Had ended with the sea.

and cannot discover the boundary

I further and further went anon,
    As such I still surveyed,
And further yet – yea, on and on,
And all the men I looked upon
    Had heart-strings fellow-made.

of his native country;

I traced the whole terrestrial round,
    Homing the other side;
Then said I, 'What is there to bound
My denizenship? It seems I have found
    Its scope to be world-wide.'

or where his duties to his fellow-creatures end;

I asked me: 'Whom have I to fight,
    And whom have I to dare,
And whom to weaken, crush, and blight?
My country seems to have kept in sight
    On my way everywhere.'

nor who are his enemies.

The Pity of It

I WALKED in loamy Wessex lanes, afar
From rail-track and from highway, and I heard
In field and farmstead many an ancient word
Of local lineage like 'Thu bist', 'Er war',

'Ich woll', 'Er sholl', and by-talk similar,
Nigh as they speak who in this month's moon gird
At England's very loins, thereunto spurred
By gangs whose glory threats and slaughters are.

Then seemed a Heart crying: 'Whosoever they be
At root and bottom of this, who flung this flame
Between kin folk kin tongued even as are we,

'Sinister, ugly, lurid, be their fame;
May their familiars grow to shun their name,
And their brood perish everlastingly.'

April 1915

In Time of 'The Breaking of Nations' *[39]

I

ONLY a man harrowing clods
    In a slow silent walk
With an old horse that stumbles and nods
    Half asleep as they stalk.

II

Only thin smoke without flame
    From the heaps of couch-grass;
Yet this will go onward the same
    Though Dynasties pass.

* *Jer. li. 20*

III

Yonder a maid and her wight
   Come whispering by:
War's annals will cloud into night
   Ere their story die.

1915

Before Marching and After

(IN MEMORIAM F.W.G.)

ORION swung southward aslant
Where the starved Egdon pine-trees had thinned,
The Pleiads aloft seemed to pant
With the heather that twitched in the wind;
But he looked on indifferent to sights such as these,
Unswayed by love, friendship, home joy or home sorrow,
And wondered to what he would march on the morrow.

The crazed household-clock with its whirr
Rang midnight within as he stood,
He heard the low sighing of her
Who had striven from his birth for his good;
But he still only asked the spring starlight, the breeze,
What great thing or small thing his history would borrow
From that Game with Death he would play on the morrow.

When the heath wore the robe of late summer,
And the fuchsia-bells, hot in the sun,
Hung red by the door, a quick comer
Brought tidings that marching was done
For him who had joined in that game overseas
Where Death stood to win, though his name was to borrow
A brightness therefrom not to fade on the morrow.

September 1915

Often When Warring

OFTEN when warring for he wist not what,
An enemy-soldier, passing by one weak,
Has tendered water, wiped the burning cheek,
And cooled the lips so black and clammed and hot;

Then gone his way, and maybe quite forgot
The deed of grace amid the roar and reek;
Yet larger vision than loud arms bespeak
He there has reached, although he has known it not.

For natural mindsight, triumphing in the act
Over the throes of artificial rage,
Has thuswise muffled victory's peal of pride,
Rended to ribands policy's specious page
That deals but with evasion, code, and pact,
And war's apology wholly stultified.

1915

'According to the Mighty Working'

I

WHEN moiling seems at cease
   In the vague void of night-time,
   And heaven's wide roomage stormless
   Between the dusk and light-time,
   And fear at last is formless,
We call the allurement Peace.

II

Peace, this hid riot, Change,
   This revel of quick-cued mumming,
   This never truly being,
   This evermore becoming,
   This spinner's wheel onfleeing
Outside perception's range.

1917

'And There Was a Great Calm'

(ON THE SIGNING OF THE ARMISTICE, 11 NOV. 1918)

I

THERE had been years of Passion – scorching, cold,
And much Despair, and Anger heaving high,
Care whitely watching, Sorrows manifold,
Among the young, among the weak and old,
And the pensive Spirit of Pity whispered, 'Why?'

II

Men had not paused to answer. Foes distraught
Pierced the thinned peoples in a brute-like blindness,
Philosophies that sages long had taught,
And Selflessness, were as an unknown thought,
And 'Hell!' and 'Shell!' were yapped at Lovingkindness.

III

The feeble folk at home had grown full-used
To 'dug-outs', 'snipers', 'Huns', from the war-adept
In the mornings heard, and at evetides perused;
To day-dreamt men in millions, when they mused –
To nightmare-men in millions when they slept.

IV

Waking to wish existence timeless, null,
Sirius they watched above where armies fell;
He seemed to check his flapping when, in the lull
Of night a boom came thencewise, like the dull
Plunge of a stone dropped into some deep well.

V

So, when old hopes that earth was bettering slowly
Were dead and damned, there sounded 'War is done!'
One morrow. Said the bereft, and meek, and lowly,
'Will men some day be given to grace? yea, wholly,
And in good sooth, as our dreams used to run?'

285

VI

Breathless they paused. Out there men raised their glance
To where had stood those poplars lank and lopped,
As they had raised it through the four years' dance
Of Death in the now familiar flats of France;
And murmured, 'Strange, this! How? All firing stopped?'

VII

Aye; all was hushed. The about-to-fire fired not,
The aimed-at moved away in trance-lipped song.
One checkless regiment slung a clinching shot
And turned. The Spirit of Irony smirked out, 'What?
Spoil peradventures woven of Rage and Wrong?'

VIII

Thenceforth no flying fires inflamed the gray,
No hurtlings shook the dewdrop from the thorn,
No moan perplexed the mute bird on the spray;
Worn horses mused: 'We are not whipped to-day;'
No weft-winged engines blurred the moon's thin horn.

IX

Calm fell. From Heaven distilled a clemency;
There was peace on earth, and silence in the sky;
Some could, some could not, shake off misery:
The Sinister Spirit sneered: 'It had to be!'
And again the Spirit of Pity whispered, 'Why?'

Christmas: 1924

'PEACE upon earth!' was said. We sing it,
And pay a million priests to bring it.
After two thousand years of mass
We've got as far as poison-gas.

1924

We Are Getting to the End

WE are getting to the end of visioning
The impossible within this universe,
Such as that better whiles may follow worse,
And that our race may mend by reasoning.

We know that even as larks in cages sing
Unthoughtful of deliverance from the curse
That holds them lifelong in a latticed hearse,
We ply spasmodically our pleasuring.

And that when nations set them to lay waste
Their neighbours' heritage by foot and horse,
And hack their pleasant plains in festering seams,
They may again, – not warely, or from taste,
But tickled mad by some demonic force. –
Yes. We are getting to the end of dreams!

Standing by the Mantelpiece[40]

(H.M.M., 1873)

THIS candle-wax is shaping to a shroud
To-night. (They call it that, as you may know) –
By touching it the claimant is avowed,
And hence I press it with my finger – so.

To-night. To me twice night, that should have been
The radiance of the midmost tick of noon,
And close around me wintertime is seen
That might have shone the veriest day of June!

But since all's lost, and nothing really lies
Above but shade, and shadier shade below,
Let me make clear, before one of us dies,
My mind to yours, just now embittered so.

Since you agreed, unurged and full-advised,
And let warmth grow without discouragement,
Why do you bear you now as if surprised,
When what has come was clearly consequent?

Since you have spoken, and finality
Closes around, and my last movements loom,
I say no more: the rest must wait till we
Are face to face again, yonside the tomb.

And let the candle-wax thus mould a shape
Whose meaning now, if hid before, you know,
And how by touch one present claims its drape,
And that it's I who press my finger – so.

Nature's Questioning

WHEN I look forth at dawning, pool,
　　　Field, flock, and lonely tree,
　　　All seem to gaze at me
Like chastened children sitting silent in a school;

Their faces dulled, constrained, and worn,
　　　As though the master's ways
　　　Through the long teaching days
Had cowed them till their early zest was overborne.

Upon them stirs in lippings mere
　　　(As if once clear in call,
　　　But now scarce breathed at all) –
'We wonder, ever wonder, why we find us here!

'Has some Vast Imbecility,
　　　Mighty to build and blend,
　　　But impotent to tend,
Framed us in jest, and left us now to hazardry?

'Or come we of an Automaton
　　　Unconscious of our pains? . . .
　　　Or are we live remains
Of Godhead dying downwards, brain and eye now gone?

'Or is it that some high Plan betides,
        As yet not understood,
        Of Evil stormed by Good,
We the Forlorn Hope over which Achievement strides?'

Thus things around. No answerer I . . .
        Meanwhile the winds, and rains,
        And Earth's old glooms and pains
Are still the same, and Life and Death are neighbours nigh.

I Look Into My Glass

I LOOK into my glass,
And view my wasting skin,
And say, 'Would God it came to pass
My heart had shrunk as thin!'

For then, I, undistrest
By hearts grown cold to me,
Could lonely wait my endless rest
With equanimity.

But Time, to make me grieve,
Part steals, lets part abide;
And shakes this fragile frame at eve
With throbbings of noontide.

The Superseded

I

As newer comers crowd the fore,
        We drop behind.
– We who have laboured long and sore
        Times out of mind,
And keen are yet, must not regret
        To drop behind.

II

Yet there are some of us who grieve
    To go behind;
Staunch, strenuous souls who scarce believe
    Their fires declined,
And know none spares, remembers, cares
    Who go behind.

III

'Tis not that we have unforetold
    The drop behind;
We feel the new must oust the old
    In every kind;
But yet we think, must we, must *we*,
    Too, drop behind?

In Tenebris I[41]

'Percussus sum sicut foenum, et aruit cor meum.' – Ps. CI

WINTERTIME nighs;
But my bereavement-pain
It cannot bring again:
    Twice no one dies.

Flower-petals flee;
But, since it once hath been,
No more that severing scene
    Can harrow me.

Birds faint in dread:
I shall not lose old strength
In the lone frost's black length:
    Strength long since fled!

Leaves freeze to dun;
But friends can not turn cold
This season as of old
    For him with none.

Tempests may scath;
But love can not make smart
Again this year his heart
Who no heart hath.

Black is night's cope;
But death will not appal
One who, past doubtings all,
Waits in unhope.

In Tenebris II

'Considerabam ad dexteram, et videbam; et non era tqui cognosceret me . . .
non est qui requirat animam meam.' – Ps. cxii

WHEN the clouds' swoln bosoms echo back the shouts of the
many and strong
That things are all as they best may be, save a few to be right ere
long,
And my eyes have not the vision in them to discern what to these
is so clear,
The blot seems straightway in me alone; one better he were not
here.

The stout upstanders say, All's well with us: ruers have nought
to rue!
And what the potent say so oft, can it fail to be somewhat true?
Breezily go they, breezily come; their dust smokes around their
career,
Till I think I am one born out of due time, who has no calling
here.

Their dawns bring lusty joys, it seems; their evenings all that is
sweet;
Our times are blessed times, they cry: Life shapes it as is most
meet,
And nothing is much the matter; there are many smiles to a tear;
Then what is the matter is I, I say. Why should such an one be
here? . . .

Let him in whose ears the low-voiced Best is killed by the clash
    of the First,
Who holds that if way to the Better there be, it exacts a full look
    at the Worst,
Who feels that delight is a delicate growth cramped by crooked-
    ness, custom, and fear,
Get him up and be gone as one shaped awry; he disturbs the
    order here.

1895–96

In Tenebris III

'Heu mihi, quia incolatus meus prolongatus est! Habitavi cum habitantibus
Cedar. Multum incola fuit anima mea.' – Ps. cxix

THERE have been times when I well might have passed and the
    ending have come –
Points in my path when the dark might have stolen on me, artless,
    unrueing –
Ere I had learnt that the world was a welter of futile doing:
Such had been times when I well might have passed, and the
    ending have come!

Say, on the noon when the half-sunny hours told that April was
    nigh,
And I upgathered and cast forth the snow from the crocus-
    border,
Fashioned and furbished the soil into a summer-seeming order,
Glowing in gladsome faith that I quickened the year thereby.

Or on that loneliest of eves when afar and benighted we stood,
She who upheld me and I, in the midmost of Egdon together,
Confident I in her watching and ward through the blackening
    heather,
Deeming her matchless in might and with measureless scope
    endued.

Or on that winter-wild night when, reclined by the chimney-
    nook quoin,

Slowly a drowse overgat me, the smallest and feeblest of folk
    there,
Weak from my baptism of pain; when at times and anon I awoke
    there –
Heard of a world wheeling on, with no listing or longing to join.

Even then! while unweeting that vision could vex or that knowl-
    edge could numb,
That sweets to the mouth in the belly are bitter, and tart, and
    untoward,
Then, on some dim-coloured scene should my briefly raised
    curtain have lowered,
Then might the Voice that is law have said 'Cease!' and the
    ending have come.

1896

Wessex Heights[42]

(1896)

THERE are some heights in Wessex, shaped as if by a kindly
    hand
For thinking, dreaming, dying on, and at crises when I stand,
Say, on Ingpen Beacon eastward, or on Wylls-Neck westwardly,
I seem where I was before my birth, and after death may be.

In the lowlands I have no comrade, not even the lone man's
    friend –
Her who suffereth long and is kind; accepts what he is too weak
    to mend:
Down there they are dubious and askance; there nobody thinks
    as I,
But mind-chains do not clank where one's next neighbour is the
    sky.

In the towns I am tracked by phantoms having weird detective
    ways –
Shadows of beings who fellowed with myself of earlier days:
They hang about at places, and they say harsh heavy things –
Men with a wintry sneer, and women with tart disparagings.

Down there I seem to be false to myself, my simple self that was,
And is not now, and I see him watching, wondering what crass
     cause
Can have merged him into such a strange continuator as this,
Who yet has something in common with himself, my chrysalis.

I cannot go to the great grey Plain; there's a figure against the
     moon,
Nobody sees it but I, and it makes my breast beat out of tune;
I cannot go to the tall-spired town, being barred by the forms
     now passed
For everybody but me, in whose long vision they stand there fast.

There's a ghost at Yell'ham Bottom chiding loud at the fall of the
     night,
There's a ghost in Froom-side Vale, thin-lipped and vague, in a
     shroud of white,
There is one in the railway train whenever I do not want it near,
I see its profile against the pane, saying what I would not hear.

As for one rare fair woman, I am now but a thought of hers,
I enter her mind and another thought succeeds me that she
     prefers;
Yet my love for her in its fulness she herself even did not know;
Well, time cures hearts of tenderness, and now I can let her go.

So I am found on Ingpen Beacon, or on Wylls-Neck to the west,
Or else on homely Bulbarrow, or little Pilsdon Crest,
Where men have never cared to haunt, nor women have walked
     with me,
And ghosts then keep their distance; and I know some liberty.

'Αγνωστωι Θεωι

LONG have I framed weak phantasies of Thee,
     O Willer masked and dumb!
     Who makest Life become, –
As though by labouring all-unknowingly,
     Like one whom reveries numb.

How much of consciousness informs Thy will,
    Thy biddings, as if blind,
    Of death-inducing kind,
Nought shows to us ephemeral ones who fill
    But moments in Thy mind.

Perhaps Thy ancient rote-restricted ways
    Thy ripening rule transcends;
    That listless effort tends
To grow percipient with advance of days,
    And with percipience mends.

For, in unwonted purlieus, far and nigh,
    At whiles or short or long,
    May be discerned a wrong
Dying as of self-slaughter; whereat I
    Would raise my voice in song.

The Something that Saved Him

    IT was when
Whirls of thick waters laved me
    Again and again,
That something arose and saved me;
    Yea, it was then.

    In that day
Unseeing the azure went I
    On my way,
And to white winter bent I,
    Knowing no May.

    Reft of renown,
Under the night clouds beating
    Up and down,
In my needfulness greeting
    Cit and clown.

Long there had been
Much of a murky colour
　　In the scene,
Dull prospects meeting duller;
　　Nought between.

Last, there loomed
A closing-in blind alley,
　　Though there boomed
A feeble summons to rally
　　Where it gloomed.

The clock rang;
The hour brought a hand to deliver;
　　I upsprang,
And looked back at den, ditch and river,
　　And sang.

Autumn in King's Hintock Park

HERE by the baring bough
　　Raking up leaves,
Often I ponder how
　　Springtime deceives, –
I, an old woman now,
　　Raking up leaves.

Here in the avenue
　　Raking up leaves,
Lords' ladies pass in view,
　　Until one heaves
Sighs at life's russet hue,
　　Raking up leaves!

Just as my shape you see
　　Raking up leaves,
I saw, when fresh and free,
　　Those memory weaves
Into grey ghosts by me,
　　Raking up leaves.

Yet, Dear, though one may sigh,
    Raking up leaves,
New leaves will dance on high –
    Earth never grieves! –
Will not, when missed am I
    Raking up leaves.

1901

Shut Out That Moon

CLOSE up the casement, draw the blind,
    Shut out that stealing moon,
She wears too much the guise she wore
    Before our lutes were strewn
With years-deep dust, and names we read
    On a white stone were hewn.

Step not forth on the dew-dashed lawn
    To view the Lady's Chair,
Immense Orion's glittering form,
    The Less and Greater Bear:
Stay in; to such sights we were drawn
    When faded ones were fair.

Brush not the bough for midnight scents
    That come forth lingeringly,
And wake the same sweet sentiments
    They breathed to you and me
When living seemed a laugh, and love
    All it was said to be.

Within the common lamp-lit room
    Prison my eyes and thought;
Let dingy details crudely loom,
    Mechanic speech be wrought:
Too fragrant was Life's early bloom,
    Too tart the fruit it brought!

1904

You on the Tower

I

'YOU on the tower of my factory –
    What do you see up there?
Do you see Enjoyment with wide wings
    Advancing to reach me here?'
– 'Yea; I see Enjoyment with wide wings
    Advancing to reach you here.'

II

'Good. Soon I'll come and ask you
    To tell me again thereon . . .
Well, what is he doing now? Hoi, there!'
    – 'He still is flying on.'
'Ah, waiting till I have full-finished.
    Good. Tell me again anon. . . .

III

'Hoi, Watchman! I'm here. When comes he?
    Between my sweats I am chill.'
    – 'Oh, you there, working still?
Why, surely he reached you a time back,
    And took you miles from your mill?
He duly came in his winging,
    And now he has passed out of view.
How can it be that you missed him?
    He brushed you by as he flew.'

Seventy-Four and Twenty

HERE goes a man of seventy-four,
Who sees not what life means for him,
And here another in years a score
Who reads its very figure and trim.

298

The one who shall walk to-day with me
Is not the youth who gazes far,
But the breezy sire who cannot see
What Earth's ingrained conditions are.

Exeunt Omnes

I

EVERYBODY else, then, going,
And I still left where the fair was? . . .
Much have I seen of neighbour loungers
　　Making a lusty showing,
　　Each now past all knowing.

II

There is an air of blankness
In the street and the littered spaces;
Thoroughfare, steeple, bridge and highway
　　Wizen themselves to lankness;
　　Kennels dribble dankness.

III

Folk all fade. And whither,
As I wait alone where the fair was?
Into the clammy and numbing night-fog
　　Whence they entered hither.
　　Soon one more goes thither!

2 June 1913

An Anniversary

IT was at the very date to which we have come,
　　In the month of the matching name,
When, at a like minute, the sun had upswum,
　　Its couch-time at night being the same.

299

And the same path stretched here that people now follow,
   And the same stile crossed their way,
And beyond the same green hillock and hollow
   The same horizon lay;
And the same man pilgrims now hereby who pilgrimed here that
    day.

Let so much be said of the date-day's sameness;
   But the tree that neighbours the track,
And stoops liked a pedlar afflicted with lameness,
   Knew of no sogged wound or wind-crack.
And the joints of that wall were not enshrouded
   With mosses of many tones,
And the garth up afar was not overcrowded
   With a multitude of white stones,
And the man's eyes then were not so sunk that you saw the
   socket-bones.

Kingston-Maurward Ewelease

At the Royal Academy

THESE summer landscapes – clump, and copse, and croft –
Woodland and meadowland – here hung aloft,
Gay with limp grass and leafery new and soft,

Seem caught from the immediate season's yield
I saw last noonday shining over the field,
By rapid snatch, while still are uncongealed

The saps that in their live originals climb;
Yester's quick greenage here set forth in mime
Just as it stands, now, at our breathing-time.

But these young foils so fresh upon each tree,
Soft verdures spread in sprouting novelty,
Are not this summer's though they feign to be.

Last year their May to Michaelmas term was run,
Last autumn browned and buried every one,
And no more know they sight of any sun.

The Upper Birch-Leaves

WARM yellowy-green
In the blue serene,
How they skip and sway
On this autumn day!
They cannot know
What has happened below, –
That their boughs down there
Are already quite bare,
That their own will be
When a week has passed, –
For they jig as in glee
To this very last.

But no; there lies
At times in their tune
A note that cries
What at first I fear
I did not hear:
'O we remember
At each wind's hollo –
Though life holds yet –
We go hence soon,
For 'tis November;
– But that *you* follow
You may forget!'

A Spellbound Palace

(HAMPTON COURT)

ON this kindly yellow day of mild low-travelling winter sun
    The stirless depths of the yews
    Are vague with misty blues:
Across the spacious pathways stretching spires of shadow run,
And the wind-gnawed walls of ancient brick are fired vermilion.

301

Two or three early sanguine finches tune
Some tentative strains, to be enlarged by May or June:
    From a thrush or blackbird
    Comes now and then a word,
While an enfeebled fountain somewhere within is heard.

    Our footsteps wait awhile,
    Then draw beneath the pile,
    When an inner court outspreads
    As 'twere History's own asile,
Where the now-visioned fountain its attenuate crystal sheds
In passive lapse that seems to ignore the yon world's clamorous
        clutch,
And lays an insistent numbness on the place, like a cold hand's
        touch.

And there swaggers the Shade of a straddling King, plumed,
        sworded, with sensual face,
And lo, too, that of his Minister, at a bold self-centred pace:
Sheer in the sun they pass; and thereupon all is still,
Save the mindless fountain tinkling on with thin enfeebled will.

On the Portrait of a Woman about to be Hanged[43]

    COMELY and capable one of our race,
    Posing there in your gown of grace,
        Plain, yet becoming;
            Could subtlest breast
            Ever have guessed
    What was behind that innocent face,
        Drumming, drumming!

    Would that your Causer, ere knoll your knell
    For this riot of passion, might deign to tell
        Why, since It made you
            Sound in the germ,
            It sent a worm
    To madden Its handiwork, when It might well
        Not have assayed you,

Not have implanted, to your deep rue,
The Clytaemnestra spirit in you,
        And with purblind vision
            Sowed a tare
            In a field so fair,
And a thing of symmetry, seemly to view,
        Brought to derision!

6 January 1923

Who's in the Next Room?

'WHO'S in the next room? – who?
        I seemed to see
Somebody in the dawning passing through,
        Unknown to me.'
'Nay: you saw nought. He passed invisibly.'

    'Who's in the next room? – who?
        I seem to hear
Somebody muttering firm in a language new
        That chills the ear.'
'No: you catch not his tongue who has entered there.'

    'Who's in the next room? – who?
        I seem to feel
His breath like a clammy draught, as if it drew
        From the Polar Wheel.'
'No: none who breathes at all does the door conceal.'

    'Who's in the next room? – who?
        A figure wan
With a message to one in there of something due?
        Shall I know him anon?'
'Yea he; and he brought such; and you'll know him anon.'

The Masked Face

I FOUND me in a great surging space,
    At either end a door,
And I said: 'What is this giddying place,
    With no firm-fixéd floor,
    That I knew not of before?'
'It is Life,' said a mask-clad face.

I asked: 'But how do I come here,
    Who never wished to come;
Can the light and air be made more clear,
    The floor more quietsome,
    And the doors set wide? They numb
Fast-locked, and fill with fear.'

The mask put on a bleak smile then,
    And said, 'O vassal-wight,
There once complained a goosequill pen
    To the scribe of the Infinite
    Of the words it had to write
Because they were past its ken.'

Afterwards

WHEN the Present has latched its postern behind my tremulous
    stay,
    And the May month flaps its glad green leaves like wings,
Delicate-filmed as new-spun silk, will the neighbours say,
    'He was a man who used to notice such things'?

If it be in the dusk when, like an eyelid's soundless blink,
    The dewfall-hawk comes crossing the shades to alight
Upon the wind-warped upland thorn, a gazer may think,
    'To him this must have been a familiar sight.'

If I pass during some nocturnal blackness, mothy and warm,
   When the hedgehog travels furtively over the lawn,
One may say, 'He strove that such innocent creatures should
    come to no harm,
   But he could do little for them; and now he is gone.'

If, when hearing that I have been stilled at last, they stand at the
    door,
   Watching the full-starred heavens that winter sees,
Will this thought rise on those who will meet my face no more,
   'He was one who had an eye for such mysteries'?

And will any say when my bell of quittance is heard in the
    gloom,
   And a crossing breeze cuts a pause in its outrollings,
Till they rise again, as they were a new bell's boom,
   'He hears it not now, but used to notice such things'?

Last Week in October

THE trees are undressing, and fling in many places –
On the gray road, the roof, the window-sill –
Their radiant robes and ribbons and yellow laces;
A leaf each second so is flung at will,
Here, there, another and another, still and still.

A spider's web has caught one while downcoming,
That stays there dangling when the rest pass on;
Like a suspended criminal hangs he, mumming
In golden garb, while one yet green, high yon,
Trembles, as fearing such a fate for himself anon.

The Weary Walker

A PLAIN in front of me,
And there's the road
Upon it. Wide country,
And, too, the road!

Past the first ridge another,
   And still the road
Creeps on. Perhaps no other
   Ridge for the road?

Ah! Past that ridge a third,
   Which still the road
Has to climb furtherward –
   The thin white road!

Sky seems to end its track;
   But no. The road
Trails down the hill at the back.
   Ever the road!

Nobody Comes

TREE-LEAVES labour up and down,
   And through them the fainting light
   Succumbs to the crawl of night.
Outside in the road the telegraph wire
   To the town from the darkening land
Intones to travellers like a spectral lyre
   Swept by a spectral hand.

A car comes up, with lamps full-glare,
   That flash upon a tree:
   It has nothing to do with me,
And whangs along in a world of its own,
   Leaving a black air;
And mute by the gate I stand again alone,
   And nobody pulls up there.

9 October 1924

Lying Awake

YOU, Morningtide Star, now are steady-eyed, over the east,
   I know it as if I saw you;

You, Beeches, engrave on the sky your thin twigs, even the least;
    Had I paper and pencil I'd draw you.

You, Meadow, are white with your counterpane cover of dew,
    I see it as if I were there;
You, Churchyard, are lightening faint from the shade of the yew,
    The names creeping out everywhere.

He Abjures Love

At last I put off love,
    For twice ten years
The daysman of my thought,
    And hope, and doing;
Being ashamed thereof,
    And faint of fears
And desolations, wrought
    In his pursuing,

Since first in youthtime those
    Disquietings
That heart-enslavement brings
    To hale and hoary,
Became my housefellows,
    And, fool and blind,
I turned from kith and kind
    To give him glory.

I was as children be
    Who have no care;
I did not shrink or sigh,
    I did not sicken;
But lo, Love beckoned me,
    And I was bare,
And poor, and starved, and dry,
    And fever-stricken.

Too many times ablaze
   With fatuous fires,
Enkindled by his wiles
   To new embraces,
Did I, by wilful ways
   And baseless ires,
Return the anxious smiles
   Of friendly faces.

No more will now rate I
   The common rare,
The midnight drizzle dew,
   The gray hour golden,
The wind a yearning cry,
   The faulty fair,
Things dreamt, of comelier hue
   Than things beholden! ...

– I speak as one who plumbs
   Life's dim profound,
One who at length can sound
   Clear views and certain.
But – after love what comes?
   A scene that lours,
A few sad vacant hours,
   And then, the Curtain.

1883

Epitaph

I NEVER cared for Life: Life cared for me
And hence I owed it some fidelity.
It now says, 'Cease; at length thou hast learnt to grind
Sufficient toll for an unwilling mind,
And I dismiss thee – not without regard
That thou didst ask no ill-advised reward,
Nor sought in me much more than thou couldst find.'

He Never Expected Much

[OR]

A CONSIDERATION

[*A reflection*] ON MY EIGHTY-SIXTH BIRTHDAY

WELL, World, you have kept faith with me,
      Kept faith with me;
Upon the whole you have proved to be
      Much as you said you were.
Since as a child I used to lie
Upon the leaze and watch the sky,
Never, I own, expected I
      That life would all be fair.

'Twas then you said, and since have said,
      Times since have said,
In that mysterious voice you shed
      From clouds and hills around:
'Many have loved me desperately,
Many with smooth serenity,
While some have shown contempt of me
      Till they dropped underground.

'I do not promise overmuch,
      Child; overmuch;
Just neutral-tinted haps and such,'
      You said to minds like mine.
Wise warning for your credit's sake!
Which I for one failed not to take,
And hence could stem such strain and ache
      As each year might assign.

So Various

YOU may have met a man – quite young –
A brisk-eyed youth, and highly strung:
> One who desires
> And inner fires
> Moved him as wires.

And you may have met one stiff and old,
If not in years; of manner cold;
> Who seemed as stone,
> And never had known
> Of mirth or moan.

And there may have crossed your path a lover,
In whose clear depths you could discover
> A staunch, robust,
> And tender trust,
> Through storm and gust.

And you may have also known one fickle,
Whose fancies changed as the silver sickle
> Of yonder moon,
> Which shapes so soon
> To demilune!

You entertained a person once
Whom you internally deemed a dunce:–
> As he sat in view
> Just facing you
> You saw him through.

You came to know a learned seer
Of whom you read the surface mere:
> Your soul quite sank;
> Brain of such rank
> Dubbed yours a blank.

Anon you quizzed a man of sadness,
Who never could have known true gladness:
    Just for a whim
    You pitied him
    In his sore trim.

You journeyed with a man so glad
You never could conceive him sad:
    He proved to be
    Indubitably
    Good company.

You lit on an unadventurous slow man,
Who, said you, need be feared by no man;
    That his slack deeds
    And sloth must needs
    Produce but weeds.

A man of enterprise, shrewd and swift,
Who never suffered affairs to drift,
    You eyed for a time
    Just in his prime,
    And judged he might climb.

You smoked beside one who forgot
All that you said, or grasped it not.
    Quite a poor thing,
    Not worth a sting
    By satirizing!

Next year you nearly lost for ever
Goodwill from one who forgot slights never;
    And, with unease,
    Felt you must seize
    Occasion to please . . .

Now . . . All these specimens of man,
So various in their pith and plan,
    Curious to say
    Were *one* man. Yca,
    I was all they.

He Resolves to Say No More[44]

O MY soul, keep the rest unknown!
It is too like a sound of moan
   When the charnel-eyed
   Pale Horse has nighed:
Yea, none shall gather what I hide!

Why load men's minds with more to bear
That bear already ails to spare?
   From now alway
   Till my last day
What I discern I will not say.

Let Time roll backward if it will;
(Magians who drive the midnight quill
   With brain aglow
   Can see it so,)
What I have learnt no man shall know.

And if my vision range beyond
The blinkered sight of souls in bond,
   – By truth made free –
   I'll let all be,
And show to no man what I see.

Moments of Vision

 THAT mirror
Which makes of men a transparency,
 Who holds that mirror
And bids us such a breast-bare spectacle see
 Of you and me?

 That mirror
Whose magic penetrates like a dart,
 Who lifts that mirror
And throws our mind back on us, and our heart,
 Until we start?

312

That mirror
   Works well in these night hours of ache;
      Why in that mirror
Are tincts we never see ourselves once take
      When the world is awake?

That mirror
   Can test each mortal when unaware;
      Yea, that strange mirror
May catch his last thoughts, whole life foul or fair
      Glassing it – where?

On a Midsummer Eve

I IDLY cut a parsley stalk,
And blew therein towards the moon;
I had not thought what ghosts would walk
With shivering footsteps to my tune.

I went, and knelt, and scooped my hand
As if to drink, into the brook,
And a faint figure seemed to stand
Above me, with the bygone look.

I lipped rough rhymes of chance, not choice,
I thought not what my words might be;
There came into my ear a voice
That turned a tenderer verse for me.

To Lizbie Browne

I

DEAR Lizbie Browne,
Where are you now?
In sun, in rain? –
Or is your brow
Past joy, past pain,
Dear Lizbie Browne?

313

II

Sweet Lizbie Browne,
How you could smile,
How you could sing! –
How archly wile
In glance-giving,
Sweet Lizbie Browne!

III

And, Lizbie Browne,
Who else had hair
Bay-red as yours,
Or flesh so fair
Bred out of doors,
Sweet Lizbie Browne?

IV

When, Lizbie Browne,
You had just begun
To be endeared
By stealth to one,
You disappeared
My Lizbie Browne!

V

Ay, Lizbie Browne,
So swift your life,
And mine so slow,
You were a wife
Ere I could show
Love, Lizbie Browne.

VI

Still, Lizbie Browne,
You won, they said,
The best of men

When you were wed . . .
Where went you then,
O Lizbie Browne?

VII

Dear Lizbie Browne,
I should have thought,
'Girls ripen fast,'
And coaxed and caught
You ere you passed,
Dear Lizbie Browne!

VIII

But, Lizbie Browne,
I let you slip;
Shaped not a sign;
Touched never your lip
With lip of mine,
Lost Lizbie Browne!

IX

So, Lizbie Browne,
When on a day
Men speak of me
As not, you'll say,
'And who was he?' –
Yes, Lizbie Browne!

To Louisa in the Lane[45]

MEET me again as at that time
In the hollow of the lane;
I will not pass as in my prime
I passed at each day's wane.
– Ah, I remember!
To do it you will have to see
Anew this sorry scene wherein you have ceased to be!

315

But I will welcome your aspen form
 As you gaze wondering round
And say with spectral frail alarm,
 'Why am I still here found?
  – Ah, I remember!
It is through him with blitheful brow
Who did not love me then, but loves and draws me now!'

And I shall answer: 'Sweet of eyes,
 Carry me with you, Dear,
To where you donned this spirit-guise;
 It's better there than here!'
  – Till I remember
Such is a deed you cannot do:
Wait must I, till with flung-off flesh I follow you.

Louie [46]

I AM forgetting Louie the buoyant;
 Why not raise her phantom, too,
  Here in daylight
  With the elect one's?
She will never thrust the foremost figure out of view!

 Mid this heat, in gauzy muslin
 See I Louie's life-lit brow
  Here in daylight
  By the elect one's. –
Long two strangers they and far apart; such neighbours now!

July 1913

In Her Precincts [47]

HER house looked cold from the foggy lea,
And the square of each window a dull black blur
 Where showed no stir:
Yes, her gloom within at the lack of me
Seemed matching mine at the lack of her.

316

The black squares grew to be squares of light
As the eveshade swathed the house and lawn,
    And viols gave tone;
There was glee within. And I found that night
The gloom of severance mine alone.

Kingston–Maurward Park

Faintheart in a Railway Train

AT nine in the morning there passed a church,
At ten there passed me by the sea,
At twelve a town of smoke and smirch,
At two a forest of oak and birch,
    And then, on a platform, she:

A radiant stranger, who saw not me.
I said, 'Get out to her do I dare?'
But I kept my seat in my search for a plea,
And the wheels moved on. O could it but be
    That I had alighted there!

At a Seaside Town in 1869 [48]

(YOUNG LOVER'S REVERIE)

I WENT and stood outside myself,
    Spelled the dark sky
    And ship-lights nigh,
And grumbling winds that passed thereby.

Then next inside myself I looked,
    And there, above
    All, shone my Love,
That nothing matched the image of.

Beyond myself again I ranged;
    And saw the free
    Life by the sea,
And folk indifferent to me.

O 'twas a charm to draw within
    Thereafter, where
    But she was; care
For one thing only, her hid there!

But so it chanced, without myself
    I had to look,
    And then I took
More heed of what I had long forsook:

The boats, the sands, the esplanade,
    The laughing crowd;
    Light-hearted, loud
Greetings from some not ill-endowed;

The evening sunlit cliffs, the talk,
    Hailings and halts,
    The keen sea-salts,
The band, the Morgenblätter Waltz.

Still, when at night I drew inside
    Forward she came,
    Sad, but the same
As when I first had known her name.

Then rose a time when, as by force,
    Outwardly wooed
    By contacts crude,
Her image in abeyance stood . . .

At last I said: This outside life
    Shall not endure;
    I'll seek the pure
Thought-world, and bask in her allure.

Myself again I crept within,
    Scanned with keen care
    The temple where
She'd shone, but could not find her there.

I sought and sought. But O her soul
    Has not since thrown
    Upon my own
One beam! Yea, she is gone, is gone.

    From an old note

At Waking [49]

WHEN night was lifting,
And dawn had crept under its shade,
    Amid cold clouds drifting
Dead-white as a corpse outlaid,
      With a sudden scare
      I seemed to behold
      My Love in bare
      Hard lines unfold.

    Yea, in a moment,
An insight that would not die
    Killed her old endowment
Of charm that had capped all nigh,
      Which vanished to none
      Like the gilt of a cloud,
      And showed her but one
      Of the common crowd.

She seemed but a sample
Of earth's poor average kind,
    Lit up by no ample
Enrichments of mine or mind.
      I covered my eyes
      As to cover the thought,
      And unrecognize
      What the morn had taught.

O vision appalling
When the one believed-in thing
    Is seen falling, falling,
With all to which hope can cling.
        Off: it is not true;
        For it cannot be
        That the prize I drew
        Is a blank to me!

Weymouth, 1869

On the Way

THE trees fret fitfully and twist,
Shutters rattle and carpets heave,
Slime is the dust of yestereve,
    And in the streaming mist
Fishes might seem to fin a passage if they list.

        But to his feet,
        Drawing nigh and nigher
        A hidden seat,
        The fog is sweet
        And the wind a lyre.

A vacant sameness grays the sky,
A moisture gathers on each knop
Of the bramble, rounding to a drop,
    That greets the goer-by
With the cold listless lustre of a dead man's eye.

        But to her sight,
        Drawing nigh and nigher
        Its deep delight,
        The fog is bright
        And the wind a lyre.

On a Heath [50]

I COULD hear a gown-skirt rustling
　　Before I could see her shape,
Rustling through the heather
　　That wove the common's drape,
On that evening of dark weather
　　When I hearkened, lips agape.

And the town-shine in the distance
　　Did but baffle here the sight,
And then a voice flew forward:
　　'Dear, is't you? I fear the night!'
And the herons flapped to norward
　　In the firs upon my right.

There was another looming
　　Whose life we did not see;
There was one stilly blooming
　　Full nigh to where walked we;
There was a shade entombing
　　All that was bright of me.

The Mound [51]

FOR a moment pause:–
　　Just here it was;
And through the thin thorn hedge, by the rays of the moon,
I can see the tree in the field, and beside it the mound –
Now sheeted with snow – whereon we sat that June
　　When it was green and round,
And she crazed my mind by what she coolly told –
　　The history of her undoing,
(As I saw it), but she called 'comradeship',
　　That bred in her no rueing:
And saying she'd not be bound

321

For life to one man, young, ripe-yeared, or old,
Left me – an innocent simpleton to her viewing;
For, though my accompt of years outscored her own,
    Hers had more hotly flown . . .
We never met again by this green mound,
To press as once so often lip on lip,
        And palter, and pause: –
        Yes; here it was!

In a Cathedral City[52]

THESE people have not heard your name;
No loungers in this placid place
Have helped to bruit your beauty's fame.

The grey Cathedral, towards whose face
Bend eyes untold, has met not yours;
Your shade has never swept its base,

Your form has never darked its doors,
Nor have your faultless feet once thrown
A pensive pit-pat on its floors.

Along the street to maids well known
Blithe lovers hum their tender airs,
But in your praise voice not a tone . . .

– Since nought bespeaks you here, or bears,
As I, your imprint through and through,
Here might I rest, till my heart shares
The spot's unconsciousness of you!

Salisbury

On the Esplanade [53]

MIDSUMMER: 10 P.M.

THE broad bald moon edged up where the sea was wide,
    Mild, mellow-faced;
Beneath, a tumbling twinkle of shines, like dyed,
    A trackway traced
To the shore, as of petals fallen from a rose to waste,
    In its overblow,
And fluttering afloat on inward heaves of the tide: –
All this, so plain; yet the rest I did not know.

The horizon gets lost in a mist new-wrought by the night:
    The lamps of the Bay
That reach from behind me round to the left and right
    On the sea-wall way
For a constant mile of curve, make a long display
    As a pearl-strung row,
Under which in the waves they bore their gimlets of light: –
All this was plain; but there was a thing not so.

Inside a window, open, with undrawn blind,
    There plays and sings
A lady unseen a melody undefined:
    And where the moon flings
Its shimmer a vessel crosses, whereon to the strings
    Plucked sweetly and low
Of a harp, they dance. Yea, such did I mark. That, behind,
My Fate's masked face crept near me I did not know!

Two Serenades [54]

I. ON CHRISTMAS EVE

LATE on Christmas Eve, in the street alone,
Outside a house, on the pavement-stone,
I sang to her, as we'd sung together
On former eves ere I felt her tether. –

323

Above the door of green by me
Was she, her casement seen by me;
    But she would not heed
    What I melodied
    In my soul's sore need –
    She would not heed.

Cassiopeia overhead,
And the Seven of the Wain, heard what I said
As I bent me there, and voiced, and fingered
Upon the strings . . . Long, long I lingered:
Only the curtains hid from her
One whom caprice had bid from her;
    But she did not come,
    And my heart grew numb
    And dull my strum;
    She did not come.

II. A YEAR LATER

I SKIMMED the strings; I sang quite low;
I hoped she would not come or know
That the house next door was the one now dittied,
Not hers, as when I had played unpitied;
– Next door, where dwelt a heart fresh stirred,
My new Love, of good will to me,
Unlike my old Love chill to me,
Who had not cared for my notes when heard:
    Yet that old Love came
    To the other's name
    As hers were the claim;
    Yea, the old Love came.

My viol sank mute, my tongue stood still,
I tried to sing on, but vain my will:
I prayed she would guess of the later, and leave me;
She stayed, as though, were she slain by the smart,
She would bear love's burn for a newer heart.
The tense-drawn moment wrought to bereave me

Of voice, and I turned in a dumb despair
At her finding I'd come to another there.
    Sick I withdrew
    At love's grim hue
    Ere my last Love knew;
    Sick I withdrew.

From an old copy

The Place on the Map

I

I LOOK upon the map that hangs by me –
Its shires and towns and rivers lined in varnished artistry –
    And I mark a jutting height
Coloured purple, with a margin of blue sea.

II

– 'Twas a day of latter summer, hot and dry;
Ay, even the waves seemed drying as we walked on, she and I,
    By this spot where, calmly quite,
She unfolded what would happen by and by.

III

This hanging map depicts the coast and place,
And re-creates therewith our unforeboded troublous case
    All distinctly to my sight,
And her tension, and the aspect of her face.

IV

Weeks and weeks we had loved beneath that blazing blue,
Which had lost the art of raining, as her eyes to-day had too,
    While she told what, as by sleight,
Shot our firmament with rays of ruddy hue.

V

For the wonder and the wormwood of the whole
Was that what in realms of reason would have joyed our double
    soul
    Wore a torrid tragic light
Under order-keeping's rigorous control.

VI

So, the map revives her words, the spot, the time,
And the thing we found we had to face before the next year's
    prime;
    The charted coast stares bright,
And its episode comes back in pantomime.

The Photograph [55]

THE flame crept up the portrait line by line
As it lay on the coals in the silence of night's profound,
    And over the arm's incline,
And along the marge of the silkwork superfine,
And gnawed at the delicate bosom's defenceless round.

Then I vented a cry of hurt, and averted my eyes;
The spectacle was one that I could not bear,
    To my deep and sad surprise;
But, compelled to heed, I again looked furtivewise
Till the flame had eaten her breasts, and mouth, and hair.

'Thank God, she is out of it now!' I said at last,
In a great relief of heart when the thing was done
    That had set my soul aghast,
And nothing was left of the picture unsheathed from the past
But the ashen ghost of the card it had figured on.

She was a woman long hid amid packs of years,
She might have been living or dead; she was lost to my sight,
   And the deed that had nigh drawn tears
Was done in a casual clearance of life's arrears;
But I felt as if I had put her to death that night! ...

     .   .   .

– Well; she knew nothing thereof did she survive,
And suffered nothing if numbered among the dead;
   Yet – yet – if on earth alive
Did she feel a smart, and with vague strange anguish strive?
If in heaven, did she smile at me sadly and shake her head?

Thoughts of Phena 56

AT NEWS OF HER DEATH

NOT a line of her writing have I,
   Not a thread of her hair,
No mark of her late time as dame in her dwelling, whereby
   I may picture her there;
   And in vain do I urge my unsight
   To conceive my lost prize
At her close, whom I knew when her dreams were upbrimming
     with light,
   And with laughter her eyes.

What scenes spread around her last days,
   Sad, shining, or dim?
Did her gifts and compassions enray and enarch her sweet ways
   With an aureate nimb?
   Or did life-light decline from her years,
   And mischances control
Her full day-star; unease, or regret, or forebodings, or fears
   Disennoble her soul?

Thus I do but the phantom retain
   Of the maiden of yore
As my relic; yet haply the best of her – fined in my brain
   It may be the more

That no line of her writing have I,
      Nor a thread of her hair,
No mark of her late time as dame in her dwelling, whereby
      I may picture her there.

March 1890

I Need Not Go [57]

      I NEED not go
      Through sleet and snow
      To where I know
      She waits for me;
      She will tarry me there
      Till I find it fair,
      And have time to spare
      From company.

      When I've overgot
      The world somewhat,
      When things cost not
      Such stress and strain,
      Is soon enough
      By cypress sough
      To tell my Love
      I am come again.

      And if some day,
      When none cries nay,
      I still delay
      To seek her side,
      (Though ample measure
      Of fitting leisure
      Await my pleasure)
      She will not chide.

      What – not upbraid me
      That I delayed me,
      Nor ask what stayed me

328

So long? Ah, no! –
New cares may claim me,
New loves inflame me,
She will not blame me,
But suffer it so.

At Mayfair Lodgings[58]

How could I be aware,
The opposite window eyeing
As I lay listless there,
That through its blinds was dying
One I had rated rare
Before I had set me sighing
For another more fair?

Had the house-front been glass,
My vision unobscuring,
Could aught have come to pass
More happiness-insuring
To her, loved as a lass
When spouseless, all-alluring?
I reckon not, alas!

So, the square window stood,
Steadily night-long shining
In my close neighbourhood,
Who looked forth undivining
That soon would go for good
One there in pain reclining,
Unpardoned, unadieu'd.

Silently screened from view
Her tragedy was ending
That need not have come due
Had she been less unbending.
How near, near were we two
At that last vital rending, –
And neither of us knew!

Unknowing[59]

WHEN, soul in soul reflected,
We breathed an aethered air,
    When we neglected
    All things elsewhere,
And left the friendly friendless
To keep our love aglow,
    We deemed it endless ...
    – We did not know!

When panting passion-goaded,
We planned to hie away,
    But, unforeboded,
    All the long day
The storm so pierced and pattered
That none could up and go,
    Our lives seemed shattered ...
    – We did not know!

When I found you helpless lying,
And you waived my long misprise,
    And swore me, dying,
    In phantom-guise
To wing to me when grieving,
And touch away my woe,
    We kissed, believing ...
    – We did not know!

But though, your powers outreckoning,
You tarry dead and dumb,
    Or scorn my beckoning,
    And will not come:
And I say, 'Why thus inanely
Brood on her memory so!'
    I say it vainly –
    I feel and know!

The Wind's Prophecy[60]

I TRAVEL on by barren farms,
And gulls glint out like silver flecks
Against a cloud that speaks of wrecks,
And bellies down with black alarms.
I say: 'Thus from my lady's arms
I go; those arms I love the best!'
The wind replies from dip and rise,
'Nay; towards her arms thou journeyest.'

A distant verge morosely gray
Appears, while clots of flying foam
Break from its muddy monochrome,
And a light blinks up far away.
I sigh: 'My eyes now as all day
Behold her ebon loops of hair!'
Like bursting bonds the wind responds,
'Nay, wait for tresses flashing fair!'

From tides the lofty coastlands screen
Come smitings like the slam of doors,
Or hammerings on hollow floors,
As the swell cleaves through caves unseen.
Say I: 'Though broad this wild terrene,
Her city home is matched of none!'
From the hoarse skies the wind replies:
'Thou shouldst have said her sea-bord one.'

The all-prevailing clouds exclude
The one quick timorous transient star;
The waves outside where breakers are
Huzza like a mad multitude.
'Where the sun ups it, mist-imbued,'
I cry, 'there reigns the star for me!'
The wind outshrieks from points and peaks:
'Here, westward, where it downs, mean ye!'

331

Yonder the headland, vulturine,
Snores like old Skrymer in his sleep,
And every chasm and every steep
Blackens as wakes each pharos-shine.
'I roam, but one is safely mine.'
I say. 'God grant she stay my own!'
Low laughs the wind as if it grinned:
'Thy Love is one thou'st not yet known.'

Rewritten from an old copy

When I Set Out for Lyonnesse[61]
(1870)

WHEN I set out for Lyonnesse,
    A hundred miles away,
    The rime was on the spray,
And starlight lit my lonesomeness
When I set out for Lyonnesse
    A hundred miles away.

What would bechance at Lyonnesse
    While I should sojourn there
    No prophet durst declare,
Nor did the wisest wizard guess
What would bechance at Lyonnesse
    While I should sojourn there.

When I came back from Lyonnesse
    With magic in my eyes,
    All marked with mute surmise
My radiance rare and fathomless,
When I came back from Lyonnesse
    With magic in my eyes!

The Discovery

I WANDERED to a crude coast
        Like a ghost;
    Upon the hills I saw fires –
        Funeral pyres
    Seemingly – and heard breaking
Waves like distant cannonades that set the land shaking.

    And so I never once guessed
        A Love-nest,
    Bowered and candle-lit, lay
        In my way,
    Till I found a hid hollow,
Where I burst on her my heart could not but follow.

She Opened the Door

    SHE opened the door of the West to me,
            With its loud sea-lashings,
            And cliff-side clashings
    Of waters rife with revelry.

    She opened the door of Romance to me,
            The door from a cell
            I had known too well,
    Too long, till then, and was fain to flee.

    She opened the door of a Love to me,
            That passed the wry
            World-welters by
    As far as the arching blue the lea.

    She opens the door of the Past to me,
            Its magic lights,
            Its heavenly heights,
    When forward little is to see!

1913

333

Green Slates

(PENPETHY

IT happened once, before the duller
    Loomings of life defined them,
I searched for slates of greenish colour
    A quarry where men mined them;

And saw, the while I peered around there,
    In the quarry standing
A form against the slate background there,
    Of fairness eye-commanding.

And now, though fifty years have flown me,
    With all their dreams and duties,
And strange-pipped dice my hand has thrown me,
    And dust are all her beauties,

Green slates – seen high on roofs, or lower
    In waggon, truck, or lorry –
Cry out: 'Our home was where you saw her
    Standing in the quarry!'

The Old Gown[62]

(SONG)

I HAVE seen her in gowns the brightest,
    Of azure, green, and red,
And in the simplest, whitest,
    Muslined from heel to head;
I have watched her walking, riding,
    Shade-flecked by a leafy tree,
Or in fixed thought abiding
    By the foam-fingered sea.

In woodlands I have known her,
    When boughs were mourning loud,
In the rain-reek she has shown her
    Wild-haired and watery-browned.

And once or twice she has cast me
   As she pomped along the street
Court-clad, ere quite she had passed me,
   A glance from her chariot-seat,

But in my memoried passion
   For evermore stands she
In the gown of fading fashion
   She wore that night when we,
Doomed long to part, assembled
   In the snug small room; yea, when
She sang with lips that trembled,
   'Shall I see his face again?'

The Frozen Greenhouse [63]

(ST JULIOT)

'THERE was a frost
Last night!' she said,
'And the stove was forgot
When we went to bed,
And the greenhouse plants
Are frozen dead!'

By the breakfast blaze
Blank-faced spoke she,
Her scared young look
Seeming to be
The very symbol
Of tragedy.

The frost is fiercer
Than then to-day,
As I pass the place
Of her once dismay,
But the greenhouse stands
Warm, tight, and gay,

While she who grieved
At the sad lot
Of her pretty plants –
Cold, iced, forgot –
Herself is colder,
And knows it not.

At the Word 'Farewell' [64]

SHE looked like a bird from a cloud
    On the clammy lawn,
Moving alone, bare-browed
    In the dim of dawn.
The candles alight in the room
    For my parting meal
Made all things withoutdoors loom
    Strange, ghostly, unreal.

The hour itself was a ghost,
    And it seemed to me then
As of chances the chance furthermost
    I should see her again.
I beheld not where all was so fleet
    That a Plan of the past
Which had ruled us from birthtime to meet
    Was in working at last:

No prelude did I there perceive
    To a drama at all,
Or foreshadow what fortune might weave
    From beginnings so small;
But I rose as if quicked by a spur
    I was bound to obey,
And stepped through the casement to her
    Still alone in the gray.

'I am leaving you . . . Farewell!' I said,
   As I followed her on
By an alley bare boughs overspread;
   'I soon must be gone!'
Even then the scale might have been turned
   Against love by a feather,
– But crimson one cheek of hers burned
   When we came in together

The Sun on the Bookcase

(STUDENT'S LOVE-SONG: 1870)

ONCE more the cauldron of the sun
Smears the bookcase with winy red,
And here my page is, and there my bed,
And the apple-tree shadows travel along.
Soon their intangible track will be run,
     And dusk grow strong
     And they have fled.

Yes: now the boiling ball is gone,
And I have wasted another day . . .
But wasted – *wasted*, do I say?
Is it a waste to have imaged one
Beyond the hills there, who, anon,
     My great deeds done,
     Will be mine alway?

The Young Churchwarden

WHEN he lit the candles there,
And the light fell on his hand,
And it trembled as he scanned
Her and me, his vanquished air
Hinted that his dream was done,
And I saw he had begun
    To understand.

337

When Love's viol was unstrung,
Sore I wished the hand that shook
Had been mine that shared her book
While that evening hymn was sung,
His the victor's as he lit
Candles where he had bidden us sit
    With vanquished look.

Now her dust lies listless there,
His afar from tending hand,
What avails the victory scanned?
Does he smile from upper air:
'Ah, my friend, your dream is done;
And 'tis *you* who have begun
    To understand!'

The Figure in the Scene

IT pleased her to step in front and sit
    Where the cragged slope was green,
While I stood back that I might pencil it
    With her amid the scene;
      Till it gloomed and rained;
But I kept on, despite the drifting wet
    That fell and stained
My draught, leaving for curious quizzings yet
    The blots engrained.

And thus I drew her there alone,
    Seated amid the gauze
Of moisture, hooded, only her outline shown,
    With rainfall marked across.
      – Soon passed our stay;
Yet her rainy form is the Genius still of the spot,
    Immutable, yea,
Though the place now knows her no more, and has known her not
    Ever since that day.

From an old note

338

Under the Waterfall[65]

'WHENEVER I plunge my arm, like this,
In a basin of water, I never miss
The sweet sharp sense of a fugitive day
Fetched back from its thickening shroud of gray.
        Hence the only prime
        And real love-rhyme
        That I know by heart,
        And that leaves no smart,
Is the purl of a little valley fall
About three spans wide and two spans tall
Over a table of solid rock,
And into a scoop of the self-same block;
The purl of a runlet that never ceases
In stir of kingdoms, in wars, in peaces;
With a hollow boiling voice it speaks
And has spoken since hills were turfless peaks.'

'And why gives this the only prime
Idea to you of a real love-rhyme?
And why does plunging your arm in a bowl
Full of spring water, bring throbs to your soul?'

'Well, under the fall, in a crease of the stone,
Though where precisely none ever has known,
Jammed darkly, nothing to show how prized,
And by now with its smoothness opalized,
        Is a drinking-glass:
        For, down that pass
        My lover and I
        Walked under a sky
Of blue with a leaf-wove awning of green,
In the burn of August, to paint the scene,
And we placed our basket of fruit and wine
By the runlet's rim, where we sat to dine;
And when we had drunk from the glass together,
Arched by the oak-copse from the weather,

I held the vessel to rinse in the fall,
Where it slipped, and sank, and was past recall,
Though we stooped and plumbed the little abyss
With long bared arms. There the glass still is.
And, as said, if I thrust my arm below
Cold water in basin or bowl, a throe
From the past awakens a sense of that time,
And the glass we used, and the cascade's rhyme.
The basin seems the pool, and its edge
The hard smooth face of the brook-side ledge,
And the leafy pattern of china-ware
The hanging plants that were bathing there.

'By night, by day, when it shines or lours,
There lies intact that chalice of ours,
And its presence adds to the rhyme of love
Persistently sung by the fall above.
No lip has touched it since his and mine
In turns therefrom sipped lovers' wine.'

Love the Monopolist [66]

(YOUNG LOVER'S REVERIE)

THE train draws forth from the station-yard,
    And with it carries me.
I rise, and stretch out, and regard
    The platform left, and see
An airy slim blue form there standing,
    And know that it is she.

While with strained vision I watch on,
    The figure turns round quite
To greet friends gaily; then is gone . . .
    The import may be slight,
But why remained she not hard gazing
    Till I was out of sight?

340

'O do not chat with others there,'
    I brood. 'They are not I.
O strain your thoughts as if they were
    Gold bands between us; eye
All neighbour scenes as so much blankness
    Till I again am by!

'A troubled soughing in the breeze
    And the sky overhead
Let yourself feel; and shadeful trees,
    Ripe corn, and apples red,
Read as things barren and distasteful
    While we are separated!

'When I come back uncloak your gloom,
    And let in lovely day;
Then the long dark as of the tomb
    Can well be thrust away
With sweet things I shall have to practise,
    And you will have to say!'
    Begun 1871 : finished —

Self-Unconscious[67]

    ALONG the way
    He walked that day,
Watching shapes that reveries limn,
    And seldom he
    Had eyes to see
The moment that encompassed him.

    Bright yellowhammers
    Made mirthful clamours,
And billed long straws with a bustling air,
    And bearing their load
    Flew up the road
That he followed, alone, without interest there.

    From bank to ground
    And over and round

They sidled along the adjoining hedge;
 Sometimes to the gutter
 Their yellow flutter
Would dip from the nearest slatestone ledge.

 The smooth sea-line
 With a metal shine,
And flashes of white, and a sail thereon,
 He would also descry
 With a half-wrapt eye
Between the projects he mused upon.

 Yes, round him were these
 Earth's artistries,
But specious plans that came to his call
 Did most engage
 His pilgrimage,
While himself he did not see at all.

 Dead now as sherds
 Are the yellow birds,
And all that mattered has passed away;
 Yet God, the Elf,
 Now shows him that self
As he was, and should have been shown, that day.

 O it would have been good
 Could he then have stood
At a clear-eyed distance, and conned the whole,
 But now such vision
 Is mere derision,
Nor soothes his body nor saves his soul.

 Not much, some may
 Incline to say,
To see therein, had it all been seen.
 Nay! he is aware
 A thing was there
That loomed with an immortal mien.

Near Bossiney

342

Near Lanivet, 1872[68]

THERE was a stunted handpost just on the crest,
    Only a few feet high:
She was tired, and we stopped in the twilight-time for her rest,
    At the crossways close thereby.

She leant back, being so weary, against its stem,
    And laid her arms on its own,
Each open palm stretched out to each end of them,
    Her sad face sideways thrown.

Her white-clothed form at this dim-lit cease of day
    Made her look as one crucified
In my gaze at her from the midst of the dusty way,
    And hurriedly 'Don't,' I cried.

I do not think she heard. Loosing thence she said,
    As she stepped forth ready to go,
'I am rested now. – Something strange came into my head;
    I wish I had not leant so!'

And wordless we moved onward down from the hill
    In the west cloud's murked obscure,
And looking back we could see the handpost still
    In the solitude of the moor.

'It struck her too,' I thought, for as if afraid
    She heavily breathed as we trailed;
Till she said, 'I did not think how 'twould look in the shade,
    When I leant there like one nailed.'

I, lightly: 'There's nothing in it. For *you*, anyhow!'
    – 'O I know there is not,' said she . . .
'Yet I wonder . . . If no one is bodily crucified now,
    In spirit one may be!'

And we dragged on and on, while we seemed to see
    In the running of Time's far glass
Her crucified, as she had wondered if she might be
    Some day. – Alas, alas!

Lines

TO A MOVEMENT IN MOZART'S E-FLAT SYMPHONY

SHOW me again the time
When in the Junetide's prime
We flew by meads and mountains northerly! –
Yea, to such freshness, fairness, fulness, fineness, freeness,
    Love lures life on.

Show me again the day
When from the sandy bay
We looked together upon the pestered sea! –
Yea, to such surging, swaying, sighing, swelling, shrinking,
    Love lures life on.

Show me again the hour
When by the pinnacled tower
We eyed each other and feared futurity! –
Yea, to such bodings, broodings, beatings, blanchings, blessings,
    Love lures life on.

Show me again just this:
The moment of that kiss
Away from the prancing folk, by the strawberry-tree! –
Yea, to such rashness, ratheness, rareness, ripeness, richness,
    Love lures life on.

Begun November 1898

We Sat at the Window[69]

(BOURNEMOUTH, 1875)

WE sat at the window looking out,
And the rain came down like silken strings
That Swithin's day. Each gutter and spout
Babbled unchecked in the busy way
    Of witless things:

344

Nothing to read, nothing to see
Seemed in that room for her and me
   On Swithin's day.

We were irked by the scene, by our own selves; yes,
For I did not know, nor did she infer
How much there was to read and guess
By her in me, and to see and crown
   By me in her.
Wasted were two souls in their prime,
And great was the waste, that July time
   When the rain came down.

A Two-Years' Idyll[70]

   YES; such it was;
  Just those two seasons unsought,
Sweeping like summertide wind on our ways;
   Moving, as straws,
  Hearts quick as ours in those days;
Going like wind, too, and rated as nought
  Save as the prelude to plays
  Soon to come – larger, life-fraught:
   Yes; such it was.

   'Nought' it was called,
  Even by ourselves – that which springs
Out of the years for all flesh, first or last,
   Commonplace, scrawled
  Dully on days that go past.
Yet, all the while, it upbore us like wings
  Even in hours overcast:
  Aye, though this best thing of things,
   'Nought' it was called!

   What seems it now?
  Lost: such beginning was all;
Nothing came after: romance straight forsook
   Quickly somehow

345

Life when we sped from our nook,
Primed for new scenes with designs smart and tall ...
    – A preface without any book,
    A trumpet uplipped, but no call;
        That seems it now.

Overlooking the River Stour

THE swallows flew in the curves of an eight
        Above the river-gleam
        In the wet June's last beam:
Like little crossbows animate
The swallows flew in the curves of an eight
        Above the river-gleam.

Planing up shavings of crystal spray
        A moor-hen darted out
        From the bank thereabout,
And through the stream-shine ripped his way;
Planing up shavings of crystal spray
        A moor-hen darted out.

Closed were the kingcups; and the mead
        Dripped in monotonous green,
        Though the day's morning sheen
Had shown it golden and honeybee'd;
Closed were the kingcups; and the mead
        Dripped in monotonous green.

And never I turned my head, alack,
        While these things met my gaze
        Through the pane's drop-drenched glaze,
To see the more behind my back ...
O never I turned, but let, alack,
        These less things hold my gaze!

The Musical Box

LIFELONG to be
Seemed the fair colour of the time;
That there was standing shadowed near
A spirit who sang to the gentle chime
Of the self-struck notes, I did not hear,
        I did not see.

    Thus did it sing
To the mindless lyre that played indoors
As she came to listen for me without:
'O value what the nonce outpours –
This best of life – that shines about
        Your welcoming!'

    I had slowed along
After the torrid hours were done.
Though still the posts and walls and road
Flung back their sense of the hot-faced sun,
And had walked by Stourside Mill, where broad
        Stream-lilies throng.

    And I descried
The dusky house that stood apart,
And her, white-muslined, waiting there
In the porch with high-expectant heart,
While still the thin mechanic air
        Went on inside.

    At whiles would flit
Swart bats, whose wings, be-webbed and tanned,
Whirred like the wheels of ancient clocks:
She laughed a hailing as she scanned
Me in the gloom, the tuneful box
        Intoning it.

347

Lifelong to be
I thought it. That there watched hard by
A spirit who sang to the indoor tune,
'O make the most of what is nigh!'
I did not hear in my dull soul-swoon –
       I did not see.

On Sturminster Foot-Bridge

(ONOMATOPOEIC)

RETICULATIONS creep upon the slack stream's face
       When the wind skims irritably past,
The current clucks smartly into each hollow place
That years of flood have scrabbled in the pier's sodden base;
       The floating-lily leaves rot fast.

On a roof stand the swallows ranged in wistful waiting rows,
       Till they arrow off and drop like stones
Among the eyot-withies at whose foot the river flows:
And beneath the roof is she who in the dark world shows
       As a lattice-gleam when midnight moans.

The Chosen[71]

Ἅτινά ἐστιν ἀλληγορούμενα

'A WOMAN for whom great gods might strive!'
       I said, and kissed her there:
And then I thought of the other five,
       And of how charms outwear.

I thought of the first with her eating eyes,
And I thought of the second with hers, green-grey,
And I thought of the third, experienced, wise,
And I thought of the fourth who sang all day.

And I thought of the fifth, whom I'd called a jade,
    And I thought of them all, tear-fraught,
And that each had shown her a passable maid,
    Yet not of the favour sought.

So I traced these words on the bark of a beech,
Just at the falling of the mast:
'After scanning five; yes, each and each,
I've found the woman desired – at last!'

' – I feel a strange benumbing spell,
    As one ill-wished!' said she.
And soon it seemed that something fell
    Was starving her love for me.

'I feel some curse. O, *five* were there?'
And wanly she swerved, and went away.
I followed sick: night numbed the air,
And dark the mournful moorland lay.

I cried: 'O darling, turn your head!'
    But never her face I viewed;
'O turn, O turn!' again I said,
    And miserably pursued.

At length I came to a Christ-cross stone
Which she had passed without discern;
And I knelt upon the leaves there strown,
And prayed aloud that she might turn.

I rose, and looked; and turn she did;
    I cried, 'My heart revives!'
'Look more,' she said. I looked as bid;
    Her face was all the five's.

All the five women, clear come back,
I saw in her – with her made one,
The while she drooped upon the track,
And her frail term seemed well-nigh run.

She'd half forgot me in her change;
   'Who are you? Won't you say
Who you may be, you man so strange,
   Following since yesterday?'

I took the composite form she was,
And carried her to an arbour small,
Not passion-moved, but even because
In one I could atone to all.

And there she lies, and there I tend,
   Till my life's threads unwind,
A various womanhood in blend –
   Not one, but all combined.

Fetching Her

   AN hour before the dawn,
       My friend,
You lit your waiting bedside-lamp
   Your breakfast-fire anon,
And outing into the dark and damp
   You saddled, and set on.

   Thuswise, before the day,
       My friend,
You sought her on her surfy shore,
   To fetch her thence away
Unto your own new-builded door
   For a staunch lifelong stay.

   You said: 'It seems to be,
       My friend,
That I were bringing to my place
   The pure brine breeze, the sea,
The mews – all her old sky and space,
   In bringing her with me!'

– But time is prompt to expugn,
       My friend,
Such magic-minted conjurings:
   The brought breeze fainted soon,
And then the sense of seamews' wings,
   And the shore's sibilant tune.

So, it had been more due,
       My friend,
Perhaps, had you not pulled this flower
   From the craggy nook it knew,
And set it in an alien bower;
   But left it where it grew!

In the Vaulted Way

IN the vaulted way, where the passage turned
To the shadowy corner that none could see,
You paused for our parting, – plaintively;
Though overnight had come words that burned
My fond frail happiness out of me.

And then I kissed you, – despite my thought
That our spell must end when reflection came
On what you had deemed me, whose one long aim
Had been to serve you; that what I sought
Lay not in a heart that could breathe such blame.

But yet I kissed you; whereon you again
As of old kissed me. Why, why was it so?
Do you cleave to me after that light-tongued blow?
If you scorned me at eventide, how love then?
The thing is dark, Dear. I do not know.

351

A Countenance

HER laugh was not in the middle of her face quite,
    As a gay laugh springs,
It was plain she was anxious about some things
    I could not trace quite.
Her curls were like fir-cones – piled up, brown –
    Or rather like tight-tied sheaves:
It seemed they could never be taken down . . .

And her lips were too full, some might say:
I did not think so. Anyway,
The shadow her lower one would cast
Was green in hue whenever she passed
    Bright sun on midsummer leaves.
Alas, I knew not much of her,
And lost all sight and touch of her!

If otherwise, should I have minded
The shy laugh not in the middle of her mouth quite,
And would my kisses have died of drouth quite
    As love became unblinded?

1884

Mismet

I

HE was leaning by a face,
He was looking into eyes,
And he knew a trysting-place,
And he heard seductive sighs;
    But the face,
    And the eyes,
    And the place,
    And the sighs,
Were not, alas, the right ones – the ones meet for him –
Though fine and sweet the features, and the feelings all abrim.

II

She was looking at a form,
She was listening for a tread,
She could feel a waft of charm
When a certain name was said;
  But the form,
  And the tread,
  And the charm,
  And name said,
Were the wrong ones for her, and ever would be so,
While the heritor of the right it would have saved her soul to
   know!

The Conformers[72]

YES; we'll wed, my little fay,
  And you shall write you mine,
And in a villa chastely gray
  We'll house, and sleep, and dine.
  But those night-screened, divine,
  Stolen trysts of heretofore,
We of choice ecstasies and fine
   Shall know no more.

The formal faced cohue
  Will then no more upbraid
With smiting smiles and whisperings two
  Who have thrown less loves in shade.
  We shall no more evade
  The searching light of the sun,
Our game of passion will be played,
   Our dreaming done.

We shall not go in stealth
  To rendezvous unknown,
But friends will ask me of your health,

And you about my own
When we abide alone,
No leapings each to each,
But syllables in frigid tone
   Of household speech.

When down to dust we glide
Men will not say askance,
As now: 'How all the country side
  Rings with their mad romance!'
But as they graveward glance
  Remark: 'In them we lose
A worthy pair, who helped advance
   Sound parish views.'

Imaginings

SHE saw herself a lady
  With fifty frocks in wear,
And rolling wheels, and rooms the best,
  And faithful maidens' care,
And open lawns and shady
  For weathers warm or drear.

She found herself a striver,
  All liberal gifts debarred,
With days of gloom, and movements stressed,
  And early visions marred,
And got no man to wive her
  But one whose lot was hard.

Yet in the moony night-time
  She steals to stile and lea
During his heavy slumberous rest
  When homecome wearily,
And dreams of some blest bright-time
  She knows can never be.

Wives in the Sere

I

NEVER a careworn wife but shows,
    If a joy suffuse her,
Something beautiful to those
    Patient to peruse her,
Some one charm the world unknows
    Precious to a muser,
Haply what, ere years were foes,
    Moved her mate to choose her.

II

But, be it a hint of rose
    That an instant hues her,
Or some early light or pose
    Wherewith thought renews her –
Seen by him at full, ere woes
    Practised to abuse her –
Sparely comes it, swiftly goes,
    Time again subdues her.

A Second Attempt[73]

THIRTY years after
I began again
An old-time passion:
And it seemed as fresh as when
The first day ventured on:
When mutely I would waft her
In Love's past fashion
Dreams much dwelt upon,
Dreams I wished she knew.

I went the course through,
From Love's fresh-found sensation –
Remembered still so well –

355

To worn words charged anew,
That left no more to tell:
Thence to hot hopes and fears,
And thence to consummation,
And thence to sober years,
Markless, and mellow-hued.

Firm the whole fabric stood,
Or seemed to stand, and sound
As it had stood before.
But nothing backward climbs,
And when I looked around
As at the former times,
There was Life – pale and hoar;
And slow it said to me,
'Twice-over cannot be!'

The Rival

I DETERMINED to find out whose it was –
The portrait he looked at so, and sighed;
Bitterly have I rued my meanness
        And wept for it since he died!

I searched his desk when he was away,
    And there was the likeness – yes, my own!
Taken when I was the season's fairest,
        And time-lines all unknown.

I smiled at my image, and put it back,
    And he went on cherishing it, until
I was chafed that he loved not the me then living,
        But that past woman still.

Well, such was my jealousy at last,
    I destroyed that face of the former me;
Could you ever have dreamed the heart of woman
        Would work so foolishly!

Had You Wept

HAD you wept; had you but neared me with a hazed uncertain
    ray,
Dewy as the face of the dawn, in your large and luminous eye,
Then would have come back all the joys the tidings had slain
    that day,
And a new beginning, a fresh fair heaven, have smoothed the
    things awry.
But you were less feebly human, and no passionate need for
    clinging
Possessed your soul to overthrow reserve when I came near;
Ay, though you suffer as much as I from storms the hours are
    bringing
Upon your heart and mine, I never see you shed a tear.

The deep strong woman is weakest, the weak one is the strong;
The weapon of all weapons best for winning, you have not used;
Have you never been able, or would you not, through the evil
    times and long?
Has not the gift been given you, or such gift have you refused?
When I bade me not absolve you on that evening or the morrow,
Why did you not make war on me with those who weep like
    rain?
You felt too much, so gained no balm for all your torrid sorrow,
And hence our deep division, and our dark undying pain.

She Charged Me [74]

SHE charged me with having said this and that
To another woman long years before,
In the very parlour where we sat, –

Sat on a night when the endless pour
Of rain on the roof and the road below
Bent the spring of the spirit more and more . . .

357

– So charged she me; and the Cupid's bow
Of her mouth was hard, and her eyes, and her face,
And her white forefinger lifted slow.

Had she done it gently, or shown a trace
That not too curiously would she view
A folly flown ere her reign had place,

A kiss might have closed it. But I knew
From the fall of each word, and the pause between,
That the curtain would drop upon us two
Ere long, in our play of slave and queen.

Alike and Unlike[75]

(GREAT-ORME'S HEAD)

WE watched the selfsame scene on that long drive,
Saw the magnificent purples, as one eye,
Of those near mountains; saw the storm arrive;
Laid up the sight in memory, you and I,
As if for joint recallings by and by.

But our eye-records, like in hue and line,
Had superimposed on them, that very day,
Gravings on your side deep, but slight on mine! –
Tending to sever us thenceforth alway;
Mine commonplace; yours tragic, gruesome, gray.

A Thunderstorm in Town[76]

(A REMINISCENCE: 1893)

SHE wore a new 'terra-cotta' dress,
And we stayed, because of the pelting storm,
Within the hansom's dry recess,
Though the horse had stopped; yea, motionless
    We sat on, snug and warm.

Then the downpour ceased, to my sharp sad pain,
And the glass that had screened our forms before
Flew up, and out she sprang to her door:
I should have kissed her if the rain
    Had lasted a minute more.

At an Inn[77]

WHEN we as strangers sought
    Their catering care,
Veiled smiles bespoke their thought
    Of what we were.
They warmed as they opined
    Us more than friends —
That we had all resigned
    For love's dear ends.

And that swift sympathy
    With living love
Which quicks the world — maybe
    The spheres above,
Made them our ministers,
    Moved them to say,
'Ah, God, that bliss like theirs
    Would flush our day!'

And we were left alone
    As Love's own pair;
Yet never the love-light shone
    Between us there!
But that which chilled the breath
    Of afternoon,
And palsied unto death
    The pane-fly's tune.

The kiss their zeal foretold,
    And now deemed come,
Came not: within his hold
    Love lingered numb.

Why cast he on our port
    A bloom not ours?
Why shaped us for his sport
    In after-hours?

As we seemed we were not
    That day afar,
And now we seem not what
    We aching are.
O severing sea and land,
    O laws of men,
Ere death, once let us stand
    As we stood then!

The Thing Unplanned[78]

THE white winter sun struck its stroke on the bridge,
    The meadow-rills rippled and gleamed
As I left the thatched post-office, just by the ridge,
And dropped in my pocket her long tender letter,
With: 'This must be snapped! it is more than it seemed;
    And now is the opportune time!'

But against what I willed worked the surging sublime
    Of the thing that I did – the thing better!

A Broken Appointment[79]

You did not come,
And marching Time drew on, and wore me numb. –
Yet less for loss of your dear presence there
Than that I thus found lacking in your make
That high compassion which can overbear
Reluctance for pure lovingkindness' sake
Grieved I, when, as the hope-hour stroked its sum,
    You did not come.

You love not me,
And love alone can lend you loyalty;
– I know and knew it. But, unto the store
Of human deeds divine in all but name,
Was it not worth a little hour or more
To add yet this: Once you, a woman, came
To soothe a time-torn man; even though it be
You love not me?

The Difference

I

SINKING down by the gate I discern the thin moon,
And a blackbird tries over old airs in the pine,
But the moon is a sorry one, sad the bird's tune,
For this spot is unknown to that Heartmate of mine.

II

Did my Heartmate but haunt here at times such as now,
The song would be joyous and cheerful the moon;
But she will see never this gate, path, or bough,
Nor I find a joy in the scene or the tune.

In Death Divided[80]

I

I SHALL rot here, with those whom in their day
      You never knew,
And alien ones who, ere they chilled to clay,
      Met not my view,
Will in your distant grave-place ever neighbour you.

II

No shade of pinnacle or tree or tower,
    While earth endures,
Will fall on my mound and within the hour
    Steal on to yours;
One robin never haunt our two green covertures.

III

Some organ may resound on Sunday noons
    By where you lie,
Some other thrill the panes with other tunes
    Where moulder I;
No selfsame chords compose our common lullaby.

IV

The simply-cut memorial at my head
    Perhaps may take
A rustic form, and that above your bed
    A stately make;
No linking symbol show thereon for our tale's sake.

V

And in the monotonous moils of strained, hard-run
    Humanity,
The eternal tie which binds us twain in one
    No eye will see
Stretching across the miles that sever you from me.

189–

The Division[81]

RAIN on the windows, creaking doors,
    With blasts that besom the green,
And I am here, and you are there,
    And a hundred miles between!

O were it but the weather, Dear,
    O were it but the miles
That summed up all our severance,
    There might be room for smiles.

But that thwart thing betwixt us twain,
    Which nothing cleaves or clears,
Is more than distance, Dear, or rain,
    And longer than the years!

1893

The Recalcitrants

LET us off and search, and find a place
Where yours and mine can be natural lives,
Where no one comes who dissects and dives
And proclaims that ours is a curious case,
Which its touch of romance can scarcely grace.

You would think it strange at first, but then
Everything has been strange in its time.
When some one said on a day of the prime
He would bow to no brazen god again
He doubtless dazed the mass of men.

None will see in us a pair whose claims
To righteous judgment we care not making;
Who have doubted if breath be worth the taking,
And have no respect for the current fames
Whence the savour has flown while abide the names.

We have found us already shunned, disdained,
And for re-acceptance have not once striven;
Whatever offence our course has given
The brunt thereof we have long sustained.
Well, let us away, scorned, unexplained.

On the Departure Platform[82]

WE kissed at the barrier; and passing through
She left me, and moment by moment got
Smaller and smaller, until to my view
    She was but a spot;

A wee white spot of muslin fluff
That down the diminishing platform bore
Through hustling crowds of gentle and rough
    To the carriage door.

Under the lamplight's fitful glowers,
Behind dark groups from far and near,
Whose interests were apart from ours,
    She would disappear,

Then show again, till I ceased to see
That flexible form, that nebulous white;
And she who was more than my life to me
    Had vanished quite . . .

We have penned new plans since that fair fond day,
And in season she will appear again –
Perhaps in the same soft white array –
    But never as then!

– 'And why, young man, must eternally fly
A joy you'll repeat, if you love her well?'
– O friend, nought happens twice thus; why,
    I cannot tell!

The Interloper[83]

'And I saw the figure and visage of Madness seeking for a home'

THERE are three folk driving in a quaint old chaise,
And the cliff-side track looks green and fair;
I view them talking in quiet glee

As they drop down towards the puffins' lair
    By the roughest of ways;
But another with the three rides on, I see,
    Whom I like not to be there!

No; it's not anybody you think of. Next
A dwelling appears by a slow sweet stream
Where two sit happy and half in the dark:
They read, helpèd out by a frail-wick'd gleam,
    Some rhythmic text;
But one sits with them whom they don't mark,
    One I'm wishing could not be there.

No: not whom you knew and name. And now
I discern gay diners in a mansion-place,
And the guests dropping wit – pert, prim, or choice,
And the hostess's tender and laughing face,
    And the host's bland brow;
But I cannot help hearing a hollow voice,
    And I'd fain not hear it there.

No: it's not from the stranger you met once. Ah,
Yet a goodlier scene than that succeeds;
People on a lawn – quite a crowd of them. Yes,
And they chatter and ramble as fancy leads;
    And they say, 'Hurrah!'
To a blithe speech made; save one, mirthless,
    Who ought not to be there.

Nay: it's not the pale Form your imaginings raise,
That waits on us all at a destined time,
It is not the Fourth Figure the Furnace showed;
O that it were such a shape sublime
    In these latter days!
It is that under which best lives corrode;
    Would, would it could not be there!

She Who Saw Not

'DID you see something within the house
That made me call you before the red sunsetting?
Something that all this common scene endows
With a richened impress there can be no forgetting?'

' – I have found nothing to see therein,
O Sage, that should have made you urge me to enter,
Nothing to fire the soul, or the sense to win:
I rate you as a rare misrepresenter!'

' – Go anew, Lady, – in by the right . . .
Well: why does your face not shine like the face of Moses?'
' – I found no moving thing there save the light
And shadow flung on the wall by the outside roses.'

' – Go yet once more, pray. Look on a seat.'
' – I go . . . O Sage, it's only a man that sits there
With eyes on the sun. Mute, – average head to feet.'
' – No more?' – 'No more. Just one the place befits there,

'As the rays reach in through the open door,
And he looks at his hand, and the sun glows through his fingers,
While he's thinking thoughts whose tenour is no more
To me than the swaying rose-tree shade that lingers.'

No more. And years drew on and on
Till no sun came, dank fogs the house enfolding;
And she saw inside, when the form in the flesh had gone,
As a vision what she had missed when the real beholding.

His Heart

A WOMAN'S DREAM

AT midnight, in the room where he lay dead
Whom in his life I had never clearly read,
I thought if I could peer into that citadel
His heart, I should at last know full and well

366

What hereto had been known to him alone,
Despite our long sit-out of years foreflown,
'And if,' I said, 'I do this for his memory's sake,
It would not wound him, even if he could wake.'

So I bent over him. He seemed to smile
With a calm confidence the whole long while
That I, withdrawing his heart, held it and, bit by bit,
Perused the unguessed things found written on it.

It was inscribed like a terrestrial sphere
With quaint vermiculations close and clear –
His graving. Had I known, would I have risked the stroke
Its reading brought, and my own heart nigh broke!

Yes, there at last, eyes opened, did I see
His whole sincere symmetric history;
There were his truth, his simple singlemindedness,
Strained, maybe, by time's storms, but there no less.

There were the daily deeds from sun to sun
In blindness, but good faith, that he had done;
There were regrets, at instances wherein he swerved
(As he conceived) from cherishings I had deserved.

There were old hours all figured down as bliss –
Those spent with me – (how little had I thought this!)
There those when, at my absence, whether he slept or waked,
(Though I knew not 'twas so!) his spirit ached.

There that when we were severed, how day dulled
Till time joined us anew, was chronicled:
And arguments and battlings in defence of me
That heart recorded clearly and ruddily.

I put it back, and left him as he lay
While pierced the morning pink and then the gray
Into each dreary room and corridor around,
Where I shall wait, but his step will not sound.

Lost Love[84]

I PLAY my sweet old airs –
    The airs he knew
    When our love was true –
    But he does not balk
    His determined walk,
And passes up the stairs.

I sing my songs once more,
    And presently hear
    His footstep near
    As if it would stay;
    But he goes his way,
And shuts a distant door.

So I wait for another morn,
    And another night
    In this soul-sick blight;
    And I wonder much
    As I sit, why such
A woman as I was born!

The Last Performance[85]

'I AM playing my oldest tunes,' declared she,
    'All the old tunes I know, –
Those I learnt ever so long ago.'
– Why she should think just then she'd play them
    Silence cloaks like snow.

When I returned from the town at nightfall
    Notes continued to pour
As when I had left two hours before:
'It's the very last time,' she said in closing;
    From now I play no more.'

368

A few morns onward found her fading,
    And, as her life outflew,
I thought of her playing her tunes right through;
And I felt she had known of what was coming,
    And wondered how she knew.

1912

The Going

WHY did you give no hint that night
That quickly after the morrow's dawn,
And calmly, as if indifferent quite,
You would close your term here, up and be gone
     Where I could not follow
     With wing of swallow
To gain one glimpse of you ever anon!

     Never to bid good-bye,
     Or lip me the softest call,
Or utter a wish for a word, while I
Saw morning harden upon the wall,
     Unmoved, unknowing
     That your great going
Had place that moment, and altered all.

Why do you make me leave the house
And think for a breath it is you I see
At the end of the alley of bending boughs
Where so often at dusk you used to be;
     Till in darkening dankness
     The yawning blankness
Of the perspective sickens me!

     You were she who abode
     By those red-veined rocks far West,
You were the swan-necked one who rode

Along the beetling Beeny Crest,
 And, reining nigh me,
 Would muse and eye me,
While Life unrolled us its very best.

Why, then, latterly did we not speak,
Did we not think of those days long dead,
And ere your vanishing strive to seek
That time's renewal? We might have said,
 'In this bright spring weather
 We'll visit together
Those places that once we visited.'

 Well, well! All's past amend,
 Unchangeable. It must go.
I seem but a dead man held on end
To sink down soon . . . O you could not know
 That such swift fleeing
 No soul foreseeing –
Not even I – would undo me so!

December 1912

Your Last Drive

HERE by the moorway you returned,
And saw the borough lights ahead
That lit your face – all undiscerned
To be in a week the face of the dead,
And you told of the charm of that haloed view
That never again would beam on you.

And on your left you passed the spot
Where eight days later you were to lie,
And be spoken of as one who was not;
Beholding it with a heedless eye
As alien from you, though under its tree
You soon would halt everlastingly.

371

I drove not with you . . . Yet had I sat
At your side that eve I should not have seen
That the countenance I was glancing at
Had a last-time look in the flickering sheen,
Nor have read the writing upon your face,
'I go hence soon to my resting-place;

'You may miss me then. But I shall not know
How many times you visit me there,
Or what your thoughts are, or if you go
There never at all. And I shall not care.
Should you censure me I shall take no heed,
And even your praises no more shall need.'

True: never you'll know. And you will not mind.
But shall I then slight you because of such?
Dear ghost, in the past did you ever find
The thought 'What profit,' move me much?
Yet abides the fact, indeed, the same, –
You are past love, praise, indifference, blame.

December 1912

The Walk

You did not walk with me
Of late to the hill-top tree
   By the gated ways,
   As in earlier days;
   You were weak and lame,
   So you never came,
And I went alone, and I did not mind,
Not thinking of you as left behind.

   I walked up there to-day
   Just in the former way;
    Surveyed around
    The familiar ground

By myself again:
What difference, then?
Only that underlying sense
Of the look of a room on returning thence.

Rain on a Grave

CLOUDS spout upon her
   Their waters amain
   In ruthless disdain, –
Her who but lately
   Had shivered with pain
As at touch of dishonour
If there had lit on her
So coldly, so straightly
   Such arrows of rain:

One who to shelter
   Her delicate head
Would quicken and quicken
   Each tentative tread
If drops chanced to pelt her
   That summertime spills
   In dust-paven rills
When thunder-clouds thicken
   And birds close their bills.

Would that I lay there
   And she were housed here!
Or better, together
Were folded away there
Exposed to one weather
We both, – who would stray there
When sunny the day there,
   Or evening was clear
   At the prime of the year.

Soon will be growing
   Green blades from her mound,
And daisies be showing
   Like stars on the ground,
Till she form part of them –
Ay – the sweet heart of them,
   Loved beyond measure
   With a child's pleasure
   All her life's round.

   31 Jan., 1913

I Found Her Out There

I FOUND her out there
On a slope few see,
That falls westwardly
To the salt-edged air,
Where the ocean breaks
On the purple strand,
And the hurricane shakes
The solid land.

I brought her here,
And have laid her to rest
In a noiseless nest
No sea beats near.
She will never be stirred
In her loamy cell
By the waves long heard
And loved so well.

So she does not sleep
By those haunted heights
The Atlantic smites
And the blind gales sweep,
Whence she often would gaze
At Dundagel's famed head,
While the dipping blaze
Dyed her face fire-red;

And would sigh at the tale
Of sunk Lyonnesse,
As a wind-tugged tress
Flapped her cheek like a flail:
Or listen at whiles
With a thought-bound brow
To the murmuring miles
She is far from now.

Yet her shade, maybe,
Will creep underground
Till it catch the sound
Of that western sea
As it swells and sobs
Whence she once domiciled,
And joy in its throbs
With the heart of a child.

Without Ceremony

IT was your way, my dear,
To vanish without a word
When callers, friends, or kin
Had left, and I hastened in
To rejoin you, as I inferred.

And when you'd a mind to career
Off anywhere – say to town –
You were all on a sudden gone
Before I had thought thereon,
Or noticed your trunks were down.

So, now that you disappear
For ever in that swift style,
Your meaning seems to me
Just as it used to be:
'Good-bye is not worth while!'

Lament

How she would have loved
A party to-day! –
Bright-hatted and gloved,
With table and tray
And chairs on the lawn
Her smiles would have shone
With welcomings . . . But
She is shut, she is shut
 From friendship's spell
 In the jailing shell
 Of her tiny cell.

Or she would have reigned
At a dinner to-night
With ardours unfeigned,
And a generous delight;
All in her abode
She'd have freely bestowed
On her guests . . . But alas,
She is shut under grass
 Where no cups flow,
 Powerless to know
 That it might be so.

And she would have sought
With a child's eager glance
The shy snowdrops brought
By the new year's advance,
And peered in the rime
Of Candlemas-time
For crocuses . . . chanced
It that she were not tranced
 From sights she loved best;
 Wholly possessed
 By an infinite rest!

And we are here staying
Amid these stale things,
Who care not for gaying,
And those junketings
That used so to joy her,
And never to cloy her
As us they cloy! . . . But
She is shut, she is shut
        From the cheer of them, dead
        To all done and said
        In her yew-arched bed.

The Haunter

HE does not think that I haunt here nightly:
        How shall I let him know
That whither his fancy sets him wandering
        I, too, alertly go? –
Hover and hover a few feet from him
        Just as I used to do,
But cannot answer the words he lifts me –
        Only listen thereto!

When I could answer he did not say them:
        When I could let him know
How I would like to join in his journeys
        Seldom he wished to go.
Now that he goes and wants me with him
        More than he used to do,
Never he sees my faithful phantom
        Though he speaks thereto.

Yes, I companion him to places
        Only dreamers know,
Where the shy hares print long paces,
        Where the night rooks go;

377

Into old aisles where the past is all to him,
    Close as his shade can do,
Always lacking the power to call to him,
    Near as I reach thereto!

What a good haunter I am, O tell him!
    Quickly make him know
If he but sigh since my loss befell him
    Straight to his side I go.
Tell him a faithful one is doing
    All that love can do
Still that his path may be worth pursuing,
    And to bring peace thereto.

The Voice

WOMAN much missed, how you call to me, call to me,
Saying that now you are not as you were
When you have changed from the one who was all to me,
But as at first, when our day was fair.

Can it be you that I hear? Let me view you, then,
Standing as when I drew near to the town
Where you would wait for me: yes, as I knew you then,
Even to the original air-blue gown!

Or is it only the breeze, in its listnessness
Travelling across the wet mead to me here,
You being ever dissolved to wan wistlessness,
Heard no more again far or near?

    Thus I; faltering forward,
    Leaves around me falling,
Wind oozing thin through the thorn from norward,
    And the woman calling.

December 1912

His Visitor [87]

I COME across from Mellstock while the moon wastes weaker
To behold where I lived with you for twenty years and more:
I shall go in the gray, at the passing of the mail-train,
And need no setting open of the long familiar door
      As before.

The change I notice in my once own quarters!
A formal-fashioned border where the daisies used to be,
The rooms new painted, and the pictures altered,
And other cups and saucers, and no cosy nook for tea
      As with me.

I discern the dim faces of the sleep-wrapt servants;
They are not those who tended me through feeble hours and
   strong,
But strangers quite, who never knew my rule here,
Who never saw me painting, never heard my softling song
      Float along.

So I don't want to linger in this re-decked dwelling,
I feel too uneasy at the contrasts I behold,
And I make again for Mellstock to return here never,
And rejoin the roomy silence, and the mute and manifold
      Souls of old.

1913

A Circular

As 'legal representative'
I read a missive not my own,
On new designs the senders give
    For clothes, in tints as shown.

Here figure blouses, gowns for tea,
And presentation-trains of state,
Charming ball-dresses, millinery,
    Warranted up to date.

And this gay-pictured, spring-time shout
Of Fashion, hails what lady proud?
Her who before last year ebbed out
　　Was costumed in a shroud.

A Dream or No

WHY go to Saint-Juliot? What's Juliot to me?
　　Some strange necromancy
　　But charmed me to fancy
That much of my life claims the spot as its key.

Yes. I have had dreams of that place in the West,
　　And a maiden abiding
　　Thereat as in hiding;
Fair-eyed and white-shouldered, broad-browed and brown-
　　　tressed.

And of how, coastward bound on a night long ago,
　　There lonely I found her,
　　The sea-birds around her,
And other than nigh things uncaring to know.

So sweet her life there (in my thought has it seemed)
　　That quickly she drew me
　　To take her unto me,
And lodge her long years with me. Such have I dreamed.

But nought of that maid from Saint-Juliot I see;
　　Can she ever have been here,
　　And shed her life's sheen here,
The woman I thought a long housemate with me?

Does there even a place like Saint-Juliot exist?
　　Or a Vallency Valley
　　With stream and leafed alley,
Or Beeny, or Bos with its flounce flinging mist?

February 1913

After a Journey [88]

HERETO I come to view a voiceless ghost;
   Whither, O whither will its whim now draw me?
Up the cliff, down, till I'm lonely, lost,
   And the unseen waters' ejaculations awe me.
Where you will next be there's no knowing,
    Facing round about me everywhere,
       With your nut-coloured hair,
And gray eyes, and rose-flush coming and going.

Yes: I have re-entered your olden haunts at last;
   Through the years, through the dead scenes I have tracked
       you;
What have you now found to say of our past –
   Scanned across the dark space wherein I have lacked you?
Summer gave us sweets, but autumn wrought division?
    Things were not lastly as firstly well
       With us twain, you tell?
But all's closed now, despite Time's derision.

I see what you are doing: you are leading me on
   To the spots we knew when we haunted here together,
The waterfall, above which the mist-bow shone
   At the then fair hour in the then fair weather,
And the cave just under, with a voice still so hollow
   That it seems to call out to me from forty years ago,
       When you were all aglow,
And not the thin ghost that I now fraily follow!

Ignorant of what there is flitting here to see,
   The waked birds preen and the seals flop lazily;
Soon you will have, Dear, to vanish from me,
   For the stars close their shutters and the dawn whitens hazily.
Trust me, I mind not, though Life lours,
   The bringing me here; nay, bring me here again!
       I am just the same as when
Our days were a joy, and our paths through flowers.

Pentargan Bay

A Death-Day Recalled

BEENY did not quiver,
  Juliot grew not gray,
Thin Vallency's river
  Held its wonted way.
Bos seemed not to utter
Dimmest note of dirge,
Targan mouth a mutter
  To its creamy surge.

Yet though these, unheeding,
  Listless, passed the hour
Of her spirit's speeding,
  She had, in her flower,
Sought and loved the places –
  Much and often pined
For their lonely faces
  When in towns confined.

Why did not Vallency
  In his purl deplore
One whose haunts were whence he
  Drew his limpid store?
Why did Bos not thunder,
  Targan apprehend
Body and Breath were sunder
  Of their former friend?

Beeny Cliff

MARCH 1870–MARCH 1913

I

O THE opal and the sapphire of that wandering western sea,
And the woman riding high above with bright hair flapping free –
The woman whom I loved so, and who loyally loved me.

II

The pale mews plained below us, and the waves seemed far away
In a nether sky, engrossed in saying their ceaseless babbling say,
As we laughed light-heartedly aloft on that clear-sunned March
day.

III

A little cloud then cloaked us, and there flew an irised rain,
And the Atlantic dyed its levels with a dull misfeatured stain,
And then the sun burst out again, and purples prinked the main.

IV

– Still in all its chasmal beauty bulks old Beeny to the sky,
And shall she and I not go there once again now March is nigh
And the sweet things said in that March say anew there by and
by?

V

What if still in chasmal beauty looms that wild weird western
shore,
The woman now is – elsewhere – whom the ambling pony bore,
And nor knows nor cares for Beeny, and will laugh there never-
more.

At Castle Boterel[89]

As I drive to the junction of lane and highway,
  And the drizzle bedrenches the waggonette,
I look behind at the fading byway,
  And see on its slope, now glistening wet,
    Distinctly yet

Myself and a girlish form benighted
  In dry March weather. We climb the road
Beside a chaise. We had just alighted
  To ease the sturdy pony's load
    When he sighed and slowed.

What we did as we climbed, and what we talked of
   Matters not much, nor to what it led, –
Something that life will not be balked of
   Without rude reason till hope is dead,
      And feeling fled.

It filled but a minute. But was there ever
   A time of such quality, since or before,
In that hill's story? To one mind never,
   Though it has been climbed, foot-swift, foot-sore,
      By thousands more.

Primaeval rocks form the road's steep border,
   And much have they faced there, first and last,
Of the transitory in Earth's long order;
   But what they record in colour and cast
      Is – that we two passed.

And to me, though Time's unflinching rigour,
   In mindless rote, has ruled from sight
The substance now, one phantom figure
   Remains on the slope, as when that night
      Saw us alight.

I look and see it there, shrinking, shrinking,
   I look back at it amid the rain
For the very last time; for my sand is sinking,
   And I shall traverse old love's domain
      Never again.

    March 1913

Places[90]

NOBODY says: Ah, that is the place
Where chanced, in the hollow of years ago,
What none of the Three Towns cared to know –

The birth of a little girl of grace –
The sweetest the house saw, first or last;
  Yet it was so
  On that day long past.

Nobody thinks: There, there she lay
In a room by the Hoe, like the bud of a flower,
And listened, just after the bedtime hour,
To the stammering chimes that used to play
The quaint Old Hundred-and-Thirteenth tune
  In Saint Andrew's tower
  Night, morn, and noon.

Nobody calls to mind that here
Upon Boterel Hill, where the waggoners skid,
With cheeks whose airy flush outbid
Fresh fruit in bloom, and free of fear,
She cantered down, as if she must fall
  (Though she never did),
  To the charm of all.

Nay: one there is to whom these things,
That nobody else's mind calls back,
Have a savour that scenes in being lack,
And a presence more than the actual brings;
To whom to-day is beneaped and stale,
  And its urgent clack
  But a vapid tale.

  Plymouth, March 1913

The Phantom Horsewoman[91]

I

QUEER are the ways of a man I know:
  He comes and stands
  In a careworn craze,
  And looks at the sands
  And the seaward haze

With moveless hands
And face and gaze,
Then turns to go . . .
And what does he see when he gazes so?

II

They say he sees as an instant thing
More clear than to-day,
A sweet soft scene
That was once in play
By that briny green;
Yes, notes alway
Warm, real, and keen,
What his back years bring –
A phantom of his own figuring.

III

Of this vision of his they might say more:
Not only there
Does he see this sight,
But everywhere
In his brain – day, night,
As if on the air
It were drawn rose-bright –
Yea, far from that shore
Does he carry this vision of heretofore:

IV

A ghost-girl-rider. And though, toil-tried,
He withers daily,
Time touches her not,
But she still rides gaily
In his rapt thought
On that shagged and shaly
Atlantic spot,
And as when first eyed
Draws rein and sings to the swing of the tide.

1913

The Spell of the Rose

'I MEAN to build a hall anon,
　　And shape two turrets there,
　　And a broad newelled stair,
And a cool well for crystal water;
　　Yes; I will build a hall anon,
　　Plant roses love shall feed upon,
　　And apple-trees and pear.'

He set to build the manor-hall,
　　And shaped the turrets there,
　　And the broad newelled stair,
And the cool well for crystal water;
　　He built for me that manor-hall,
　　And planted many trees withal,
　　But no rose anywhere.

And as he planted never a rose
　　That bears the flowers of love,
　　Though other flowers throve
Some heart-bane moved our souls to sever
　　Since he had planted never a rose;
　　And misconceits raised horrid shows,
　　And agonies came thereof.

'I'll mend these miseries,' then said I,
　　And so, at dead of night,
　　I went and, screened from sight,
That nought should keep our souls in severance,
　　I set a rose-bush, 'This,' said I,
　　'May end divisons dire and wry,
　　And long-drawn days of blight.'

But I was called from earth – yea, called
　　Before my rose-bush grew;
　　And would that now I knew

What feels he of the tree I planted,
   And whether, after I was called
   To be a ghost, he, as of old,
     Gave me his heart anew!

Perhaps now blooms that queen of trees
   I set but saw not grow,
   And he, beside its glow –
Eyes couched of the mis-vision that blurred me –
   Ay, there beside that queen of trees
   He sees me as I was, though sees
     Too late to tell me so!

St Launce's Revisited[92]

   SLIP back, Time!
Yet again I am nearing
Castle and keep, uprearing
   Gray, as in my prime.

   At the inn
Smiling nigh, why is it
Not as on my visit
   When hope and I were twin?

   Groom and jade
Whom I found here, moulder;
Strange the tavern-holder,
   Strange the tap-maid.

   Here I hired
Horse and man for bearing
Me on my wayfaring
   To the door desired.

   Evening gloomed
As I journeyed forward
To the faces shoreward,
   Till their dwelling loomed.

If again
Towards the Atlantic sea there
I should speed, they'd be there
    Surely now as then? . . .

Why waste thought,
When I know them vanished
Under earth; yea, banished
    Ever into nought!

Where the Picnic Was

WHERE we made the fire
In the summer time
Of branch and briar
On the hill to the sea,
I slowly climb
Through winter mire,
And scan and trace
The forsaken place
Quite readily.

Now a cold wind blows,
And the grass is gray,
But the spot still shows
As a burnt circle – aye,
And stick-ends, charred,
Still strew the sward
Whereon I stand,
Last relic of the band
Who came that day!

Yes, I am here
Just as last year,
And the sea breathes brine
From its strange straight line
Up hither, the same
As when we four came.

– But two have wandered far
From this grassy rise
Into urban roar
Where no picnics are,
And one – has shut her eyes
For evermore.

*   *   *

The Prospect

THE twigs of the birch imprint the December sky
  Like branching veins upon a thin old hand;
I think of summer-time, yes, of last July,
  When she was beneath them, greeting a gathered band
    Of the urban and bland.

Iced airs wheeze through the skeletoned hedge from the north,
  With steady snores, and a numbing that threatens snow,
And skaters pass; and merry boys go forth
  To look for slides. But well, well do I know
    Whither I would go!

December 1912

The Change

OUT of the past there rises a week –
  Who shall read the years O! –
Out of the past there rises a week
  Enringed with a purple zone.
Out of the past there rises a week
When thoughts were strung too thick to speak,
And the magic of its lineaments remains with me alone.

In that week there was heard a singing –
  Who shall spell the years, the years! –
In that week there was heard a singing,
  And the white owl wondered why.
In that week, yea, a voice was ringing,
  And forth from the casement were candles flinging
Radiance that fell on the deodar and lit up the path thereby.

Could that song have a mocking note? –
   Who shall unroll the years O! –
Could that song have a mocking note
   To the white owl's sense as it fell?
Could that song have a mocking note
   As it trilled out warm from the singer's throat,
And who was the mocker and who mocked when two felt all
     was well?

In a tedious trampling crowd yet later –
   Who shall bare the years, the years! –
In a tedious trampling crowd yet later,
   When silvery singings were dumb;
In a crowd uncaring what time might fate her,
   Mid murks of night I stood to await her,
And the twanging of iron wheels gave out the signal that she was
     come.

She said with a travel-tired smile –
   Who shall lift the years O! –
She said with a travel-tired smile,
   Half scared by scene so strange;
She said, outworn by mile on mile,
   The blurred lamps wanning her face the while,
'O Love, I am here; I am with you!' . . . Ah, that there should
     have come a change!

O the doom by someone spoken –
   Who shall unseal the years, the years! –
O the doom that gave no token,
   When nothing of bale saw we:
O the doom by someone spoken,
   O the heart by someone broken,
The heart whose sweet reverberances are all time leaves to me.

Jan.–Feb. 1913

It Never Looks Like Summer

'IT never looks like summer here
    On Beeny by the sea.'
But though she saw its looks as drear,
    Summer it seemed to me.

It never looks like summer now
    Whatever weather's there;
But ah, it cannot anyhow,
    On Beeny or elsewhere!

Boscastle
8 March 1913

Where They Lived[93]

DISHEVELLED leaves creep down
    Upon that bank to-day,
Some green, some yellow, and some pale brown;
    The wet bents bob and sway;
The once warm slippery turf is sodden
    Where we laughingly sat or lay.

The summerhouse is gone,
    Leaving a weedy space;
The bushes that veiled it once have grown
    Gaunt trees that interlace,
Through whose lank limbs I see too clearly
    The nakedness of the place.

And where were hills of blue,
    Blind drifts of vapour blow,
And the names of former dwellers few,
    If any, people know,
And instead of a voice that called, 'Come in, Dears,'
    Time calls, 'Pass below!'

The Dream Is – Which?

I AM laughing by the brook with her,
    Splashed in its tumbling stir;
And then it is a blankness looms
    As if I walked not there,
Nor she, but found me in haggard rooms,
    And treading a lonely stair.

With radiant cheeks and rapid eyes
    We sit where none espies;
Till a harsh change comes edging in
    As no such scene were there,
But winter, and I were bent and thin,
    And cinder-gray my hair.

We dance in heys around the hall,
    Weightless as thistleball;
And then a curtain drops between,
    As if I danced not there,
But wandered through a mounded green
    To find her, I knew where.

March 1913

Old Excursions

'WHAT'S the good of going to Ridgeway,
    Cerne, or Sydling Mill,
    Or to Yell'ham Hill,
Blithely bearing Casterbridge-way
    As we used to do?
She will no more climb up there,
Or be visible anywhere
    In those haunts we knew.'

But to-night, while walking weary,
    Near me seemed her shade,
    Come as 'twere to upbraid

394

This my mood in deeming dreary
    Scenes that used to please;
And, if she did come to me,
Still solicitous, there may be
    Good in going to these.

So, I'll care to roam to Ridgeway,
    Cerne, or Sydling Mill,
    Or to Yell'ham Hill,
Blithely bearing Casterbridge-way
    As we used to do,
Since her phasm may flit out there,
And may greet me anywhere
    In those haunts we knew.

April 1913

The West-of-Wessex Girl[94]

A VERY West-of-Wessex girl,
    As blithe as blithe could be,
    Was once well-known to me,
And she would laud her native town,
    And hope and hope that we
Might sometime study up and down
    Its charms in company.

But never I squired my Wessex girl
    In jaunts to Hoe or street
    When hearts were high in beat,
Nor saw her in the marbled ways
    Where market-people meet
That in her bounding early days
    Were friendly with her feet.

Yet now my West-of-Wessex girl,
    When midnight hammers slow
    From Andrew's, blow by blow,

As phantom draws me by the hand
    To the place – Plymouth Hoe –
Where side by side in life, as planned,
    We never were to go!

Begun in Plymouth, March 1913

Looking at a Picture on an Anniversary

BUT don't you know it, my dear,
    Don't you know it,
That this day of the year
(What rainbow-rays embow it!)
We met, strangers confessed,
    But parted – blest?

Though at this query, my dear,
    There in your frame
Unmoved you still appear,
You must be thinking the same,
But keep that look demure
    Just to allure.

And now at length a trace
    I surely vision
Upon that wistful face
Of old-time recognition,
Smiling forth, 'Yes, as you say,
    It is the day.'

For this one phase of you
    Now left on earth
This great date must endue
With pulsings of rebirth? –
I see them vitalize
    Those two deep eyes!

But if this face I con
    Does not declare
Consciousness living on
    Still in it, little I care
    To live myself, my dear,
        Lone-labouring here!

Spring 1913

The Chimes Play 'Life's a Bumper!' 95

'AWAKE! I'm off to cities far away,'
I said; and rose, on peradventures bent.
The chimes played 'Life's a Bumper!' long that day
To the measure of my walking as I went:
Their sweetness frisked and floated on the lea,
As they played out 'Life's a Bumper!' there to me.

'Awake!' I said. 'I go to take a bride!'
– The sun arose behind me ruby-red
As I journeyed townwards from the countryside,
The chiming bells saluting near ahead.
Their sweetness swelled in tripping tings of glee
As they played out 'Life's a Bumper!' there to me.

'Again arise.' I seek a turfy slope,
And go forth slowly on an autumn noon,
And there I lay her who has been my hope,
And think, 'O may I follow hither soon!'
While on the wind the chimes come cheerily,
Playing out 'Life's a Bumper!' there to me.

1913

Paths of Former Time

No; no;
  It must not be so:
They are the ways we do not go.

Still chew
The kine, and moo
In the meadows we used to wander through;

Still purl
The rivulets and curl
Towards the weirs with a musical swirl;

Haymakers
As in former years
Rake rolls into heaps that the pitchfork rears;

Wheels crack
On the turfy track
The waggon pursues with its toppling pack,

'Why then shun –
Since summer's not done –
All this because of the lack of one?'

Had you been
Sharer of that scene
You would not ask while it bites in keen

Why it is so
We can no more go
By the summer paths we used to know!

1913

Something Tapped

SOMETHING tapped on the pane of my room
  When there was never a trace
Of wind or rain, and I saw in the gloom
  My weary Belovéd's face.

'O I am tired of waiting,' she said,
  'Night, morn, noon, afternoon;
So cold it is in my lonely bed,
  And I thought you would join me soon!'

I rose and neared the window-glass,
    But vanished thence had she:
Only a pallid moth, alas,
    Tapped at the pane for me.

August 1913

The Curtains Now Are Drawn

(SONG)

I

THE curtains now are drawn,
And the spindrift strikes the glass,
Blown up the jaggèd pass
By the surly salt sou'-west,
And the sneering glare is gone
Behind the yonder crest,
    While she sings to me:
'O the dream that thou art my Love, be it thine,
And the dream that I am thy Love, be it mine,
And death may come, but loving is divine.'

II

I stand here in the rain,
With its smite upon her stone,
And the grasses that have grown
Over women, children, men,
And their texts that 'Life is vain:'
But I hear notes as when
    Once she sang to me:
'O the dream that thou art my Love, be it thine,
And the dream that I am thy Love, be it mine,
And death may come, but loving is divine.'

1913

On the Doorstep

THE rain imprinted the step's wet shine
With target-circles that quivered and crossed
As I was leaving this porch of mine;
When from within there swelled and paused
    A song's sweet note;
    And back I turned, and thought,
     'Here I'll abide.'

The step shines wet beneath the rain,
Which prints its circles as heretofore;
I watch them from the porch again,
But no song-notes within the door
    Now call to me
    To shun the dripping lea;
    And forth I stride.

Jan. 1914

My Spirit Will Not Haunt the Mound

MY spirit will not haunt the mound
    Above my breast,
But travel, memory-possessed,
To where my tremulous being found
    Life largest, best.

My phantom-footed shape will go
    When nightfall grays
Hither and thither along the ways
I and another used to know
    In backward days.

Two Lips

I KISSED them in fancy as I came
    Away in the morning glow;
I kissed them through the glass of her picture-frame:
    She did not know.

I kissed them in love, in troth, in laughter,
    When she knew all; long so!
That I should kiss them in a shroud thereafter
    She did not know.

A Poet[96]

ATTENTIVE eyes, fantastic heed,
Assessing minds, he does not need,
Nor urgent writs to sup or dine,
Nor pledges in the rosy wine.

For loud acclaim he does not care
By the august or rich or fair,
Nor for smart pilgrims from afar,
Curious on where his hauntings are.

But soon or later, when you hear
That he has doffed this wrinkled gear,
Some evening, at the first star-ray,
Come to his graveside, pause and say:

'Whatever his message – glad or grim –
Two bright-souled women clave to him;'
Stand and say that while day decays;
It will be word enough of praise.

    July 1914

The Wistful Lady

'LOVE, while you were away there came to me –
        From whence I cannot tell –
A plaintive lady pale and passionless,
Who laid her eyes upon me critically,
And weighed me with a wearing wistfulness,
        As if she knew me well.'

'I saw no lady of that wistful sort
        As I came riding home.
Perhaps she was some dame the Fates constrain
By memories sadder than she can support,
Or by unhappy vacancy of brain,
        To leave her roof and roam?'

'Ah, but she knew me. And before this time
        I have seen her, lending ear
To my light outdoor words, and pondering each,
Her frail white finger swayed in pantomime,
As if she fain would close with me in speech,
        And yet would not come near.

'And once I saw her beckoning with her hand
        As I came into sight
At an upper window. And I at last went out;
But when I reached where she had seemed to stand,
And wandered up and down and searched about,
        I found she had vanished quite.'

Then thought I how my dead Love used to say,
        With a small smile, when she
Was waning wan, that she would hover round
And show herself after her passing day
To any newer Love I might have found,
        But show her not to me.

After the Visit[97]

(TO F.E.D.)

COME again to the place
Where your presence was as a leaf that skims
Down a drouthy way whose ascent bedims
    The bloom on the farer's face.

Come again, with the feet
That were light on the green as a thistledown ball,
And those mute ministrations to one and to all
    Beyond a man's saying sweet.

Until then the faint scent
Of the bordering flowers swam unheeded away,
And I marked not the charm in the changes of day
    As the cloud-colours came and went.

Through the dark corridors
Your walk was so soundless I did not know
Your form from a phantom's of long ago
    Said to pass on the ancient floors,

Till you drew from the shade,
And I saw the large luminous living eyes
Regard me in fixed inquiring-wise
    As those of a soul that weighed,

Scarce consciously,
The eternal question of what Life was,
And why we were there, and by whose strange laws
    That which mattered most could not be.

To Meet, or Otherwise[98]

WHETHER to sally and see thee, girl of my dreams,
    Or whether to stay
And see thee not! How vast the difference seems
    Of Yea from Nay

Just now. Yet this same sun will slant its beams
    At no far day
On our two mounds, and then what will the difference weigh!

Yet I will see thee, maiden dear, and make
    The most I can
Of what remains to us amid this brake
    Cimmerian
Through which we grope, and from whose thorns we ache,
    While still we scan
Round our frail faltering progress for some path or plan.

By briefest meeting something sure is won;
    It will have been:
Nor God nor Demon can undo the done,
    Unsight the seen,
Make muted music be as unbegun,
    Though things terrene
Groan in their bondage till oblivion supervene.

So, to the one long-sweeping symphony
    From times remote
Till now, of human tenderness, shall we
    Supply one note,
Small and untraced, yet that will ever be
    Somewhere afloat
Amid the spheres, as part of sick Life's antidote.

A Jog-Trot Pair[99]

WHO were the twain that trod this track
    So many times together
        So many times together
            Hither and back,
In spells of certain and uncertain weather?

Commonplace in conduct they
    Who wandered to and fro here
        Day by day:
Two that few dwellers troubled themselves to know here.

The very gravel-path was prim
    That daily they would follow:
        Borders trim:
Never a wayward sprout, or hump, or hollow.

Trite usages in tamest style
    Had tended to their plighting.
        'It's just worth while,
Perhaps,' they had said. 'And saves much sad good-nighting.'

And petty seemed the happenings
    That ministered to their joyance:
        Simple things,
Onerous to satiate souls, increased their buoyance.

Who could those common people be,
    Of days the plainest, barest?
        They were we;
Yes; happier than the cleverest, smartest, rarest.

The Shadow on the Stone [100]

I WENT by the Druid stone
    That broods in the garden white and lone,
And I stopped and looked at the shifting shadows
    That at some moments fall thereon
    From the tree hard by with a rhythmic swing,
    And they shaped in my imagining
To the shade that a well-known head and shoulders
    Threw there when she was gardening.

I thought her behind my back,
    Yea, her I long had learned to lack,
And I said: 'I am sure you are standing behind me,
    Though how do you get into this old track?'
    And there was no sound but the fall of a leaf
    As a sad response; and to keep down grief
I would not turn my head to discover
    That there was nothing in my belief.

Yet I wanted to look and see
That nobody stood at the back of me;
But I thought once more: 'Nay, I'll not unvision
A shape which, somehow, there may be.'
So I went on softly from the glade,
And left her behind me throwing her shade,
As she were indeed an apparition –
My head unturned lest my dream should fade.

Begun 1913 : finished 1916

The Marble Tablet [101]

THERE it stands, though alas, what a little of her
    Shows in its cold white look!
Not her glance, glide, or smile; not a tittle of her
    Voice like the purl of a brook;
      Not her thoughts, that you read like a book.

It may stand for her once in November
    When first she breathed, witless of all;
Or in heavy years she would remember
    When circumstance held her in thrall;
      Or at last, when she answered her call!

Nothing more. The still marble, date-graven,
    Gives all that it can, tersely lined;
That one has at length found the haven
    Which every one other will find;
      With silence on what shone behind.

St Juliot : 8 September 1916

The Monument-Maker [102]

I CHISELLED her monument
    To my mind's content,
Took it to the church by night,
When her planet was at its height,

And set it where I had figured the place in the daytime.
    Having niched it there
I stepped back, cheered, and thought its outlines fair,
    And its marbles rare.

Then laughed she over my shoulder as in our Maytime:
    'It spells not me!' she said:
'Tells nothing about my beauty, wit, or gay time
    With all those, quick and dead,
    Of high or lowlihead,
        That hovered near,
Including you, who carve there your devotion;
    But you felt none, my dear!'

And then she vanished. Checkless sprang my emotion
    And forced a tear
At seeing I'd not been truly known by her,
And never prized! – that my memorial here,
    To consecrate her sepulchre,
        Was scorned, almost,
        By her sweet ghost:
Yet I hoped not quite, in her very innermost!

1916

Quid Hic Agis?[103]

I

WHEN I weekly knew
An ancient pew,
And murmured there
The forms of prayer
And thanks and praise
In the ancient ways,
And heard read out
During August drought
That chapter from Kings
Harvest-time brings;

– How the prophet, broken
By griefs unspoken,
Went heavily away
To fast and to pray,
And, while waiting to die,
The Lord passed by,
And a whirlwind and fire
Drew nigher and nigher,
And a small voice anon
Bade him up and be gone, –
I did not apprehend
As I sat to the end
And watched for her smile
Across the sunned aisle,
That this tale of a seer
Which came once a year
Might, when sands were heaping,
Be like a sweat creeping,
Or in any degree
Bear on her or on me!

II

When later, by chance
Of circumstance,
It befel me to read
On a hot afternoon
At the lectern there
The selfsame words
As the lesson decreed,
To the gathered few
From the hamlets near –
Folk of flocks and herds
Sitting half aswoon,
Who listened thereto
As women and men
Not overmuch
Concerned at such –
So, like them then,

I did not see
What drought might be
With me, with her,
As the Kalendar
Moved on, and Time
Devoured our prime.

III

But now, at last,
When our glory has passed,
And there is no smile
From her in the aisle,
But where it once shone
A marble, men say,
With her name thereon
Is discerned to-day;
And spiritless
In the wilderness
I shrink from sight
And desire the night,
(Though, as in old wise,
I might still arise,
Go forth, and stand
And prophesy in the land),
I feel the shake
Of wind and earthquake,
And consuming fire
Nigher and nigher,
And the voice catch clear,
'What doest thou here?'

The Spectator: 1916. During the War

The Clock of the Years[104]

'A spirit passed before my face; the hair of my flesh stood up.'

AND the Spirit said,
'I can make the clock of the years go backward,
But am loth to stop it where you will.'
And I cried, 'Agreed
To that. Proceed:
It's better than dead!'

He answered, 'Peace;'
And called her up – as last before me;
Then younger, younger she freshed, to the year
I first had known
Her woman-grown,
And I cried, 'Cease! –

'Thus far is good –
It is enough – let her stay thus always!'
But alas for me – He shook his head:
No stop was there
And she waned child-fair,
And to babyhood.

Still less in mien
To my great sorrow became she slowly,
And smalled till she was nought at all
In his checkless griff;
And it was as if
She had never been.

'Better,' I plained,
'She were dead as before! The memory of her
Had lived in me; but it cannot now!'
And coldly his voice:
'It was your choice
To mar the ordained.'

1916

A Procession of Dead Days [105]

I SEE the ghost of a perished day;
I know his face, and the feel of his dawn:
'Twas he who took me far away
   To a spot strange and gray:
Look at me, Day, and then pass on,
But come again: yes, come anon!

Enters another into view;
His features are not cold or white,
But rosy as a vein seen through:
   Too soon he smiles adieu.
Adieu, O ghost-day of delight;
But come and grace my dying sight.

Enters the day that brought the kiss:
He brought it in his foggy hand
To where the mumbling river is,
   And the high clematis;
It lent new colour to the land,
And all the boy within me manned.

Ah, this one. Yes, I know his name,
He is the day that wrought a shine
Even on a precinct common and tame,
   As 'twere of purposed aim.
He shows him as a rainbow sign
Of promise made to me and mine.

The next stands forth in his morning clothes,
And yet, despite their misty blue,
They mark no sombre custom-growths
   That joyous living loathes,
But a meteor act, that left in its queue
A train of sparks my lifetime through.

I almost tremble at his nod –
This next in train – who looks at me

As I were slave, and he were god
   Wielding an iron rod.
I close my eyes; yet still is he
In front there, looking mastery.

In semblance of a face averse
The phantom of the next one comes:
I did not know what better or worse
   Chancings might bless or curse
When his original glossed the thrums
Of ivy, bringing that which numbs.

Yes; trees were turning in their sleep
Upon their windy pillows of gray
When he stole in. Silent his creep
   On the grassed eastern steep . . .
I shall not soon forget that day,
And what his third hour took away!

If You Had Known [106]

   IF you had known
When listening with her to the far-down moan
Of the white-selvaged and empurpled sea,
And rain came on that did not hinder talk,
Or damp your flashing facile gaiety
In turning home, despite the slow wet walk
By crooked ways, and over stiles of stone;
   If you had known

   You would lay roses,
Fifty years thence, on her monument, that discloses
Its graying shape upon the luxuriant green;
Fifty years thence to an hour, by chance led there,
What might have moved you? – yea, had you foreseen
That on the tomb of the selfsame one, gone where
The dawn of every day is as the close is,
   You would lay roses!

1920

An Upbraiding

NOW I am dead you sing to me
　　The songs we used to know,
But while I lived you had no wish
　　Or care for doing so.

Now I am dead you come to me
　　In the moonlight, comfortless;
Ah, what would I have given alive
　　To win such tenderness!

When you are dead, and stand to me
　　Not differenced, as now,
But like again, will you be cold
　　As when we lived, or how?

A Duettist to Her Pianoforte [107]

SONG OF SILENCE

(E.L.H. - H.C.H.)

SINCE every sound moves memories,
　　How can I play you
Just as I might if you raised no scene,
By your ivory rows, of a form between
My vision and your time-worn sheen,
　　As when each day you
Answered our fingers with ecstasy?
So it's hushed, hushed, hushed, you are for me!

And as I am doomed to counterchord
　　Her notes no more
In those old things I used to know,
In a fashion, when we practised so,
'Good-night! – Good-bye!' to your pleated show
　　Of silk, now hoar,
Each nodding hammer, and pedal and key,
For dead, dead, dead, you are to me!

413

I faint would second her, strike to her stroke,
  As when she was by,
Aye, even from the ancient clamorous 'Fall
Of Paris', or 'Battle of Prague' withal,
To the 'Roving Minstrels', or 'Elfin Call'
  Sung soft as a sigh:
But upping ghosts press achefully,
And mute, mute, mute, you are for me!

Should I fling your polyphones, plaints, and quavers
  Afresh on the air,
Too quick would the small white shapes be here
Of the fellow twain of hands so dear:
And a black-tressed profile, and pale smooth ear;
  – Then how shall I bear
Such heavily-haunted harmony?
Nay: hushed, hushed, hushed, you are for me!

Penance

'WHY do you sit, O pale thin man,
  At the end of the room
By that harpsichord, built on the quaint old plan?
  – It is cold as a tomb,
And there's not a spark within the grate;
   And the jingling wires
   Are as vain desires
   That have lagged too late.'

'Why do I? Alas, far times ago
  A woman lyred here
In the evenfall; one who fain did so
  From year to year;
And, in loneliness bending wistfully,
   Would wake each note
   In sick sad rote,
   None to listen to see!

'I would not join. I would not stay,
     But drew away,
Though the winter fire beamed brightly ... Aye!
     I do to-day
What I would not then; and the chill old keys,
     Like a skull's brown teeth
     Loose in their sheath,
     Freeze my touch; yes, freeze.'

The Strange House

(MAX GATE, A.D.2000)

'I HEAR the piano playing –
     Just as a ghost might play.'
' – O, but what are you saying?
     There's no piano to-day;
Their old one was sold and broken;
     Years past it went amiss.'
' – I heard it, or shouldn't have spoken:
     A strange house, this!

'I catch some undertone here,
     From some one out of sight.'
' – Impossible; we are alone here,
     And shall be through the night.'
' – The parlour-door – what stirred it?'
     ' – No one: no soul's in range.'
' – But, anyhow, I heard it,
     And it seems strange!

'Seek my own room I cannot –
     A figure is on the stair!'
' – What figure? Nay, I scan not
     Any one lingering there.
A bough outside is waving,
     And that's its shade by the moon.'
' – Well, all is strange! I am craving
     Strength to leave soon.'

'– Ah, maybe you've some vision
 Of showings beyond our sphere;
Some sight, sense intuition
 Of what once happened here?
The house is old; they've hinted
 It once held two love-thralls,
And they may have imprinted
   Their dreams on its walls?

'They were – I think 'twas told me –
 Queer in their works and ways;
The teller would often hold me
 With weird tales of those days.
Some folk can not abide here,
 But we – we do not care
Who loved, laughed, wept, or died here,
   Knew joy, or despair.'

When Oats Were Reaped

THAT day when oats were reaped, and wheat was ripe, and
   barley ripening,
   The road-dust hot, and the bleaching grasses dry,
   I walked along and said,
While looking just ahead to where some silent people lie:

'I wounded one who's there, and now know well I wounded her;
   But, ah, she does not know that she wounded me!'
   And not an air stirred,
Nor a bill of any bird; and no response accorded she.

August 1913

You Were the Sort that Men Forget

YOU were the sort that men forget;
       Though I – not yet! –
Perhaps not ever. Your slighted weakness
   Adds to the strength of my regret!

You'd not the art – you never had
       For good or bad –
To make men see how sweet your meaning,
   Which, visible, had charmed them glad.

You would, by words inept let fall,
       Offend them all,
Even if they saw your warm devotion
   Would hold your life's blood at their call.

You lacked the eye to understand
       Those friends off hand
Whose mode was crude, though whose dim purport
   Outpriced the courtesies of the bland.

I am now the only being who
       Remembers you
It may be. What a waste that Nature
   Grudged soul so dear the art its due!

Tolerance

'IT is a foolish thing,' said I,
'To bear with such, and pass it by;
Yet so I do, I know not why!'

And at each cross I would surmise
That if I had willed not in that wise
I might have spared me many sighs.

But now the only happiness
In looking back that I possess –
Whose lack would leave me comfortless –

Is to remember I refrained
From masteries I might have gained,
And for my tolerance was disdained;

For see, a tomb. And if it were
I had bent and broke, I should not dare
To linger in the shadows there.

He Prefers Her Earthly

THIS after-sunset is a sight for seeing,
Cliff-heads of craggy cloud surrounding it.
  – And dwell you in that glory-show?
You may; for there are strange strange things in being,
    Stranger than I know.

Yet if that chasm of splendour claim your presence
Which glows between the ash cloud and the dun,
  How changed must be your mortal mould!
Changed to a firmament-riding earthless essence
    From what you were of old:

All too unlike the fond and fragile creature
Then known to me ... Well, shall I say it plain?
  I would not have you thus and there,
But still would grieve on, missing you, still feature
    You as the one you were.

The Five Students [108]

THE sparrow dips in his wheel-rut bath,
    The sun grows passionate-eyed,
And boils the dew to smoke by the paddock-path;
    As strenuously we stride, –
Five of us; dark He, fair He, dark She, fair She, I,
    All beating by.

The air is shaken, the high-road hot,
    Shadowless swoons the day,
The greens are sobered and cattle at rest; but not
    We on our urgent way, –
Four of us; fair She, dark She, fair He, I, are there,
    But one – elsewhere.

Autumn moulds the hard fruit mellow,
    And forward still we press
Through moors, briar-meshed plantations, clay-pits yellow,
    As in the spring hours – yes,
Three of us: fair He, fair She, I, as heretofore,
    But – fallen one more.

The leaf drops: earthworms draw it in
    At night-time noiselessly,
The fingers of birch and beech are skeleton-thin,
    And yet on the beat are we, –
Two of us; fair She, I. But no more left to go
    The track we know.

Icicles tag the church-aisle leads,
    The flag-rope gibbers hoarse,
The home-bound foot-folk wrap their snow-flaked heads,
    Yet I still stalk the course –
One of us . . . Dark and fair He, dark and fair She, gone:
    The rest – anon.

During Wind and Rain [109]

THEY sing their dearest songs –
    He, she, all of them – yea,
Treble and tenor and bass,
    And one to play;
With the candles mooning each face . . .
    Ah, no; the years O!
How the sick leaves reel down in throngs!

They clear the creeping moss –
Elders and juniors – aye,
Making the pathways neat
 And the garden gay;
And they build a shady seat . . .
 Ah, no; the years, the years;
See, the white storm-birds wing across!

They are blithely breakfasting all –
Men and maidens – yea,
Under the summer tree,
 With a glimpse of the bay,
While pet fowl come to the knee . . .
 Ah, no; the years O!
And the rotten rose is ript from the wall.

They change to a high new house,
He, she, all of them – aye,
Clocks and carpets and chairs
 On the lawn all day,
And brightest things that are theirs . . .
 Ah, no; the years, the years;
Down their carved names the rain-drop ploughs.

GENERAL PREFACE TO THE
WESSEX EDITION OF 1912

In accepting a proposal for a definite edition of these productions in prose and verse I have found an opportunity of classifying the novels under heads that show approximately the author's aim, if not his achievement, in each book of the series at the date of its composition. Sometimes the aim was lower than at other times; sometimes, where the intention was primarily high, force of circumstances (among which the chief were the necessities of magazine publication) compelled a modification, great or slight, of the original plan. Of a few, however, of the longer novels, and of many of the shorter tales, it may be assumed that they stand today much as they would have stood if no accidents had obstructed the channel between the writer and the public. That many of them, if any, stand as they would stand if written *now* is not to be supposed.

In the classification of these fictitious chronicles – for which the name of 'The Wessex Novels' was adopted, and is still retained – the first group is called 'Novels of Character and Environment', and contains those which approach most nearly to uninfluenced works; also one or two which, whatever their quality in some few of their episodes, may claim a veri-similitude in general treatment and detail.

The second group is distinguished as 'Romances and Fantasies', a sufficiently descriptive definition. The third class – 'Novels of Ingenuity' – show a not infrequent disregard of the probable in the chain of events, and depend for their interest mainly on the incidents themselves. They might also be characterized as 'Experiments', and were written for the nonce simply; though despite the artificiality of their fable some of their scenes are not without fidelity to life.

It will not be supposed that these differences are distinctly perceptible in every page of every volume. It was inevitable that blendings and alternations should occur in all. Moreover, as it was not thought desirable in every instance to change the arrangement of the shorter stories to which readers have grown accustomed, certain of these may be found under headings to which an acute judgment might deny appropriateness.

It has sometimes been conceived of novels that evolve their action on a circumscribed scene – as do many (though not all) of these – that they cannot be so inclusive in their exhibition of human nature as novels wherein the scenes cover large extents of country, in which events figure and towns and cities, even wander over the four quarters of the globe. I am not concerned to argue this point further than to suggest that the conception is an untrue one in respect of the elementary passions. But I would state that the geographical limits of the stage here trodden were not absolutely forced upon the writer by circumstances; he forced them upon himself from judgment. I considered that our magnificent heritage from the Greeks in dramatic literature found sufficient room for a large proportion of its action in an extent of their country not much larger than the half-dozen counties here reunited under the old name of Wessex, that the domestic emotions have throbbed in Wessex nooks with as much intensity as in the palaces of Europe, and that, anyhow, there was quite enough human nature in Wessex for one man's literary purpose. So far was I possessed by this idea that I kept within the frontiers when it would have been easier to overlap them and give more cosmopolitan features to the narrative.

Thus, though the people in most of the novels (and in much of the shorter verse) are dwellers in a province bounded on the north by the Thames, on the south by the English Channel, on the east by a line running from Hayling Island to Windsor Forest, and on the west by the Cornish coast, they were meant to be typically and essentially those of any and every place where – beings in whose hearts and minds that which is apparently local should be really universal.

But whatever the success of this intention, and the value of these novels as delineations of humanity, they have at least a humble supplementary quality of which I may be justified in

Thought's the slave of life, and life time's fool

reminding the reader, though it is one that was quite unintentional and unforeseen. At the dates represented in the various narrations things were like that in Wessex: the inhabitants lived in certain ways, engaged in certain occupations, kept alive certain customs, just as they are shown doing in these pages. And in particularizing such I have often been reminded of Boswell's remarks on the trouble to which he was put and the pilgrimages he was obliged to make to authenticate some detail, though the labour was one which would bring him no praise. Unlike his achievement, however, on which an error would as he says have brought discredit, if these country customs and vocations, obsolete and obsolescent, had been detailed wrongly, nobody would have discovered such errors to the end of Time. Yet I have instituted inquiries to correct tricks of memory, and striven against temptations to exaggerate, in order to preserve for my own satisfaction a fairly true record of a vanishing life.

It is advisable also to state here, in response to inquiries from readers interested in landscape, prehistoric antiquities, and especially old English architecture, that the description of these backgrounds has been done from the real – that is to say, has something real for its basis, however illusively treated. Many features of the first two kinds have been given under their existing names; for instance, the Vale of Blackmoor or Blakemore, Hambledon Hill, Bulbarrow, Nettlecombe Tout, Dogbury Hill, High-Stoy, Bubb-Down Hill, The Devil's Kitchen, Cross-in-Hand, Long-Ash Lane, Benvill Lane, Giant's Hill, Crimmer-crock Lane, and Stonehenge. The rivers Froom, or Frome, and Stour, are, of course, well known as such. And the further idea was that large towns and points tending to mark the outline of Wessex – such as Bath, Plymouth, The Start, Portland Bill, Southampton, etc. – should be named clearly. The scheme was not greatly elaborated, but, whatever its value, the names remain still.

In respect of places described under fictitious or ancient names in the novels – for reasons that seemed good at the time of writing them – and kept up in the poems – discerning people have affirmed in print that they clearly recognize the originals: such as Shaftesbury in 'Shaston', Sturminster Newton in

'Stourcastle', Dorchester in 'Casterbridge', Salisbury Plain in 'The Great Plain', Cranborne Chase in 'The Chase', Beaminster in 'Emminster', Bere Regis in 'Kingsbere', Woodbury Hill in 'Greenhill', Wool Bridge in 'Wellbridge', Harfoot or Harput Lane in 'Stagfoot Lane', Hazlebury in 'Nuttlebury', Bridport in 'Port Bredy', Maiden Newton in 'Chalk Newton', a farm near Nettlecombe Tout in 'Flintcomb Ash', Sherborne in 'Sherton Abbas', Milton Abbey in 'Middleton Abbey', Cerne Abbas in 'Abbot's Cernel', Eveshot in 'Evershed', Taunton in 'Toneborough', Bournemouth in 'Sandbourne', Winchester in 'Wintoncester', Oxford in 'Christminster', Reading in 'Aldbrickham', Newbury in 'Kennetbridge', Wantage in 'Alfredston', Basingstoke in 'Stoke Barehills', and so on. Subject to the qualifications above given, that no detail is guaranteed – that the portraiture of fictitiously named towns and villages was only suggested by certain real places, and wantonly wanders from inventorial descriptions of them – I do not contradict these keen hunters for the real; I am satisfied with their statements as at least an indication of their interest in the scenes.

Thus much for the novels. Turning now to the verse – to myself the more individual part of my literary fruitage – I would say that, unlike some of the fiction, nothing interfered with the writer's freedom in respect of its form or content. Several of the poems – indeed many – were produced before novel-writing had been thought of as a pursuit; but few saw the light till all the novels had been published. The limited stage to which the majority of the latter confine their exhibitions has not been adhered to here in the same proportion, the dramatic part especially having a very broad theatre of action. It may thus relieve the circumscribed areas treated in the prose, if such relief be needed. To be sure, one might argue that by surveying Europe from a celestial point of vision – as in *The Dynasts* – that continent becomes virtually a province – a Wessex, an Attica, even a mere garden – and hence is made to conform to the principle of the novels, however far it outmeasures their region. But that may be as it will.

The few volumes filled by the verse cover a producing period of some eighteen years first and last, while the seventeen or more volumes of novels represent correspondingly about four-and-twenty years. One is reminded by this disproportion in time and result how much more concise and quintessential expression becomes when given in rhythmic form than when shaped in the language of prose.

One word on what has been called the present writer's philosophy of life, as exhibited more particularly in this metrical section of his compositions. Positive views on the Whence and the Wherefore of things have never been advanced by this pen as a consistent philosophy. Nor is it likely, indeed, that imaginative writings extending over more than forty years would exhibit a coherent scientific theory of the universe even if it had been attempted – of that universe concerning which Spencer owns to the 'paralysing thought' that possibly there exists no comprehension of it anywhere. But such objectless consistency never has been attempted, and the sentiments in the following pages have been stated truly to be mere impressions of the moment, and not convictions or arguments.

That these impressions have been condemned as 'pessimistic' – as if that were a very wicked adjective – shows a curious muddle-mindedness. It must be obvious that there is a higher characteristic of philosophy than pessimism, or than meliorism, or even than the optimism of these critics – which is truth. Existence is either ordered in a certain way, or it is not so ordered, and conjectures which harmonize best with experience are removed above all comparison with other conjectures which do not so harmonize. So that to say one view is worse than other views without proving it erroneous implies the possibility of a false view being better or more expedient than a true view; and no pragmatic proppings can make that *idolum specus* stand on its feet, for it postulates a prescience denied to humanity.

And there is another consideration. Differing natures find their tongue in the presence of differing spectacles. Some natures become vocal at tragedy, some are made vocal by comedy, and it seems to me that to whichever of these aspects of life a writer's instinct for expression the more readily responds, to that he should allow it to respond. That before a contrasting side of things he remains undemonstrative need not be assumed to mean that he remains unperceiving.

It was my hope to add to these volumes of verse as many more as would make a fairly comprehensive cycle of the whole. I had wished that those in dramatic, ballad, and narrative form should include most of the cardinal situations which occur in social and public life, and those in lyric form a round of emotional experiences of some completeness. But

> The petty done, the undone vast!

The more written the more seems to remain to be written; and the night cometh. I realize that these hopes and plans, except possibly to the extent of a volume or two, must remain unfulfilled.

October 1911   T.H.

NOTES

DOMICILIUM

1 (p. 51). Hardy's earliest known poem, written between 1857–1860.
Heathcroppers = wild ponies.

TO AN ACTRESS

2 (p. 54). The actress may have been Mrs Mary Scott-Siddons, whom Hardy
saw play Rosalind in *As You Like It* in April 1867.

ONE WE KNEW

3 (p. 58). M.H. = Mary Head Hardy, the poet's grandmother, whose
reminiscences, tales and legends were the material for much of Hardy's
poetry and prose.

THE CHOIRMASTER'S BURIAL

4 (p. 59). The choirmaster was the poet's grandfather, Thomas Hardy,
founder of the village choir at Stinsford church. The 'tenor man' was
Hardy's father. The incident is also recorded in *The Early Life of Thomas
Hardy*.

A CHURCH ROMANCE

5 (p. 60). Hardy's father played the violin in the Stinsford ('Mellstock')
village choir. *The Early Life of Thomas Hardy* says: 'Mrs Hardy (the poet's
mother) once described him to her son as he was when she first set eyes on
him in the now removed west gallery of Stinsford church, appearing to her
more travelled glance (she had lived for a time in London, Weymouth, and
other towns) and somewhat satirical vision, "rather amusingly old-fashioned,
in spite of being decidedly good-looking – wearing the blue swallow-tail coat
with gilt embossed buttons then customary, a red and black flowered waist-
coat, Wellington boots, and French-blue trousers." '

THE GHOST OF THE PAST

6 (p. 61). Memories of the poet's birthplace at Higher Bockhampton.

MIDDLE-AGE ENTHUSIASMS

7 (p. 65). M.H. = Mary Hardy, the poet's favourite sister.

ON ONE WHO LIVED AND DIED WHERE HE WAS BORN

8 (p. 66). The poet's father, Thomas Hardy (1811–1892).

NOTES

BEREFT

9 (p. 69). The speaker may be the poet's mother, who survived his father by twelve years.

AFTER THE LAST BREATH

10 (p. 70). J.H. = Jemima Hardy, the poet's mother.

LOGS ON THE HEARTH

11 (p. 73). The sister was Mary Hardy (1841–1915).

MOLLY GONE

12 (p. 73). Molly = the poet's sister, Mary Hardy.

IN THE GARDEN

13 (p. 74). M.H. = the poet's sister, Mary Hardy.

PAYING CALLS

14 (p. 75). The scene of this poem is Stinsford churchyard.

VOICES FROM THINGS GROWING IN A CHURCHYARD

15 (p. 77). *The Later Years of Thomas Hardy* comments: 'Fanny Hurd's real name was Fanny Hurden, and Hardy remembered her as a delicate child who went to school with him. She died when she was about eighteen, and her grave and a headstone with her name are to be seen in Stinsford churchyard. The others mentioned in this poem were known to him by name and repute.' Thomas Voss is mentioned in *Under the Greenwood Tree*.

A SHEEP FAIR

16 (p. 83). Pummery = Poundberry, a hill outside Dorchester.

VAGRANT'S SONG

17 (p. 84). 'Che-hane' (dial.) has been conjectured to mean, 'I'm safe'.

THE JUBILEE OF A MAGAZINE

18 (p. 87). The magazine was the *Cornhill*, whose editor, Leslie Stephen (father of Virginia Woolf), helped to launch Hardy as a successful novelist. The magazine carried an emblem of 'the sower, reaper, thresher' on its cover.

APOSTROPHE TO AN OLD PSALM TUNE

19 (p. 96). The sixty-ninth Psalm, whose tune was rearranged by W. H. Monk (1823–1889), musical editor of *Hymns Ancient and Modern*. Hardy

must have first heard the new arrangement played by Emma Gifford at St Juliot in 1870, when they first met. 'Your raiser was borne off' refers to Emma's death; the 'new stirrer of tones' would be his second wife, Florence Dugdale.

REMINISCENCES OF A DANCING MAN

20 (p. 97). Hardy was a great frequenter of London dance-halls when he worked as an assistant architect in Blomfield's London office between 1862 and 1867. See *The Early Life of Thomas Hardy*, pp. 44-5.

SONG TO AN OLD BURDEN

21 (p. 102). The references in the first stanza are to Hardy's father and grand-father; in the second, to his mother Jemima Hardy.

THE BRIDE-NIGHT FIRE

22 (p. 102). Hardy's first published poem, which appeared in the *Gentleman's Mazazine*, November 1875. In *Goodbye to All That* Robert Graves records: 'Hardy was at the critics again . . . one man had recently singled out as an example of gloom a poem he had written about a woman whose house was burned down on her wedding-night. "Of course it is a humorous piece," said Hardy, "and the man must have been thick-witted not to see that."'

THE RUINED MAID

23 (p. 112). spudding up docks = digging up weeds
    barton = farm

A MAN

24 (p. 129). The dedication may mean 'Hardy of Mellstock' (i.e. Stinsford), either the father or grandfather of the poet.

THE ABBEY-MASON

25 (p. 130). Writing on 22 July 1898, to Mrs Henniker, Hardy remarks of Gloucester Cathedral: 'a most interesting building, for it was there that the Perpendicular style was invented: you can see how it grew in the old masons' minds.' The poem, however, is fiction.
    Parpend ashlars = squared throughstones binding a wall.

THE CHAPEL-ORGANIST

26 (p. 142). The chapel is probably the Dorford Baptist Church between Dorchester and Fordington.
    Havenpool = Poole.

HONEYMOON TIME AT AN INN

27 (p. 147). A. J. Guerard remarks of this poem that it 'is very queer indeed. The fifth line of the first stanza repeats the first line. This occurs again, with a

slight change in wording, in the seventh stanza. This leaves us with a theoretical possibility, for a forty-eight line poem, of forty-six different types of metrical line. *And this is precisely what we have!* Except for the lines noted above, no two are rhythmically alike.'

('The Illusion of Simplicity: The Shorter Poems of Thomas Hardy', *Sewanee Review*, Summer 1964).

AT WYNYARD'S GAP

28 (p. 151). A one-act verse play. A pencil note of Hardy's on the proofs of this poem seems to indicate that he intended it to be acted.

THE COLLECTOR CLEANS HIS PICTURE

29 (p. 162). The speaker of the poem is William Barnes, vicar of Winterborne Came, near Hardy's home at Max Gate. The invented words with Anglo-Saxon roots like 'brushcraft', 'artfeat', 'easel-lumber' would be typical of the Dorset poet.
luthern = dormer-window.

LAST LOOK ROUND ST MARTIN'S FAIR

30 (p. 174). This fair used to be held at Martinstown near Dorchester.

WINTER NIGHT IN WOODLAND

31 (p. 181). The penultimate line of the poem names the members of the 'Mellstock Quire' in *Under the Greenwood Tree*.
swingel = flail

FRIENDS BEYOND

32 (p. 182). The scene is Stinsford churchyard. The characters are based on actual persons, most of whom appear in *Under the Greenwood Tree*. The 'Mellstock Quire' also figures in the next four poems.

THE PINE PLANTERS

33 (p. 197). See *The Woodlanders*, Chapter VIII.

THE LAST SIGNAL

34 (p. 209). Winterborne Came Rectory, where William Barnes was Rector, is barely half a mile from Hardy's home at Max Gate. Hardy often visited the old poet. *The Early Life of Thomas Hardy* has this comment on the poem: 'Hardy's walk across the fields to attend the poet's funeral was marked by the singular incident to which he alludes in the poem entitled "The Last Signal"'.

GOD'S FUNERAL

35 (p. 230). First published in the *Fortnightly Review*, March 1912, with the subtitle 'An Allegorical Conception of the Present State of Theology'.

Hardy had offered the editor an alternative title: ' "The Funeral of Jahveh" – the subject being the gradual decline and extinction in the human race of a belief in an anthromorphic god of the King of Dahomey type – a fact recognized by all bodies of theologians for many years.'

THE MOTHER MOURNS

36 (p. 243). From Hardy's notebook, 17 November 1883: 'Poem. We have reached a degree of intelligence which Nature never contemplated when framing her laws, and for which she consequently has provided no adequate satisfactions.' 7 April 1889: 'A woeful fact – that the human race is too extremely developed for its corporeal conditions, the nerves being evolved to an activity abnormal in such an environment. Even the higher animals are in excess in this respect. It may be questioned if Nature, or what we call Nature, so far back as when she crossed the line from invertebrates to vertebrates, did not exceed her mission. The planet does not supply the materials for happiness to higher existences.'

A REFUSAL

37 (p. 248). 'The grave Dean of Westminster' was Herbert E. Ryle. His letter in *The Times* for 19 July 1924 gave his reasons for refusing permission to place a tablet to Byron in Poet's Corner: 'Unfortunately Byron, partly by his own openly dissolute life and partly by the influence of the licentious verse, earned a world-wide reputation for immorality among English-speaking people.'

BUDMOUTH DEARS

38 (p. 271). Budmouth = Weymouth.

IN TIME OF 'THE BREAKING OF NATIONS'

39 (p. 282). On this poem Hardy commented: 'I have a faculty . . . for burying an emotion in my heart or brain for forty years, and for exhuming it at the end of that time as fresh as when interred. For instance, the poem entitled "The Breaking of Nations" contains a feeling that moved me in 1870, during the Franco-Prussian War, when I chanced to be looking at such an agricultural incident in Cornwall. But I did not write the verses till during the war with Germany of 1914, and onwards.' *The Early Life of Thomas Hardy* remarks: 'On the day that the bloody battle of Gravelotte was fought they [Hardy and Emma Gifford] were reading Tennyson in the grounds of the rectory [at St Juliot]. It was at this time and spot that Hardy was struck by the incident of the old horse harrowing the arable field in the valley below, which, when in far later years it was recalled to him by a still bloodier war, he made into the little poem of three verses.'

STANDING BY THE MANTELPIECE

40 (p. 287). H.M.M = Horace Mosley Moule, Hardy's friend and mentor, who committed suicide at Cambridge in 1873.

Moule is the speaker of the poem, and he appears to be addressing a woman – probably the 'un-named lady of title' to whom, according to a conversation of Hardy's with Sydney Cockerell, Moule had been engaged. In her book, *Folkways in Thomas Hardy*, Ruth A. Firmor says that the column of tallow left standing after most of a candle has been consumed, shaped like a shroud or coffin, is an omen of death. In the poem Moule seems to be addressing his fiancée after having decided to take his life following the breaking of their engagement.

IN TENEBRIS

41 (p. 290). Between 1895 and 1896 Hardy was in the depths of depression, partly because of the death of his father in 1892, partly because of the reception of *Jude the Obscure*, and partly because of the bitterness of his marriage.

WESSEX HEIGHTS

42 (p. 293). On 6 December 1914, the second Mrs Hardy (Florence Dugdale) wrote to Lady Hoare: 'When I read "Wessex Heights" it makes me miserable. It wrings my heart to think that he [i.e. Hardy] ever suffered so much. It was written in '96, before I knew him, but the four people mentioned are actual women. One was dead and three living when it was written – now only one is living.'

The identities of these four women are speculative. They may be Emma Gifford ('no comrade'); Hardy's mother has been suggested for 'the figure against the moon'; the 'ghost in Yell'ham Bottom' and 'in Froom-Side Vale' may be Tryphena Sparks; 'the one rare fair woman' is almost certainly Mrs Henniker.

ON THE PORTRAIT OF A WOMAN ABOUT TO BE HANGED

43 (p. 302). The woman was Edith Thompson, who was hanged with her lover Frederick Bywaters for murdering her husband. The poem was published in 1923.

HE RESOLVES TO SAY NO MORE

44 (p. 312). This poem closes Hardy's last and posthumous collection of poems, and was written in the year before his death.

TO LOUISA IN THE LANE

45 (p. 315). The girl was Louisa Harding, a farmer's daughter, one of Hardy's adolescent loves; though no more passed between them than 'a murmured "Good Evening"'. She never married and was buried in Stinsford churchyard in 1913. Hardy wanted to erect a tombstone for her but feared her family would not like it.

LOUIE

46 (p. 316). See note 45 above.

'The elect one' = Emma Gifford, also buried in Stinsford churchyard.

IN HER PRECINCTS

47 (p. 316). The poem refers to Mrs Julia Augusta Martin, the lady of the manor at Kingston Maurward, who took an interest in Hardy when he was a small boy. Hardy had a sentimental attachment to her.

AT A SEASIDE TOWN IN 1869

48 (p. 317). The town is Weymouth, where Hardy was working for the architect G. R. Crickmay. At this time he was probably engaged to Tryphena Sparks.

AT WAKING

49 (p. 319) See note 48 above.

ON A HEATH

50 (p. 321). The scene of the poem is probably Egdon Heath (i.e. Puddletown Heath). In *Talks with Thomas Hardy*, V. H. Collins records the following conversation about the final stanza: 'C: Who or what is it that is referred to in the last stanza? – H: There is a third person. – C: "Another looming", "one still blooming", "a shade entombing" – are there not three different things? – H: No, only one.'

The reference is probably to Emma Gifford, whom Hardy had met while still engaged to Tryphena Sparks. The indefatigable Lois Deacon and Terry Coleman believe that 'another looming / Whose life we did not see' refers to Tryphena's hypothetic pregnancy.

THE MOUND

51 (p. 321). This poem may refer to Tryphena Sparks.

IN A CATHEDRAL CITY

52 (p. 322). The woman addressed in the poem may be Tryphena Sparks.

ON THE ESPLANADE

53 (p. 323). The scene of the poem is Weymouth. 'My Fate's masked face' may be a reference to Emma Gifford, whom Hardy had yet to meet.

TWO SERENADES

54 (p. 323). The poem may refer to Hardy's transference of his affections from Tryphena to Emma Gifford.

THE PHOTOGRAPH

55 (p. 326). The photograph may have been one of Tryphena Sparks.

THOUGHTS OF PHENA

56 (p. 327). From Hardy's journal, dated 5 March 1890 (quoted in *The Early Life of Thomas Hardy*): 'In the train on the way to London. Wrote the first

four or six lines of "Not a line of her writing have I." It was a curious instance of sympathetic telepathy. The woman whom I was thinking of – a cousin – was dying at the time, and I quite in ignorance of it. She died six days later. The remainder of the piece was not written till after her death.'

This is the only poem of Hardy's that mentions Tryphena Sparks by name.

I NEED NOT GO

57 (p. 328). The dead woman in the poem is probably Tryphena.

AT MAYFAIR LODGINGS

58 (p. 329). The identity of the woman in the poem is unknown. V. H. Collins (op. cit.) records a conversation about this poem. He asked Hardy 'Why and how "need not the tragedy have come due"? Because she would have married him, and there would not now have been the tragedy of her dying apart from him?' Hardy answered, 'Yes'.

UNKNOWING

59 (p. 330). The poem may refer to Tryphena Sparks.

THE WIND'S PROPHECY

60 (p. 331). The poem refers to Hardy's first journey to Cornwall in March 1870 when he travelled to St Juliot to make drawings for the restoration of its church, and there first met Emma Gifford. He was still engaged to Tryphena Sparks at the time.

WHEN I SET OUT FOR LYONNESSE

61 (p. 332). This poem, like the six that follow, refers to Hardy's first visit to Cornwall in March 1870, when he met Emma Gifford at St Juliot.

THE OLD GOWN

62 (p. 334). Memories of Emma Gifford. The first and last stanzas refer to Hardy's first visit to St Juliot in 1870, but the second stanza may refer to Hardy's visit with Emma to a Royal Garden Party at Windsor in 1902. There were not enough conveyances to take all the guests from the station to the castle. Mrs Hardy took a place in one of the royal carriages, but when the other guests, noticing how frail Hardy looked, urged him to get in beside her she settled the matter by saying: 'Mr Hardy ride? Why, that walk up the hill in the sun will do him a lot of good!'

THE FROZEN GREENHOUSE

63 (p. 335). The poem refers to the last day of Hardy's first visit to St Juliot rectory.

AT THE WORD 'FAREWELL'

64 (p. 336). See note 63 above.

UNDER THE WATERFALL

65 (p. 339). *The Early Life of Thomas Hardy* describes the incident: 'Often we [Hardy and Emma] walked to Boscastle Harbour down the beautiful Valency Valley where we had to jump over stones and climb over a low wall by rough steps, or get through a narrow pathway, to come on great wide spaces suddenly, with a sparkling little brook going the same way, in which we once lost a tiny picnic-tumbler, and there it is to this day no doubt between two of the boulders.' Hardy also drew a sketch of Emma looking for the glass, and dated it 19 August 1870.

LOVE THE MONOPOLIST

66 (p. 340). The scene is probably Launceston, then the nearest railhead to St Juliot.

SELF-UNCONSCIOUS

67 (p. 341). Emma Gifford lived near Bossiney when Hardy was courting her in 1870. V. H. Collins (op. cit.) asked Hardy what the line 'As he was, and should have been shown, that day' meant. The reply was: 'If he had realized, when young, what he was, he would have acted differently. That is the tragedy of youth: when we know, it is too late to alter things.'

NEAR LANIVET, 1872

68 (p. 343). In 1872 Hardy and Emma visited Bodmin to discuss their engagement with Emma's father, who was far from enthusiastic about Hardy as a suitor. The 'stunted handpost', a carved stone cross, still exists at Peperry Cross.

WE SAT AT THE WINDOW

69 (p. 344). The Hardys were married in August 1874, and stayed a short while in Bournemouth the following year.

A TWO-YEARS' IDYLL

70 (p. 345). This, and the three following poems, refer to the Hardys' stay at Sturminster Newton, the happiest period of their marriage.

THE CHOSEN

71 (p. 348). Of the five women in the poem, 'the first with her eating eyes' is probably Florence Dugdale, Hardy's second wife; 'the fourth who sang all day' must be Emma Gifford; while 'the fifth, whom I'd called a jade' may be Tryphena Sparks. The identity of the other two is speculative.

THE CONFORMERS

72 (p. 353). cohue = mob or crowd (Fr).

A SECOND ATTEMPT

73 (p. 355). The poem probably refers to Emma Gifford. The MS gives 'about 1900' as the date of composition, so 'Thirty years after' points to 1870, in which year Hardy met Emma.

SHE CHARGED ME

74 (p. 357). 'Another woman' may refer to Mrs Henniker. See note 75 below.

ALIKE AND UNALIKE

75 (p. 358). Entry in Hardy's diary for 18 May 1893: 'Left Euston by 9 o'clock morning train with E. for Llandudno, *en route* for Dublin. After arrival at Llandudno drove around Great Orme's Head. Magnificent deep purple-grey mountains, the fine colour being on account of an approaching storm.' They were on their way to visit the Lord Lieutenant of Ireland, Lord Houghton, and his sister, Mrs Henniker. The speaker of the poem is Emma Gifford.

A THUNDERSTORM IN TOWN

76 (p. 358). The woman in the poem is probably Mrs Henniker.

AT AN INN

77 (p. 359). This poem also probably refers to Mrs Henniker.

THE THING UNPLANNED

78 (p. 360). 'The thatched post-office, just by the ridge' was the one at Lower Bockhampton. The poem either refers to Tryphena Sparks or, more probably, Mrs Henniker.

A BROKEN APPOINTMENT

79 (p. 360). The poem probably refers to Mrs Henniker.

IN DEATH DIVIDED

80 (p. 361). The reference is probably to Mrs Henniker, though Tryphena Sparks has been suggested.

THE DIVISION

81 (p. 362). Also probably associated with Mrs Henniker.

ON THE DEPARTURE PLATFORM

82 (p. 364). The poem probably refers to Florence Dugdale, who became Hardy's second wife, and whom he met through Mrs Henniker in 1904.

THE INTERLOPER

83 (p. 364). According to R. L. Purdy's *Thomas Hardy: A Bibliographical Study*, ' "The Interloper" was the threat of madness which hung over Hardy's first wife at St Juliot, Sturminster Newton, &c.'

V. H. Collins (op. cit.) records the following conversation with Hardy on 27 December 1920: 'C: What is "that under which the best lives corrode"? – H: Madness. – C: In each case? – H: Yes. I knew the family. – Mrs H: [i.e. Florence Dugdale] I always thought the poem was obscure. – H: (reads it) Certainly it is not clear. No one could possibly guess. – C: I asked several people, and they were all puzzled. One of my colleagues, Mr Williams – himself a poet – suggested that it was no definite thing, but a sort of undermining rot which destroys everything. – H: That was a remarkably good guess. He got as near it as one possibly could . . . Write down "Insanity"; that is a better word than "Madness". I wonder how I could make it clear.'

LOST LOVE

84 (p. 368). The speaker of the poem is Emma Gifford.

THE LAST PERFORMANCE

85 (p. 368). Shortly before her death in 1912 Hardy's wife 'one day suddenly sat down to the piano and played a long series of her favourite tunes, saying at the end she would never play any more. The poem called "The Last Performance" approximately describes this incident' (*The Later Years of Thomas Hardy*).

POEMS OF 1912–13

86 (p. 370). This sequence is Hardy's elegy for Emma Gifford, his first wife, who died suddenly and unexpectedly on 27 November 1912. The epigraph is from Virgil's *Aeneid*, IV, 24: 'adgnosco veteris vestigia flammae' – 'I recognize the traces of an old fire'.

In March 1913 Hardy revisited St Juliot, where he had courted Emma, returning home by way of Plymouth, where she was born. The sequence was originally published in *Satires of Circumstance* (1914). In the original version the sequence ended with 'A Phantom Horsewoman', but in the *Collected Poems* of 1919 Hardy added three further poems: 'The Spell of the Rose', 'St Launce Revisited', and 'The Picnic'.

HIS VISITOR

87 (p. 379). Florence Dugdale came to Max Gate within a month of Emma's death to help run the household.

AFTER A JOURNEY

88 (p. 381). In March 1913 Hardy made a pilgrimage to Cornwall to revisit the scenes of his courtship of Emma Gifford. The next seven poems treat of this pilgrimage.

AT CASTLE BOTEREL

89 (p. 383). Castle Boterel = Boscastle, a small town on the coast, a mile or two from St Juliot.

PLACES

90 (p. 384). Emma Gifford was born at Plymouth, the scene of the poem. Hardy never visited it during her lifetime.

THE PHANTOM HORSEWOMAN

91 (p. 385). The original version of 'Poems 1912–13' ended with this poem.

ST LAUNCE'S REVISITED

92 (p. 388). St Launce's = Launceston. In 1870, when Hardy first visited St Juliot, it was the nearest railhead.

WHERE THEY LIVED

93 (p. 393). The MS of this poem was dated 'March 1913' and then altered to 'October 1913'. Hardy had revisited St Juliot Rectory, whose summerhouse is referred to in this poem, in March 1913.

THE WEST OF WESSEX GIRL

94 (p. 395). The poem refers to Emma Gifford, born at Plymouth.

THE CHIMES PLAY 'LIFE'S A BUMPER!'

95 (p. 397). The bells are those of St Peter's church in Dorchester.

A POET

96 (p. 401). 'Two bright-souled women clave to him'. The reference is to Emma Gifford and Florence Dugdale. Hardy had married the latter in February 1914.

AFTER THE VISIT

97 (p. 403). F.E.D. = Florence Emily Dugdale. The poem was published in 1910, but the dedication was not added until it appeared in *Satires of Circumstance*, by which time Florence Dugdale had become Hardy's second wife.

TO MEET, OR OTHERWISE

98 (p. 403). First published a year after the death of Emma Gifford, this poem is addressed to Florence Dugdale.

A JOG-TROT PAIR

99 (p. 404). 'The twain' are Hardy and his second wife.

THE SHADOW ON THE STONE

100 (p. 405). 'The Druid stone' was a large monolith Hardy discovered three feet underground at Max Gate in 1891, and had set up in the garden. Hardy is said to have found Emma Gifford burning all his love letters to her behind this stone.

THE MARBLE TABLET

101 (p. 406). Hardy erected a memorial tablet to Emma Gifford in the church at St Juliot in 1913, near the harmonium on which she used to play the music for the church services.

THE MONUMENT-MAKER

102 (p. 406). See note 101 above.

QUID HIC AGIS?

103 (p. 407). 'The chapter from Kings' = 1 Kings xix. The reference in the first stanza is to Hardy's mother, in the second to Emma Gifford. In the third stanza 'the marble' refers to the tablet that Hardy erected to Emma in St Juliot church.

THE CLOCK OF THE YEARS

104 (p. 410). griff = claw.

A PROCESSION OF DEAD DAYS

105 (p. 411). Memories of Emma Gifford. The first four stanzas refer to their courtship and engagement; the fifth to their wedding; and the remaining stanzas to the troubles of their marriage, and Emma's death – she died at 'the third hour' – about 9 a.m. on 27 November 1912.

IF YOU HAD KNOWN

106 (p. 412). The first stanza refers to Hardy's courtship of Emma Gifford in Cornwall in 1870.

A DUETTIST TO HER PIANOFORTE

107 (p. 413). E.L.H. = Emma Lavinia Gifford; H.C.H. = Mrs Helen C. Holder, her sister.

THE FIVE STUDENTS

108 (p. 418). 'Dark he' is probably Hardy's friend and mentor Horace Moule, who committed suicide in 1873; 'fair he' may be T. W. Hooper Tolbort, mentioned with Moule as one of Hardy's 'two literary friends' in *The Early Life of Thomas Hardy*; 'dark she' is Tryphena Sparks, who died in 1890; 'fair she' is Emma Gifford.

DURING WIND AND RAIN

109 (p. 419). The poem visualizes scenes in Emma Gifford's early life (see *Some Recollections by Emma Hardy*, ed. Robert Gittings, Oxford University Press, 1961). It is set in Plymouth, where Emma was born and the Gifford family lived.

In compiling these notes the editor has been much indebted to J. O. Bailey's invaluable *The Poetry of Thomas Hardy: A Handbook and Commentary*, University of North Carolina Press, 1970.

The following five prefaces are the only ones Hardy wrote to individual volumes of his poetry.

Preface to *Wessex Poems and Other Verses*

OF the miscellaneous collection of verse that follows, only four pieces have been published, though many were written long ago, and others partly written. In some few cases the verses were turned into prose and printed as such, it having been un-anticipated at that time that they might see the light.·

Whenever an ancient and legitimate word of the district, for which there was no equivalent in received English, suggested itself as the most natural, nearest, and often only expression of a thought, it has been made use of, on what seemed good grounds.

The pieces are in a large degree dramatic or personative in conception; and this even where they are not obviously so.

The dates attached to some of the poems do not apply to the rough sketches given in illustration,* which have been recently made, and, as may be surmised, are inserted for personal and local reasons rather than for their intrinsic qualities.

September 1898   T.H.

Preface to *Poems of the Past and Present*

HEREWITH I tender my thanks to the editors and proprietors of *The Times*, the *Morning Post*, the *Daily Chronicle*, the *Westminster Gazette*, *Literature*, the *Graphic*, *Cornhill*, *Sphere*, and other papers, for permission to reprint from their pages such of the following pieces of verse as have already been published.

Of the subject-matter of this volume – even that which is in other than narrative form – much is dramatic or impersonative

---

* The early editions were illustrated by the writer.

even where not explicitly so. Moreover, that portion which may be regarded as individual comprises a series of feelings and fancies written down in widely differing moods and circumstances, and at various dates. It will probably be found, therefore, to possess little cohesion of thought or harmony of colouring. I do not greatly regret this. Unadjusted impressions have their value, and the road to a true philosophy of life seems to lie in humbly recording diverse readings of its phenomena as they are forced upon us by chance and change.

August 1901   T.H.

Preface to *Time's Laughing-Stocks*

IN collecting the following poems I have to thank the editors and proprietors of the periodicals in which certain of them have appeared for permission to reclaim them.

Now that the miscellany is brought together, some lack of concord in pieces written at widely severed dates, and in contrasting moods and circumstances, will be obvious enough. This I cannot help, but the sense of disconnection, particularly in respect of those lyrics penned in the first person, will be immaterial when it is borne in mind that they are to be regarded, in the main, as dramatic monologues by different characters.

As a whole they will, I hope, take the reader forward, even if not far, rather than backward. I should add that some lines in the early-dated poems have been rewritten, though they have been left substantially unchanged.

September 1909   T.H.

'Apology' from *Late Lyrics and Earlier*

ABOUT half the verses that follow were written quite lately. The rest are older, having been held over in MS. when past volumes were published, on considering that these would contain a sufficient number of pages to offer readers at one time, more especially during the distractions of the war. The unusually far back

442

poems to be found here are, however, but some that were over-looked in gathering previous collections. A freshness in them, now unattainable, seemed to make up for their inexperience and to justify their inclusion. A few are dated; the dates of others are not discoverable.

The launching of a volume of this kind in neo-Georgian days by one who began writing in mid-Victorian, and has published nothing to speak of for some years, may seem to call for a few words of excuse or explanation. Whether or no, readers may feel assured that a new book is submitted to them with great hesitation at so belated a date. Insistent practical reasons, however, among which were requests from some illustrious men of letters who are in sympathy with my productions, the accident that several of the poems have already seen the light, and that dozens of them have been lying about for years, compelled the course adopted, in spite of the natural disinclination of a writer whose works have been so frequently regarded askance by a pragmatic section here and there, to draw attention to them once more.

I do not know that it is necessary to say much on the contents of the book, even in deference to suggestions that will be mentioned presently. I believe that those readers who care for my poems at all – readers to whom no passport is required – will care for this new instalment of them, perhaps the last, as much as for any that have preceded them. Moreover, in the eyes of a less friendly class the pieces, though a very mixed collection indeed, contain, so far as I am able to see, little or nothing in technic or teaching that can be considered a Star-Chamber matter, or so much as agitating to a ladies' school; even though, to use Wordsworth's observation in his Preface to *Lyrical Ballads*, such readers may suppose 'that by the act of writing in verse an author makes a formal engagement that he will gratify certain known habits of association: that he not only thus apprises the reader that certain classes of ideas and expressions will be found in his book, but that others will be carefully excluded.'

It is true, nevertheless, that some grave, positive, stark, delineations are interspersed among those of the passive, lighter, and traditional sort presumably nearer to stereotyped tastes. For –

while I am quite aware that a thinker is not expected, and, indeed, is scarcely allowed, now more than heretofore, to state all that crosses his mind concerning existence in this universe, in his attempts to explain or excuse the presence of evil and the incongruity of penalizing the irresponsible – it must be obvious to open intelligences that, without denying the beauty and faithful service of certain venerable cults, such disallowance of 'obstinate questionings' and 'blank misgivings' tends to a paralysed intellectual stalemate. Heine observed nearly a hundred years ago that the soul has her eternal rights; that she will not be darkened by statutes, nor lullabied by the music of bells. And what is to-day, in allusions to the present author's pages, alleged to be 'pessimism' is, in truth, only such 'questionings' in the exploration of reality, and is the first step towards the soul's betterment, and the body's also.

If I may be forgiven for quoting my own words, let me repeat what I printed in this relation more than twenty years ago, and wrote much earlier, in a poem entitled 'In Tenebris':

If way to the Better there be, it exacts a full look at the Worst:

that is to say, by the exploration of reality, and its frank recognition stage by stage along the survey, with an eye to the best consummation possible: briefly, evolutionary meliorism. But it is called pessimism nevertheless; under which word, expressed with condemnatory emphasis, it is regarded by many as some pernicious new thing (though so old as to underlie the Gospel scheme, and even to permeate the Greek drama); and the subject is charitably left to decent silence, as if further comment were needless.

Happily there are some who feel such Levitical passing-by to be, alas, by no means a permanent dismissal of the matter; that comment on where the world stands is very much the reverse of needless in these disordered years of our prematurely afflicted century: that amendment and not madness lies that way. And looking down the future these few hold fast to the same: that whether the human and kindred animal races survive till the exhaustion or destruction of the globe, or whether these races perish and are succeeded by others before that conclusion comes, pain to all upon it, tongued or dumb, shall be kept down to a minimum by loving-kindness, operating through scientific knowledge, and actuated by the modicum of free will conjecturally possessed by organic life when the mighty necessitating forces – unconscious or other – that have 'the balancing of the clouds', happen to be in equilibrium, which may or may not be often.

To conclude this question I may add that the argument of the so-called optimists is neatly summarized in a stern pronouncement against me by my friend Mr Frederic Harrison in a late essay of his, in the words: 'This view of life is not mine.' The solemn declaration does not seem to me to be so annihilating to the said 'view' (really a series of fugitive impressions which I have never tried to co-ordinate) as is complacently assumed. Surely it embodies a too human fallacy quite familiar in logic. Next, a knowing reviewer, apparently a Roman Catholic young man, speaks, with some rather gross instances of the *suggestio falsi* in his whole article, of 'Mr Hardy refusing consolation', the 'dark gravity of his ideas', and so on. When a Positivist and a Romanist agree there must be something wonderful in it, which should make a poet sit up. But . . . O that 'twere possible!

I would not have alluded in this place or anywhere else to such casual personal criticisms – for casual and unreflecting they must be – but for the satisfaction of two or three friends in whose opinion a short answer was deemed desirable, on account of the continual repetition of these criticisms, or more precisely, quizzings. After all, the serious and truly literary inquiry in this connection is: Should a shaper of such stuff as dreams are made on disregard considerations of what is customary and expected, and apply himself to the real function of poetry, the application of ideas to life (in Matthew Arnold's familiar phrase)? This bears more particularly on what has been called the 'philosophy' of these poems – usually reproved as 'queer'. Whoever the author may be that undertakes such application of ideas in this 'philosophic' direction – where it is specially required – glacial judgments must inevitably fall upon him amid opinion whose arbiters largely decry individuality, to whom *ideas* are oddities to smile at, who are moved by a yearning the reverse of that of the Athenian inquirers on Mars Hill; and stiffen their features not only at sound of a new thing, but at a restatement of old things in new terms. Hence should anything of this sort in the following adumbrations seem 'queer' – should any of them seem to good Panglossians to embody strange and disrespectful conceptions of this best of all possible worlds, I apologize; but cannot help it.

Such divergences, which, though piquant for the nonce, it would be affectation to say are not saddening and discouraging likewise, may, to be sure, arise sometimes from superficial aspect only, writer and reader seeing the same thing at different angles. But in palpable cases of divergency they arise, as already said, whenever a serious effort is made towards that which the authority I have cited – who would now be called old-fashioned, possibly even parochial – affirmed to be what no good critic could deny as the poet's province, the application of ideas to life. One might shrewdly guess, by the by, that in such recommendation the famous writer may have overlooked the cold-shouldering results upon an enthusiastic disciple that would be pretty certain to follow his putting the high aim in practice, and have forgotten the disconcerting experience of Gil Blas with the Archbishop.

To add a few more words to what has already taken up too many, there is a contingency liable to miscellanies of verse that I have never seen mentioned, so far as I can remember; I mean the chance little shocks that may be caused over a book of various character like the present and its predecessors by the juxtaposition of unrelated, even discordant, effusions; poems perhaps years apart in the making, yet facing each other. An odd result of this has been that dramatic anecdotes of a satirical and humorous intention following verse in graver voice, have been read as misfires because they raise the smile that they were intended to raise, the journalist, deaf to the sudden change of key, being unconscious that he is laughing with the author and not at him. I admit that I did not foresee such contingencies as I ought to have done, and that people might not perceive when the tone altered. But the difficulties of arranging the themes in a graduated kinship of moods would have been so great that irrelation was almost unavoidable with efforts so diverse. I must trust for right note-catching to those finely-touched spirits who can divine without half a whisper, whose intuitiveness is proof against all the accidents of inconsequence. In respect of the less alert, however, should any one's train of thought be thrown out of gear by a consecutive piping of vocal reeds in jarring tonics, without a semiquaver's rest between, and be led thereby to miss the writer's arm and meaning in one out of two contiguous compositions, I shall deeply regret it.

Having at last, I think, finished with the personal points that I was recommended to notice, I will forsake the immediate object of this Preface; and leaving *Late Lyrics* to whatever fate it deserves, digress for a few moments to more general considerations. The thoughts of any man of letters concerned to keep poetry alive cannot but run uncomfortably on the precarious prospects of English verse at the present day. Verily the hazards and casualties surrounding the birth and setting forth of almost every modern creation in numbers are ominously like those of one of Shelley's paper-boats on a windy lake. And a forward conjecture scarcely permits the hope of a better time, unless men's tendencies should change. So indeed of all art, literature, and 'high thinking', nowadays. Whether owing to the barbarizing of taste in the younger minds by the dark madness of the late war, the unabashed cultivation of selfishness in all classes, the plethoric growth of knowledge simultaneously with the stunting of wisdom, 'a degrading thirst after outrageous stimulation' (to quote Wordsworth again), or from any other cause, we seem threatened with a new Dark Age.

I formerly thought, like other much exercised writers, that so far as literature was concerned a partial cause might be impotent or mischievous criticism; the satirizing of individuality, the lack of whole-seeing in contemporary estimates of poetry and kindred work, the knowingness affected by junior reviewers, the overgrowth of meticulousness in their peerings for an opinion, as if it were a cultivated habit in them to scrutinize the tool-marks and be blind to the building, to hearken for the key-creaks and be deaf to the diapason, to judge the landscape by a nocturnal exploration with a flash-lantern. In other words, to carry on the old game of sampling the poem or drama by quoting the worst line or worst passage only, in ignorance or not of Coleridge's proof that a versification of any length neither can be nor ought to be all poetry; of reading meanings into a book that its author never dreamt of writing there. I might go on interminably.

But I do not now think any such temporary obstructions to be the cause of the hazard, for these negligences and ignorances, though they may have stifled a few true poets in the run of generations, disperse like stricken leaves before the wind of next week, and are no more heard of again in the region of letters than their writers themselves. No: we may be convinced that something of the deeper sort mentioned must be the cause.

In every poetry, pure literature in general, religion – I include religion, in its essential and undogmatic sense, because poetry and religion touch each other, or rather modulate into each other; are, indeed, often but different names for the same thing – these, I say, the visible signs of mental and emotional life, must like all other things keep moving, becoming; even though at present, when belief in witches of Endor is displacing the Darwinian theory and 'the truth that shall make you free', men's minds appear, as above noted, to be moving backwards rather than on. I speak somewhat sweepingly, and should except many thoughtful writers in verse and prose; also men in certain worthy but small bodies of various denominations, and perhaps in the homely quarter where advance might have been the very least expected a few years back – the English Church – if one reads it rightly as showing evidence of 'removing those things that are shaken', in accordance with the wise Epistolary recommendation to the Hebrews. For since the historic and once august hierarchy of Rome some generation ago lost its chance of being the religion of the future by doing otherwise, and throwing over the little band of New Catholics who were making a struggle for continuity by applying the principle of evolution to their own faith, joining hands with modern science, and outflanking the hesitating English instinct towards liturgical restatement (a flank march which I at the time quite expected to witness, with the gathering of many millions of waiting agnostics into its fold); since then, one may ask, what other purely English establishment than the Church, of sufficient dignity and footing, with such strength of old association, such scope for transmutability, such architectural spell, is left in this country to keep the shreds of morality together?*

It may indeed be a forlorn hope, a mere dream, that of an alliance between religion, which must be retained unless the world is to perish, and complete rationality, which must come, unless also the world is to perish, by means of the interfusing effect of poetry – 'the breath and finer spirit of all knowledge; the impassioned expression of science', it was defined by an English poet who was quite orthodox in his ideas. But if it be true, as Comte argued, that advance is never in a straight line, but in a looped orbit, we may, in the aforesaid ominous moving backward, be doing it *pour mieux sauter*, drawing back for a spring. I repeat that I forlornly hope so, notwithstanding the supercilious regard of hope by Schopenhauer, von Hartmann, and other philosophers down to Einstein who have my respect. But one dares not prophesy. Physical, chronological, and other contingencies keep me in these days from critical studies and literary circles

> Where once we held debate, a band
> Of youthful friends, on mind and art

(if one may quote Tennyson in this century). Hence I cannot know how things are going so well as I used to know them, and the aforesaid limitations must quite prevent my knowing henceforward.

I have to thank the editors and owners of *The Times*, *Fortnightly*, *Mercury*, and other periodicals in which a few of the

*However, one must not be too sanguine in reading signs, and since the above was written evidence that the Church will go far in the removal of 'things that are shaken' has not been encouraging.

poems have appeared for kindly assenting to their being re-claimed for collected publication.

February 1922   T.H.

Introductory Note to *Winter Words*

[*Winter Words*, though prepared for the press, would have undergone further revision, had the author lived to issue it on the birthday of which he left the number uninserted below.]

So far as I am aware, I happen to be the only English poet who has brought out a new volume of his verse on his . . . birthday, whatever may have been the case with the ancient Greeks, for it must be remembered that poets did not die young in those days.

This, however, is not the point of the present few preliminary words. My last volume of poems was pronounced wholly gloomy and pessimistic by reviewers – even by some of the more able class. My sense of the oddity of this verdict may be imagined when, in selecting them, I had been, as I thought, rather too liberal in admitting flippant, not to say farcical, pieces into the collection. However, I did not suppose that the licensed tasters had wilfully misrepresented the book, and said nothing, knowing well that they could not have read it.

As labels stick, I foresee readily enough that the same perennial inscription will be set on the following pages, and therefore take no trouble to argue on the proceeding, notwithstanding the surprises to which I could treat my critics by uncovering a place here and there to them in the volume.

This being probably my last appearance on the literary stage, I would say, more seriously, that though alas, it would be idle to pretend that the publication of these poems can have much interest for me, the track having been adventured so many times before to-day, the pieces themselves have been prepared with reasonable care, if not quite with the zest of a young man new to print.

I also repeat what I have often stated on such occasions, that no harmonious philosophy is attempted in these pages – or in any bygone pages of mine, for that matter.

T.H.

INDEX OF TITLES

INDEX

INDEX OF FIRST LINES

457

INDEX